MW00626179

PROBABILITY MODELS
A STUDY GUIDE FOR EXAM P
with 123 exercises

λ

Poisson Labs

PREFACE

The purpose of this book is to help you pass the Society of Actuaries' exam on Probability. The book covers all of the material on the official syllabus, as of August 2015. Just as importantly, it covers the material in enough depth that you can actually use the book as a primary text. Most importantly, it includes 123 challenging problems and solutions, and a practice exam comparable to the real thing.

In order to get the most out of the book, we suggest the following:

- Read a section and take notes, every day.
- Make flash cards, and review them every day.
- Do the problem sets a day or two after reading the relevant section. Try not to look at your notes unless you have to. The harder you try to remember, the faster you will learn.
- If you get a problem wrong, keep track of why. Was it a lapse of attention? Did you forget something important? Or was there a computational trick you hadn't learned? Make and review flash cards for the tricks and formulas you don't know.
- Keep track of which problems you find easy and which are hard.
- Once you have done all of the problem sets, do random selections of all of the problems you found hard, 15 - 25 at a time. Allow yourself 6 minutes for each problem. Work at a steady pace. Don't rush! We suggest doing this approximately twice a week until all the hard problems are all done.
- Once you can get at least 90% on random selections of problems, take the practice exam, under timed conditions. Again, keep track of the wrong answers and dissect the solutions. If you can get a score better than 85% on the practice exam, you are doing great!

The aim is to collect enough information to let you focus your learning where you need it most. We can recommend Poisson

Labs' *Prompt and Practical* flash card and practice exam systems to optimize learning. *Prompt* takes advantage of *spaced-repetition*, which automatically schedules flash cards so that easy flash cards are seen less and difficult flash cards are seen more often. The *Practical* practice exam system has hundreds of exam difficulty problems, and is tightly integrated with *Prompt*. *Prompt and Practical* will give you the confidence you need.

CONTENTS

1

ELEMENTARY PROBABILITY

EVENTS

In probability theory, we are interested in quantifying the 'information' contained in an experiment. These real-life experiments have outcomes that are not known to us before we perform them. We model these experiments with *probability distributions* or *probability models*. Broadly speaking, a probability model for an experiment is composed of a listing of all of the possible outcomes for an experiment, together with a listing of the likelihoods for each of the outcomes.

Definition 1.1. The set Ω of all possible outcomes for an experiment is called a *sample space*, and the elements of Ω are called *outcomes*.

Example 1.2. An experiment consists of a die. The sample space Ω is

$$\Omega = \{1, 2, 3, 4, 5, 6\}.$$

Example 1.3. An experiment consists of rolling a die twice. The sample space Ω is

$$\Omega = \{(x_1, x_2) \colon x_i \in \{1, 2, 3, 4, 5, 6\}\}.$$

Another experiment consists of rolling two dice. The sample space Ω is

$$\Omega = \{(x_1, x_2) \colon x_i \in \{1, 2, 3, 4, 5, 6\}\}.$$

These two experiments both have the same outcomes, even though the experiments are structured differently.

Example 1.4. An experiment consists of counting the number of cars passing through a busy intersection in one minute. The sample space Ω is the set of natural numbers.

In this example, Ω is undoubtedly much too large. There is effectively no chance that, for example, $1,000,000,000$ cars will pass through the intersection in one minute. However, there is no harm in including large numbers, especially in cases when it is unclear how large the largest outcome can be.

Definition 1.5. An *event* is a collection of outcomes. In particular, an event ω is a subset of the sample space Ω. We call Ω the *certain* event, and call the empty set $\emptyset$ the *impossible* event.

We are typically not interested in 'arbitrary' events—events defined as a collection of outcomes. We are typically interested in defining the outcomes that are 'acceptable' by defining an event that includes the acceptable outcomes. In other words, events are tools we use to define the kinds of outcomes we are interested in.

Example 1.6. An experiment consists of rolling two dice. The event that corresponds to the phrase "rolls a double" is

$$\left\{(x,x) : x \in \{1,2,3,4,5,6\}\right\}.$$

This example illustrates our previous remark. The phrase "rolls a double" is a verbal description of an event. It only includes outcomes where the first and second dice agree. Given a logical proposition $P(x)$ about outcomes, we can build an event for it as

$$\{x \colon P(x)\}.$$

This is known as *set-builder notation*. We often like to use what we call event-builder notation.

Definition 1.7. Given a logical proposition $P(x)$, we write the event that corresponds to it as

$$[P(x)].$$

We call this *event-builder notation*. In a slight abuse of our new notation, if we are given an event A, we express it in event-builder notation as $[A] = A$.

Because events are collections, we can use the language of set theory to compare events.

Definition 1.8. Let A and B be events. If every element of A is an element of B, we write $A \subset B$, and say that A is a *subset* of B. A is a *proper subset* of B if $A \subset B$ and $A \neq B$.

Example 1.9. Let A and B be events. If $A \subset B$ and $B \subset A$, then $A = B$.

Proof. Two sets are equal when they contain the same elements. Suppose that $A \subset B$ and $B \subset A$ but $A \neq B$. Since $A \subset B$, every element of A is an element of B. If $A \neq B$, then A is a proper subset of B. In particular, there is some element $b \in B$ such that $b \notin A$. This implies that $B \not\subset A$, in contradiction to our hypothesis. ■

Because events are collections, we can use the language of set theory to create new events from old.

Definition 1.10. The *union* of events A and B is the event

$$A \cup B = \left\{x \colon x \in A \text{ or } x \in B\right\}.$$

Verbally, the union of events A and B is described as set of outcomes that are either in A or in B. Because of the close correspondence between sets and logical propositions, we sometimes write

$$\left[A \vee B\right] = [A] \cup [B].$$

Example 1.11. Figure 1 on the following page, the union of A and B is shaded in grey.

Definition 1.12. The *intersection* of events A and B is the event

$$A \cap B = \left\{x \colon x \in A \text{ and } x \in B\right\}.$$

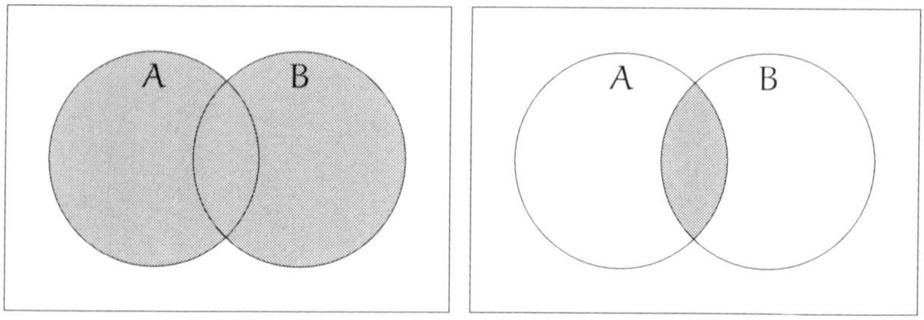

Figure 1: On the left, the union of A and B is shaded. On the right, the intersection of A and B is shaded.

Verbally, the intersection of the events A and B consists of outcomes x that are in A and also in B. In the context of probability theory, $A \cap B$ is often written AB. Because of the close correspondence between sets and logical propositions, we sometimes write

$$[A \wedge B] = [A] \cap [B].$$

Example 1.13. Figure 1, the intersection of A and B is shaded in grey.

Definition 1.14. The events A and B are *mutually exclusive* if $A \cap B = \emptyset$.

Example 1.15. An experiment consists of rolling a die. Let A be the event of rolling an even number, and let B be the event of rolling an odd number. Then

$$A = \{2,4,6\} \qquad B = \{1,3,5\}$$

and

$$A \cap B = \emptyset.$$

Definition 1.16. A *partition* of the sample space Ω is a collection of mutually exclusive events $\{A_i\}$ such that

$$\Omega = \bigcup_i A_i.$$

Example 1.17. The *distributive laws* for events are

$$A \cup (B \cap C) = (A \cup B) \cap (A \cup C)$$
$$A \cap (B \cup C) = (A \cap C) \cup (A \cap C).$$

Proof. We will prove the first distributive law and leave the proof of the latter as an exercise. Let $x \in A \cup (B \cap C)$. Then x is either in A or in $B \cap C$. We have two cases to consider. Suppose that $x \in A$. Then $x \in A \cup B$ and $x \in A \cup C$. This implies that $x \in (A \cup B) \cap (A \cup C)$. Now we consider the latter case. Let $x \in (B \cap C)$. Then $x \in B$ and $x \in C$. This implies that $x \in (A \cup B)$ and $x \in (A \cup C)$, so that $x \in (A \cup B) \cap (A \cup C)$.

So far, we have shown that every element of $A \cup (B \cap C)$ is an element of $(A \cup B) \cap (A \cup C)$. We now prove the other inclusion. Let $x \in (A \cup B) \cap (A \cup C)$. Then $x \in (A \cup B)$ and $x \in (A \cup C)$. There are two cases to consider. Suppose that $x \in A$. Then $x \in A \cup (B \cap C)$. Now, suppose that $x \notin A$. Since $x \in (A \cup B)$, under the assumption that $x \notin A$, $x \in B$. Similarly, if x is not in A, x must be in C. If x is not in A, $x \in B \cap C$, and $x \in A \cup (B \cap C)$.

This last argument shows that every element of $(A \cup B) \cap (A \cup C)$ is an element of $A \cup (B \cap C)$. Together, these arguments show that

$$A \cup (B \cap C) = (A \cup B) \cap (A \cup C). \qquad \blacksquare$$

Example 1.18. We have seen that proofs of elementary set theoretical identities are both trivial and lengthy. Venn diagrams can make verifying identities much easier. But Venn diagrams are not proofs, they are just tools to help us construct proofs or solve problems. Consider the Venn diagram in figure 2 on the following page. The diagram condenses the cases a formal proof requires into an easy to read diagram.

Definition 1.19. The *complement* of an event A is the event

$$A' = \left[(x \in \Omega) \wedge (x \notin A)\right].$$

Verbally, the complement of A is the event that consists of every outcome not in A. Similarly, we can define the set $A \setminus B = A \cap B'$. We see that $A' = \Omega \setminus A$.

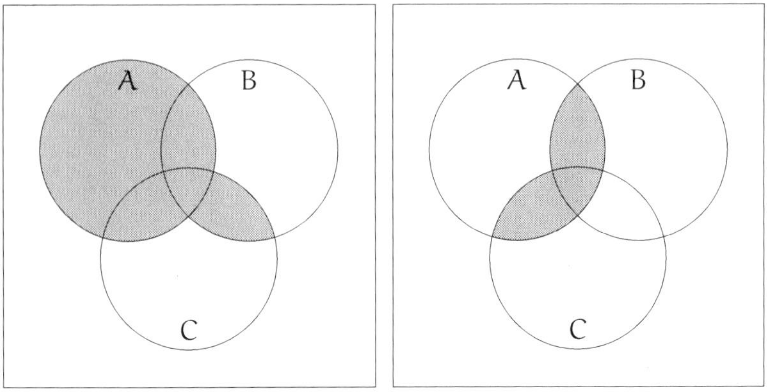

Figure 2: On the left, $A \cup (B \cap C)$ is shaded. The diagram allows us to visually verify that $A \cup (B \cap C)$ is the same region as the intersection of $A \cup B$ and $A \cup C$. Similarly, on the right, $A \cap (B \cup C)$ is shaded.

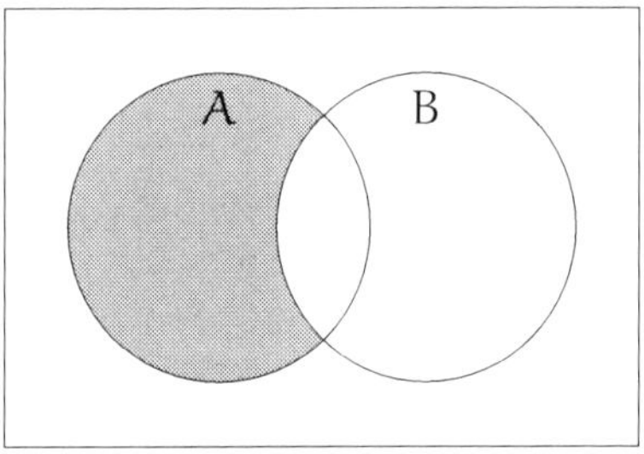

Figure 3: $A \setminus B$ is shaded.

Example 1.20. Figure 3 illustrates $A \setminus B$.

Example 1.21. Let A and B be events. *DeMorgan's laws* for events are

$$(A \cup B)' = A' \cap B' \qquad (A \cap B)' = A' \cup B'.$$

Figure 4 on the facing page illustrates the sets involved.

AXIOMS OF PROBABILITY

As we have previously discussed, a probability model for an experiment is composed of a sample space, which lists all of

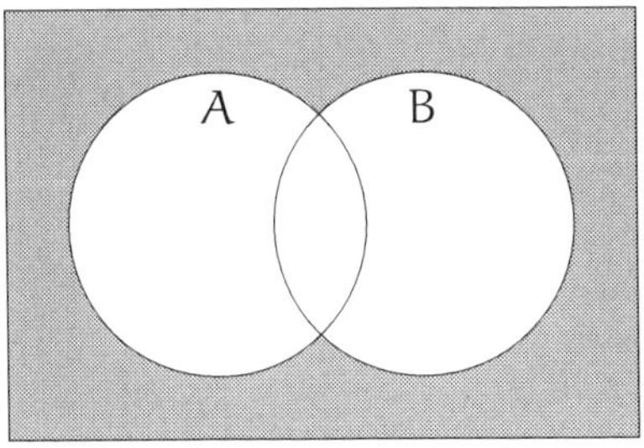

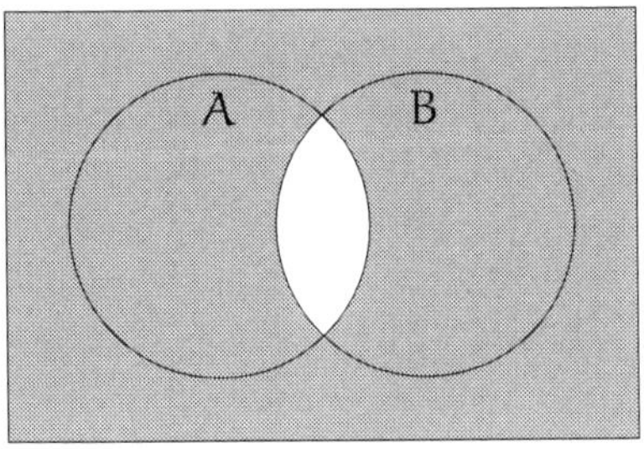

Figure 4: On the left, $(A \cup B)'$ is shaded. The Venn diagram allows us to visually confirm that this area is the same as the intersection of A' and B'. On the right, $(A \cap B)'$ is shaded. This Venn diagram allows us to visually check that the region is the same as $A' \cup B'$.

the possible outcomes for the experiment, and a listing of the likelihoods for each of the outcomes. We discussed the sample space, and events, in the previous section. In this section, we will formalize the notion of a probability measure, which is, intuitively the listing of likelihoods for events.

Definition 1.22. Let Σ be the collection of events for a probability model. A *probability measure* $\mathbf{P}\colon \Sigma \to [0,1]$ that satisfies

i. $\mathbf{P}[\Omega] = 1$

ii. For any collection $\{A_n\}$ of pairwise mutually exclusive events,

$$\mathbf{P}\left[\bigcup_n A_n\right] = \sum_{n=1} \mathbf{P}[A_n] .$$

For technical reasons, we cannot typically let Σ be the entire family of subsets of Ω. We call $\mathbf{P}$ a probability measure because, intuitively, it measures the probability that an event occurs. But some sets are too complicated to have a consistent notion of measurement imposed on them. In practice, we will never see any sets so wild that they cannot be measured. Focusing on the real numbers for a moment, every open interval is measurable.

If a set A is measurable, then its complement A' is measurable. And if $\{A_n\}$ is a countable collection of measurable sets, then both

$$\bigcup_n A_n \quad \text{and} \quad \bigcap_n A_n$$

are measurable. In general, a family Σ of subsets of Ω which satisfies these properties is called a σ-algebra, and the elements of Σ are *defined* as the measurable sets. We see that a collection of measurable sets is very rich, and in a strong sense, it is impossible to even construct a non-measurable set.[1] For this reason, we see that restricting ourselves to Σ instead of $\wp\{\Omega\}$ is not a strong limitation. From now on, when we say that a set is an event, we mean that it is an element of Σ.

We will now illustrate elementary properties of probability measures.

Theorem 1.23. *For an event* A, $\mathbf{P}[A'] = 1 - \mathbf{P}[A]$.

Proof. Let A be an event. Clearly, A and A' are mutually exclusive, and $A \cup A' = \Omega$. Then

$$\mathbf{P}[A] + \mathbf{P}[A'] = \mathbf{P}[A \cup A'] = \mathbf{P}[\Omega] = 1.$$

From this, we conclude $\mathbf{P}[A'] = 1 - \mathbf{P}[A]$. ■

As an immediate consequence of this theorem, we conclude that since $\mathbf{P}[\Omega] = 1$ and $\varnothing = \Omega'$, $\mathbf{P}[\varnothing] = 0$.

Example 1.24. An unfair coin results in heads with probability 0.3. What is the probability of flipping a tails?

Solution. Let H be the event of flipping heads. We are told that $\mathbf{P}[H] = 0.3$. We conclude that $\mathbf{P}[H'] = 1 - \mathbf{P}[H] = 0.7$. ■

Theorem 1.25. *For events* A *and* B, *if* $A \subset B$, $\mathbf{P}[A] \leq \mathbf{P}[B]$.

Proof. Since $A \subset B$, we can write B as the disjoint union $A \cup (B \setminus A)$. This means we can write

$$\mathbf{P}[B] = \mathbf{P}[A \cup (B \setminus A)] = \mathbf{P}[A] + \mathbf{P}[B \setminus A].$$

Since $\mathbf{P}[B \setminus A] \geq 0$, $\mathbf{P}[B] \geq \mathbf{P}[A] + 0 = \mathbf{P}[A]$. ■

1 On the other hand, it is possible to prove that non-measurable sets exist.

Theorem 1.26. *For events* A *and* B*,*

$$\mathbf{P}[A \cup B] = \mathbf{P}[A] + \mathbf{P}[B] - \mathbf{P}[AB].$$

Proof. We can write $A \cup B$ as the disjoint union $(A \setminus B) \cup B$. Because of this, we can write

$$\mathbf{P}[A \cup B] = \mathbf{P}[A \setminus B] + \mathbf{P}[B]. \tag{1.27}$$

On the other hand, we can express A as the disjoint union $A = (A \setminus B) \cup AB$, so that we write

$$\mathbf{P}[A] = \mathbf{P}[A \setminus B] + \mathbf{P}[AB].$$

We solve for $\mathbf{P}[AB] = \mathbf{P}[A] - \mathbf{P}[AB]$, and substitute into (1.27), so that

$$\mathbf{P}[A \cup B] = \mathbf{P}[A] + \mathbf{P}[B] - \mathbf{P}[AB]$$

as desired. ■

Example 1.28 (Bonferroni's Inequality). Let A and B be events. Prove that

$$\mathbf{P}[AB] \geq \mathbf{P}[A] + \mathbf{P}[B] - 1.$$

Solution. Consider that

$$1 \geq \mathbf{P}[A \cup B] = \mathbf{P}[A] + \mathbf{P}[B] - \mathbf{P}[AB].$$

This implies that

$$\mathbf{P}[AB] \geq \mathbf{P}[A] + \mathbf{P}[B] - 1.$$ ■

CONDITIONAL PROBABILITY

Extracting information from probability models is a major focus of probability theory. We expect that as an experiment unfolds and reveals information, that we can make more specific and accurate inferences about the final result. For example, suppose that a patient visits a hospital complaining of ankle pain. The patient's specific complaints will affect the relative likelihood of the diagnosis. On the basis that the patient has ankle pain, it is unlikely that the patient is having a heart attack. On that same basis, it is much more likely that the patient has a sprained ankle. If the patient further reveals that he slipped and twisted his ankle, the diagnosis of a sprained ankle would be even more likely.

The basic building block modeling this phenomenon is the concept of conditional probability.

Definition 1.29. Given events A and B, the *conditional probability* of A given B is

$$\mathbf{P}[A|B] = \frac{\mathbf{P}[AB]}{\mathbf{P}[B]},$$

when $\mathbf{P}[B] \neq 0$. This definition is meaningless when $\mathbf{P}[B] = 0$.

The idea behind the definition of the conditional probability is that if we know that the event B occurred, then the relevant sample space is B instead of Ω, and that the conditional probability is a probability measure on B.

Example 1.30. An experiment consists of flipping a coin once. Let H represent the event of flipping heads, and T represent the event of flipping tails. What is $\mathbf{P}[T|H]$?

Solution. Since the events are mutually exclusive,

$$\mathbf{P}[T|H] = \frac{\mathbf{P}[TH]}{\mathbf{P}[H]} = \frac{0}{\frac{1}{2}} = 0. \qquad \blacksquare$$

Conditional probabilities capture information about the dependence of events. As we saw in the previous example, the event of flipping a tail is impossible, conditional on the event of flipping a head. In the following, we see an example where an event makes a related event more likely.

Example 1.31. An experiment consists of rolling a die once. Let D_i represent the event that the outcome is divisible by i. What is $\mathbf{P}[D_4|D_2]$?

Solution. The event D_4 is $\{4\}$, while the event D_2 is $\{2,4,6\}$. We calculate

$$\mathbf{P}\left[D_4|D_2\right] = \frac{\mathbf{P}\left[D_4 D_2\right]}{\mathbf{P}\left[D_2\right]} = \frac{\mathbf{P}\left[\{4\}\right]}{\mathbf{P}\left[\{2,4,6\}\right]} = \frac{\frac{1}{6}}{\frac{1}{2}} = \frac{1}{3}. \qquad \blacksquare$$

Revealing that the result of the throw is even *doubles* the probability that it is a four.

Theorem 1.32. *As a consequence of the definition of conditional probabilities, for events* A *and* B, *we have the* product law

$$\mathbf{P}\left[AB\right] = \mathbf{P}\left[A|B\right]\mathbf{P}\left[B\right].$$

Example 1.33. A jar contains 5 red balls and 4 blue balls. Two balls are simultaneously taken from the jar. What is the probability that they are both red?

Solution. Let R_i denote the event that the ith ball we look at is red. The probability that both balls are red is

$$\mathbf{P}\left[R_1 R_2\right] = \mathbf{P}\left[R_2|R_1\right]\mathbf{P}\left[R_1\right] = \left(\frac{4}{8}\right)\left(\frac{5}{9}\right) = \frac{5}{18}. \qquad \blacksquare$$

Example 1.34. Players A and B take turns rolling a die. The first to roll a 6 wins. A rolls first. What is the probability that B wins?

Solution. Let A and B the events that A wins and B wins, respectively. Let A_1 be the event that A wins on the first throw. If A does not win, B must win, and vice-versa. This implies that

$$1 = \mathbf{P}\left[A\right] + \mathbf{P}\left[B\right].$$

Because the players take turns, given that A does not win on the first throw, on B's first throw, she is in the same situation as A was in his first throw. In other words, $\mathbf{P}\left[B|A_1'\right] = \mathbf{P}\left[A\right]$. This motivates us to condition on A_1'

$$\begin{aligned} &= \mathbf{P}\left[A\right] + \mathbf{P}\left[B|A_1'\right]\mathbf{P}\left[A_1'\right] \\ &= \mathbf{P}\left[A\right] + \mathbf{P}\left[A\right]\mathbf{P}\left[A_4'\right] \\ &= \mathbf{P}\left[A\right]\left(1 + \mathbf{P}\left[A_1'\right]\right) \end{aligned}$$

so that

$$\mathbf{P}[A] = \frac{1}{1 + \mathbf{P}[A_1']} = \frac{6}{11}.$$

Finally,

$$\mathbf{P}[B] = 1 - \mathbf{P}[A] = \frac{5}{11}. \qquad \blacksquare$$

At this point, you might be wondering how we knew to condition, on which event to condition, and other similar questions. We found a *symmetry*. If a player is rolling the dice, he will either lose eventually, or win on this throw, on the next throw, or on the throw after that, and so on. This is true whether player A or B is currently throwing. Conditioning on A not winning in the first throw let us assume that B got a throw at all. The product rule let us escape the assumption that A did not win in the first throw, by multiplying by the probability that A did not win in the first throw.

The law of total probability is an important tool for calculating probabilities from conditional probabilities.

Theorem 1.35 (Law of Total Probability). *Let $\{B_i\}$ be a countable partition of the sample space Ω, and let A be an arbitrary event. Then*

$$\mathbf{P}[A] = \sum_{i=1}^{\infty} \mathbf{P}[A|B_i]\,\mathbf{P}[B_i]\,.$$

Proof. We can write

$$\begin{aligned} \mathbf{P}[A] &= \mathbf{P}[A \cap \Omega] \\ &= \mathbf{P}\left[A \cap \left(\bigcup_i B_i\right)\right] \\ &= \mathbf{P}\left[\bigcup_i (A \cap B_i)\right] \end{aligned}$$

Since the events B_i are disjoint, the events $A \cap B_i$ are disjoint, and

$$= \sum_{i=1}^{\infty} \mathbf{P}[A \cap B_i]$$
$$= \sum_{i=1}^{\infty} \mathbf{P}[A|B_i]\, \mathbf{P}[B_i]\,. \qquad \blacksquare$$

The law of total probability can help us calculate the probabilities for complex, multi-step experiments.

Example 1.36. Urn A contains 8 red balls and 6 black balls. Urn B contains 4 red balls and 10 black balls. A fair coin is tossed, and if it lands heads, a ball is drawn from urn A. Otherwise, a ball is drawn from urn B. What is the probability of drawing a red ball?

Solution. Let A represent the event that we draw from urn A, and let B represent the event that we draw from urn B. Finally, let R represent the event of drawing a red ball. By the law of total probability,

$$\begin{aligned}\mathbf{P}[R] &= \mathbf{P}[R|A]\,\mathbf{P}[A] + \mathbf{P}[R|B]\,\mathbf{P}[B] \\ &= \left(\frac{8}{14}\right)\left(\frac{1}{2}\right) + \left(\frac{4}{14}\right)\left(\frac{1}{2}\right) \\ &= \frac{3}{7}.\end{aligned} \qquad \blacksquare$$

The previous example would be very tedious to solve if we had to solve it by enumerating the sample space and calculating the probabilities of each of the events.

INDEPENDENCE

As we have seen, conditioning helps us quantify the effect of knowing that an event has occurred, by quantifying the dependence between events. Some events are made necessary by the occurrence of other events, and some are made impossible. But sometimes, an event reveals no information about another event. In these cases, we say that they are independent events.

Definition 1.37. The events A and B are *independent* if

$$\mathbf{P}[A|B] = \mathbf{P}[A] .$$

When events are independent, knowledge that one event has occurred does not affect the probability that the other has occurred. As a consequence of the definition of independence, we have

Theorem 1.38. *For independent events* A *and* B*,*

$$\mathbf{P}[AB] = \mathbf{P}[A]\,\mathbf{P}[B] .$$

Proof. By the product rule,

$$\mathbf{P}[A|B] = \frac{\mathbf{P}[AB]}{\mathbf{P}[B]} ,$$

so that, by independence, we can write

$$\mathbf{P}[A]\,\mathbf{P}[B] = \mathbf{P}[A|B]\,\mathbf{P}[B] = \mathbf{P}[AB] . \qquad \blacksquare$$

Example 1.39. Let $A \subset B$, and let $\mathbf{P}[B] \leq 1$. Can A and B be independent?

Solution. Suppose that A and B are independent. Then

$$\mathbf{P}[A] = \mathbf{P}[A|B] = \frac{\mathbf{P}[AB]}{\mathbf{P}[B]} = \frac{\mathbf{P}[A]}{\mathbf{P}[B]} .$$

On the other hand, since $\mathbf{P}[B] < 1$,

$$\mathbf{P}[A] \leq \frac{\mathbf{P}[A]}{\mathbf{P}[B]} ,$$

with equality if and only if $\mathbf{P}[A] = 0$. ■

Example 1.40. Due to physical considerations, we assume that the outcomes of distinct dice rolls are independent events. In particular, there is no known physical mechanism by which one dice roll can affect the outcome of the next. Indeed, independence is an extra-mathematical assumption about an experiment, which we model in terms of probabilities.

Example 1.41. The event of drawing a diamond from a deck of cards is independent of drawing a king. We can verify this directly. The probability of drawing a diamond is $13/52$, and the probability of drawing a king is $4/52$. The product of these probabilities is

$$\frac{13}{52} \times \frac{4}{52} = \frac{52}{52^2} = \frac{1}{52},$$

which we recognize as the probability of drawing the king of diamonds.

Example 1.42. A computer network is designed so that there are n links between the points A and B. The probability that a link will fail is $p = 0.05$, independently of the other link. The connection between A and B is broken if all of the links fail. It is found that the probability that the connection is not broken is 0.999875. What is n?

Solution. The probability that all of the links fail is $1 - 0.999875 = 0.000125$. Since the links fail independently, the probability that they all fail is p^n, so that $p^n = 0.000125$. We solve for n by taking logarithms[2]

$$n \log p = \log 0.000125,$$

so that $n = 3$. ■

In this last example, we assumed that the three computer links would fail independently of each other. The meaning of this statement seems intuitively obvious. We can easily imagine that there is no physical mechanism by which the failure of one link can cause the failure of another. But we have not defined independence for families of events in a mathematically rigorous fashion.

2 We follow Paul Halmos, Walter Rudin, and other modern mathematicians in denoting the natural logarithm by log instead of the perhaps more familiar ln. This notation is motivated by the 'usual' notation of $\log_b$ for the logarithm with base b. Since e is the 'natural' base for $\log_b$, it is natural to omit the base when it is e. This notation is common in real and complex analysis, as well as advanced probability theory.

Definition 1.43. A family $\mathcal{X}$ of events are *mutually independent* if for any subset $\mathcal{A} \subset \mathcal{X}$,

$$\mathbf{P}\left[\bigcap_{A \in \mathcal{A}} A\right] = \prod_{A \in \mathcal{A}} \mathbf{P}[A] .$$

Pairwise independence—that is, independence between all pairs of events—is not sufficient to guarantee mutual independence. It is straight-forward to construct a family of events that is pairwise independent but not mutually independent.

Example 1.44. A fair coin is flipped twice. Let A be the event of heads on the first flip, B be the event of heads on the second flip, and let C be the event that only one heads is flipped. A and B are clearly independent. We can show that A and C are independent, since

$$\mathbf{P}[A|C] = \frac{\mathbf{P}[AC]}{\mathbf{P}[C]} = \frac{\mathbf{P}[AB']}{\mathbf{P}[AB'] + \mathbf{P}[A'B]} = \frac{1}{2} = \mathbf{P}[A] .$$

A similar argument shows that B and C are independent. But

$$\mathbf{P}[ABC] = 0 \neq \mathbf{P}[A]\,\mathbf{P}[B]\,\mathbf{P}[C] .$$

BAYES THEOREM

We have discussed that the conditional probability of A given B quantifies the degree of dependence of A on B. We would like to see how this dependence relates to the dependence of B on A. Questions like these arise naturally in many circumstances, because the relationship can allow us to 'reverse engineer' an experiment to find the quantities we are really interested in.

Consider an experiment with measurement error. Suppose that we are interested in the result of a coin flip, but that our detector sometimes gives incorrect reports. If the coin flip is heads, then 90% of the time, the detector is right. If the coin flip is tails, then 85% of the time, the detector is right. If the detector reports a heads, what is the probability that a heads was actually flipped?

As we have seen, the conditional probability of A given B is defined as

$$\mathbf{P}[A|B] = \frac{\mathbf{P}[AB]}{\mathbf{P}[B]}$$

and the product rule lets us calculate

$$\mathbf{P}[AB] = \mathbf{P}[A|B]\,\mathbf{P}[B]\,.$$

But by symmetry, the product rule lets us calculate $\mathbf{P}[AB]$ as

$$\mathbf{P}[B|A]\,\mathbf{P}[A]\,,$$

so that

$$\mathbf{P}[A|B]\,\mathbf{P}[B] = \mathbf{P}[B|A]\,\mathbf{P}[A]$$

and

$$\mathbf{P}[B|A] = \frac{\mathbf{P}[A|B]\,\mathbf{P}[B]}{\mathbf{P}[A]}.$$

This is the most general form of *Bayes theorem.*

Example 1.45. The probability that a mathematics major graduates is 0.5. The probability that a student is a mathematics major is 0.1. The probability that a student graduates is 0.7. What is the probability that a student is a mathematics major, given that they graduated?

Solution. Let M be the event that a student is a mathematics major, and G be the event that a student graduates. We are given that

$$\mathbf{P}[M] = 0.1 \qquad \mathbf{P}[G] = 0.8 \qquad \mathbf{P}[G|M] = 0.5$$

We apply Bayes theorem, so that

$$\mathbf{P}[M|G] = \frac{\mathbf{P}[G|M]\,\mathbf{P}[M]}{\mathbf{P}[G]} = 6.25\%.$$

■

Bayes theorem is particularly powerful, and most commonly used, when combined with the law of total probability.

Example 1.46. Suppose that we are interested in the result of a coin flip, but that our detector sometimes gives incorrect reports. If the coin flip is heads, then 90% of the time, the detector is right. If the coin flip is tails, then 85% of the time, the detector is right. If the detector reports a heads, what is the probability that a heads was actually flipped?

Solution. Let H be the event that the coin flip was heads, and T be the event that the coin flip was tails. Let D_H be the event that the detector reports heads, and D_T be the event that the detector reports tails. We are given

$$\mathbf{P}\left[D_H|H\right] = 0.9 \qquad \mathbf{P}\left[H\right] = 0.5$$
$$\mathbf{P}\left[D_T|T\right] = 0.85 \qquad \mathbf{P}\left[T\right] = 0.5$$

We use Bayes theorem

$$\mathbf{P}\left[H|D_H\right] = \frac{\mathbf{P}\left[D_H|H\right]\mathbf{P}\left[H\right]}{\mathbf{P}\left[D_H\right]}$$

and the law of total probability

$$= \frac{\mathbf{P}\left[D_H|H\right]\mathbf{P}\left[H\right]}{\mathbf{P}\left[D_H|H\right]\mathbf{P}\left[H\right] + \mathbf{P}\left[D_H|T\right]\mathbf{P}\left[T\right]}.$$

We calculate $\mathbf{P}\left[D_H|T\right] = 1 - \mathbf{P}\left[D_T|T\right] = 0.15$, so that $\mathbf{P}\left[H|D_H\right] \approx 0.86$. ■

EXERCISES

1° At a certain company, the probability that an employee does not have life insurance, given that he has a pension plan, is 11/13. The probability that an employee does not have a pension plan, given that he has life insurance, is 7/9. If every employee has a pension plan, life insurance, or both, what is the probability that an employee has life insurance, given that they only have one product?

2° In a survey of 2250 people, it is found that

i. 1452 get news from the Internet.

ii. 1244 get news from television.

iii. 1291 get news from newspapers.

iv. 769 get news from both the Internet and newspapers.

v. 606 gets news from both television and newspapers.

vi. 276 get news only from television.

vii. 281 get news from all three.

What is the probability that an Internet user gets the news from exactly two sources?

3° Kelly and Jerome are playing ping pong. If Kelly serves, the probability that she will serve next is $3/4$. If Jerome serves, the probability that he will have the next serve is $2/3$. Jerome serves first. What is the probability that Jerome will have the fourth serve?

4° Sunny days are forecast with probability 30% and cloudy days are forecast on the rest of the days. Forecasts are estimated to be correct 70% of the time. A pale man puts is concerned about his exposure to UV rays, and puts on sun block every day it is forecast to be sunny. He also flips a coin to decide if he will put on sunblock when it is forecast to be cloudy. What is the probability that he man does not wear sunblock during a sunny day?

5° Suppose that A and B are independent, and that $\mathbf{P}[A] = 0.3$ and $\mathbf{P}[A \cup B] = 0.8$. What is $\mathbf{P}[B]$?

6° The events A, B, and C are independent with $\mathbf{P}[A] = 0.3$, $\mathbf{P}[B] = 0.4$, and $\mathbf{P}[C] = 0.5$. What is the probability that exactly two of the events A, B, and C will occur?

7° Given $\mathbf{P}[A|B] = 0.5$, $\mathbf{P}[B|A] = 0.4$, and $\mathbf{P}[A] + \mathbf{P}[B] = 0.5$, find $\mathbf{P}[A]$.

8° An aeronautics company tests each component it makes three times. The probability that a component passes the first test is 90%. The probability that it passes the second test, given that it passes the first, is 95%, and the probability that it passes the third test given that it passes the first two is 98%.

What is the probability that a component fails the second test, given that it fails at all?

9° A home insurance has low-risk, medium-risk, and high-risk clients, who respectively have probabilities 0.00125, 0.01, and 0.03 of filing a claim. 65% of the clients are low-risk, 25% are medium-risk, and the rest are high-risk. What percentage of claims are filed by high-risk clients?

10° An analyst classifies accidents into low severity, medium severity, and high severity accidents, and finds that the probability of a hospitalization after a low severity accident is 10%, the probability of a hospitalization after a medium severity accident is 30%, and the probability of a hospitalization after a high severity accident is 95%. The probability that an accident is low severity is 65%. The probability that an accident is medium severity is 25%. The probability that an accident is high severity is 10%.

Given that no hospitalization occurred, what is the probability that the accident was medium severity?

SOLUTIONS

1° Let P be the event of having a pension plan, and let L represent having life insurance. We draw the diagram

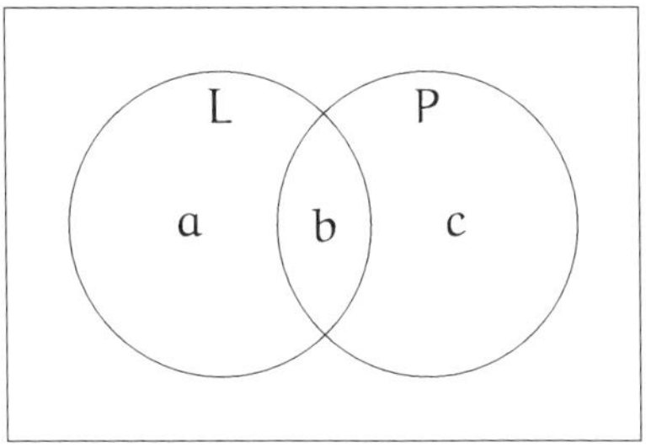

We are given that

$$\mathbf{P}\left[L'|P\right] = \frac{11}{13} = \frac{c}{b+c},$$

which implies that

$$11b + 11c = 13c$$
$$\frac{11}{2}b = c$$

Similarly, we are given

$$\mathbf{P}\left[P'|L\right] = \frac{7}{9} = \frac{a}{a+b},$$

which implies that

$$7a + 7b = 9a$$
$$\frac{7}{2}b = a.$$

Since each employee has at least one product,

$$1 = \mathbf{P}\left[L \cup P\right] = a + b + c = \frac{7}{2}b + b + \frac{11}{2}b.$$

We solve for $b = 0.1$, $a = 0.35$, and $c = 0.55$. Finally, the probability we seek is

$$\mathbf{P}\left[LP' | LP' \cup L'P\right] = \frac{a}{a+c} = 0.3889.$$

2° Draw the Venn diagram, and fill it in.

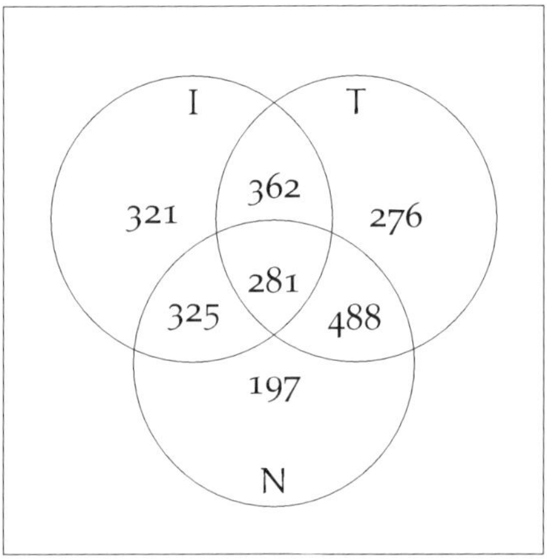

From (vii), we see that the triple intersection contains 281. From (vii.) and (iv), we see that 488 use the Internet and news papers, but not television. From (vii) and (v), we see that 325 get the news from only television and news papers. From (vi), we see that 276 get the news only from television, and from ii, we see that 362 use television and the Internet alone. The probability we seek is $(488 + 362)/1452 \approx 0.59$.

3° Perhaps the most straight-forward way to solve this problem is to draw the tree diagram to systematically enumerate the events.

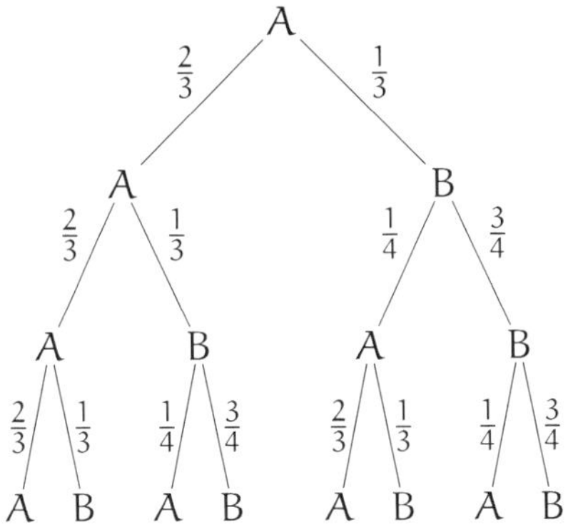

We can calculate

$$\mathbf{P}[A_4] = \left(\frac{2}{3}\right)^3 + 2\left(\frac{2}{3}\right)\left(\frac{1}{3}\right)\left(\frac{1}{4}\right) + \left(\frac{1}{3}\right)\left(\frac{3}{4}\right)\left(\frac{1}{4}\right) \approx 0.47.$$

4° Since the man wears sunblock every day that sun is forecast, it is only possible for him to not wear sunblock during a sunny day if a cloudy day is forecast, and the forecast is wrong. Symbolically, let S be the event that it is a sunny day, let F be the event that a sunny day was forecast, and let B be the event that the man is wearing sunblock. Note that S and B are conditionally independent, since, conditional on F, the man flips a coin to decide whether to wear sunblock. Then

$$\begin{aligned}\mathbf{P}[SB'] &= \mathbf{P}[SB'F] + \mathbf{P}[SB'F'] \\ &= \mathbf{P}[SB'F'] \\ &= \mathbf{P}[SB'|F']\,\mathbf{P}[F'] \\ &= \mathbf{P}[S|F']\,\mathbf{P}[B'|F']\,\mathbf{P}[F'] \\ &= 0.105.\end{aligned}$$

5° We write

$$\begin{aligned}\mathbf{P}[A \cup B] &= \mathbf{P}[A] + \mathbf{P}[B] - \mathbf{P}[AB] \\ &= \mathbf{P}[A] + \mathbf{P}[B] - \mathbf{P}[A]\,\mathbf{P}[B] \\ &= \mathbf{P}[A] + \mathbf{P}[B]\,(1 - \mathbf{P}[A])\end{aligned}$$

so that

$$\mathbf{P}[B] = \frac{\mathbf{P}[A \cup B] - \mathbf{P}[A]}{1 - \mathbf{P}[A]} \approx 0.714.$$

6° We seek the probability

$$\mathbf{P}[ABC' \cup AB'C \cup A'BC]\,.$$

Perhaps the easiest way to find an easy to calculate expression for this probability is to draw the Venn diagram for the event $ABC' \cup AB'C \cup A'BC$.

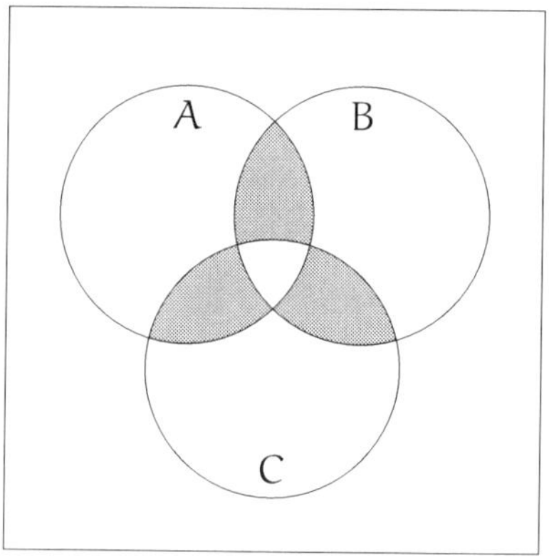

Based on this diagram, we see that the probability we seek is

$$\begin{aligned}&(\mathbf{P}[AB] - \mathbf{P}[ABC]) + (\mathbf{P}[BC] - \mathbf{P}[ABC]) + (\mathbf{P}[CA] - \mathbf{P}[ABC]) \\ &\quad = \mathbf{P}[AB] + \mathbf{P}[BC] + \mathbf{P}[CA] - 3\mathbf{P}[ABC] \\ &\quad = 0.29.\end{aligned}$$

7° We have

$$\mathbf{P}[A|B]\,\mathbf{P}[B] = \mathbf{P}[AB] = \mathbf{P}[B|A]\,\mathbf{P}[A],$$

so that

$$0.5\mathbf{P}[B] = \mathbf{P}[AB] = 0.4\mathbf{P}[A]$$

and

$$\mathbf{P}[B] = 0.8\mathbf{P}[A].$$

We now substitute and simplify

$$\begin{aligned} 0.5 &= \mathbf{P}[A] + \mathbf{P}[B] \\ &= \mathbf{P}[A] + 0.8\mathbf{P}[A] \\ &= 1.8\mathbf{P}[A], \end{aligned}$$

so that $\mathbf{P}[A] = 0.278$.

8° Let A denote the event that a component passes the first test, B denote the event that it passes the second test, and C denote the event that it passes the third test. Finally, let F be the event $A' \cup B' \cup C'$ – the event that the component fails some test. We begin by calculating

$$\mathbf{P}[B'|A] = 1 - \mathbf{P}[B|A] = 0.05,$$

which implies that

$$\mathbf{P}[B'A] = \mathbf{P}[B'|A]\,\mathbf{P}[A] = 0.045.$$

Now we calculate

$$\mathbf{P}[F] = 1 - \mathbf{P}[C|AB]\,\mathbf{P}[B|A]\,\mathbf{P}[A] = 0.1621.$$

Finally, we calculate

$$\mathbf{P}[B'A|F] = \frac{\mathbf{P}[B'AF]}{\mathbf{P}[F]} \approx 0.278.$$

9° We must calculate $\mathbf{P}[H|C]$. We summarize the data we are given as

$$\mathbf{P}[C|L] = 0.00125 \qquad \mathbf{P}[L] = 0.65$$
$$\mathbf{P}[C|M] = 0.01 \qquad \mathbf{P}[M] = 0.25$$
$$\mathbf{P}[C|H] = 0.03 \qquad \mathbf{P}[H] = 0.1$$

We apply Bayes theorem to calculate

$$\mathbf{P}[H|C] = \frac{\mathbf{P}[C|H]\,\mathbf{P}[H]}{\mathbf{P}[C|H]\,\mathbf{P}[H] + \mathbf{P}[C|M]\,\mathbf{P}[M] + \mathbf{P}[C|L]\,\mathbf{P}[L]} = 0.475.$$

10° Let L represent a low severity accident, M represent a medium severity accident, and S denote a high severity accident. Finally, let H represent a hospitalization. We are given the data:

$$\mathbf{P}[H|L] = 0.1 \qquad \mathbf{P}[L] = 0.65 \qquad \mathbf{P}[H'|L] = 0.9$$
$$\mathbf{P}[H|M] = 0.3 \qquad \mathbf{P}[M] = 0.25 \qquad \mathbf{P}[H'|M] = 0.7$$
$$\mathbf{P}[H|S] = 0.95 \qquad \mathbf{P}[S] = 0.1 \qquad \mathbf{P}[H'|S] = 0.05$$

We apply Bayes theorem to find

$$\begin{aligned}\mathbf{P}[M|H'] &= \frac{\mathbf{P}[H'|M]\,\mathbf{P}[M]}{\mathbf{P}[H'|L]\,\mathbf{P}[L] + \mathbf{P}[H'|M]\,\mathbf{P}[M] + \mathbf{P}[H'|S]\,\mathbf{P}[S]} \\ &= \frac{0.7 \times 0.25}{0.9 \times 0.65 + 0.7 \times 0.25 + 0.05 \times 0.1} \\ &= 0.22875\end{aligned}$$

2

COMBINATORIAL PROBABILITY

In chapter 1, we focused mainly on calculating the probabilities of events in terms of the probabilities of other events. In this chapter, we introduce *combinatorial probability*, which we can think of as the theory of calculating probabilities by counting. When combinatorial probability is applicable, it lets us calculate the probabilities of events directly, by counting the elements in an event, and dividing by the number of elements in the sample space. Of course, this procedure is only valid when each outcome for an experiment is equally likely. All of the results from chapter 1 remain valid, and will still be useful to us for calculating the probabilities of complex events, given that we can calculate the probabilities of simpler events using combinatorial methods. We will begin by formalizing this discussion.

Definition 2.1. Suppose that we are calculating the probability of an event A. An outcome ω is *admissible* if $\omega \in A$.

Definition 2.2. Let A be an event with finitely many elements. Its *cardinality* $|A|$ is the number of elements in A.

Definition 2.3. If the sample space Ω has finite cardinality, and each outcome is equally likely, then the probability that an event A occurs is

$$\mathbf{P}[A] = \frac{|A|}{|\Omega|}.$$

COUNTING PRINCIPLES

This and the following sections are meant to be an introduction to basic combinatorial analysis. We begin by introducing various counting principle, and use them to count the number of various kinds of mathematical objects. For the purposes of the exam, it is important to understand *both* the formulas we derive, and the techniques we used to derive them. Problems in combinatorics can always be made harder, by adding a twist. Only the careful use of the counting principles can let us combine the tools we will learn into a solution.

Definition 2.4 (Addition Principle)**.** For disjoint, finite events A and B, $|A \cup B| = |A| + |B|$.

There is a strong tradition of using the language of choices to express these principles. For disjoint A and B, if we can choose from A in $|A|$ ways or choose from B in $|B|$ ways, then we can choose from $A \cup B$ in $|A| + |B|$ ways.

Example 2.5. A French restaurant has 12 choices for an entrée, and an Indian restaurant has 8 choices for an entrée. None of the entres are served at both restaurants. How many entres can you choose from if you must choose between the French and Indian restaurants?

Solution. Let F be the set of entres we may choose from if we go to the French restaurant, and let I be the entres we may choose from if we go to the Indian restaurant. Then $|F \cup I| = |F| + |I| = 20$. ■

Definition 2.6 (Multiplication Principle)**.** For finite events A and B, the cardinality of

$$A \times B = \{(a, b) \colon a \in A, b \in B\}$$

is $|A \times B| = |A| \times |B|$.

Recall that the event $A \times B$ is called the *Cartesian product* of A and B. We can cast this principle in terms of choices, as well. If we must make a sequence of choices, by choosing an element of A, and then an element of B, then there are $|A| \times |B|$ ways of making the sequence of choices.

Example 2.7. A French restaurant offers a special that lets you choose any entre for each of two courses. They serve you your first choice, and then, when you are done, they serve you your second choice. They offer 12 different entres. In how many ways can you choose your meal?

Solution. We see that we must make two choices. We may choose from any of the 12 entres in our first choice, and we may choose from any of the 12 for our second choice. The multiplication principle implies that there are 144 ways to choose your meal. ■

Example 2.8. Two fair dice are thrown. Let $p(k)$ be the probability that the sum of their face values is k. Find an expression for $p(k)$.

Solution. We begin by enumerating the possible rolls and values for k.

	1	2	3	4	5	6
1	7	8	9	10	11	12
2	6	7	8	9	10	11
3	5	6	7	8	9	10
4	4	5	6	7	8	9
5	3	4	5	6	7	8
6	2	3	4	5	6	7

We see that there are 6 ways to roll 7, and that there are 5 ways to roll 6, and 4 ways to roll 5, and so on. In fact, if $k \leq 7$, there are $k-1$ ways to roll k. By symmetry, if $k > 7$, there are $13-k$ ways to roll k. We see there are 36 equally probable dice rolls, so that

$$p(k) = \begin{cases} \frac{k-1}{36}, & \text{if } k \leq 7 \\ \frac{13-k}{36}, & \text{if } k > 7. \end{cases}$$ ■

We have another principle we would like to introduce, but is not a mathematical statement. It is an observation, and a warning to be careful. The *Consequence Principle* is that *choices may have consequences*. A choice you make can limit, or expand, your later options. In order to count your options when a choice can limit later options, count the options under each choice with consequences, and add the number of options together.

Example 2.9. A French restaurant offers 12 choices for an entre, and offers a special that lets you choose distinct entres for each of two courses. An Indian restaurant offers 8 entres, and has a special that lets you choose any entre for each of two courses. In how many ways can you buy a special?

Solution. We must make two choices in succession, and each of them has consequences. First, we must choose which restaurant to go to and then we must choose our entres. Let F be the meals you can order if you go to the French restaurant, and let I be the meals you can order if you go to the Indian restaurant.

If you go to the French restaurant, you can choose your first course in any of 12 ways. Since the choices must be distinct, you can choose your second course in any of 11 ways. By the multiplication principle, $|F| = 132$.

If you go to the Indian restaurant, you can choose your first course in any of 8 ways. The Indian restaurant does not require that both courses are distinct, so you can order your second course in 8 ways. By the multiplication principle, $|I| = 64$.

The total number of meals we can choose from, then, is $|F \cup I| = |F| + |I| = 196$. ■

Theorem 2.10 (Inclusion-Exclusion Principle). *Given sets finite sets* A *and* B,

$$|A \cup B| = |A| + |B| - |AB|.$$

We have already seen a very similar result, when we proved the addition rule for probabilities. Most generally, the inclusion-exclusion principle applies to measures of all kinds. When we proved it previously, we proved it for all probability measures. Now, we prove it for the counting measure $|\cdot|$. However, we will do it in a combinatorial style.

Proof. Let A and B be finite sets. We estimate that $|A \cup B| \leq |A| + |B|$. However, this is an over-estimate, since if A and B are not disjoint, the elements of $A \cap B$ are counted twice. This implies that $|A \cup B| = |A| + |B| - |AB|$. ■

Definition 2.11. A function f is an *injection* if $f(x) = f(y)$ implies that $x = y$. When f is an injection from A to B, we say that f is a function from A *into* B. A function $f\colon A \to B$ is a *surjection* if for each $b \in B$, there is an $a \in A$ such that $f(a) = b$. If f is a surjection, we say that it is a function from A *onto* B. A *bijection* is a function f that is both an injection and a surjection.

Example 2.12. It is a basic result that a function is a bijection if and only if it is invertible.

Definition 2.13 (The Equality Principle). If there is a bijection between the elements of A and the elements of B, then $|A| = |B|$.

PERMUTATIONS AND COMBINATIONS

Definition 2.14. A *permutation* of a finite set A an ordered arrangement of the elements of A.

In other words, a permutation is a sequence that contains each element of A exactly once. It is straight-forward to show that there is a bijection between the set of permutations of A and the space of bijections of A to A. The bijection between the permutations on A and the space of bijections of A to A is very natural, and other texts—especially those on algebra—define a permutation on A as a bijection from A to itself. The intuition behind this correspondence is straight-forward. If a function f is a bijection from A into itself, then the only thing it can 'do' is re-arrange elements of A.

Theorem 2.15. *There is a bijection between the set of permutations of A and the set of bijections from A to A.*

Proof. We define a bijection f as the function which maps a_1 to a_2, a_2 to a_3, …, $a_{|A|}$ to a_1. f is clearly injective and surjective, so it is a bijection. Given a bijection f, we can recover a permutation by beginning at a value a_1 and sequentially calculating its image under f, thereby defining $a_i = f^{i-1}(a_1)$. We can define $\pi = (a_1, a_2, \ldots, a_{|A|})$.

We will now show that π is a permutation by showing that each element is distinct. Suppose $a_i = a_j$, and suppose, without loss of generality, that $i \leq j$. We can write $f^{i-1}(a_1) = f^{j-1}(a_1) = \left(f^{j-i} \circ f^{i-1}\right)(a_1)$, so that $f^{j-i} = f^0$ and $i = j$. Since there are $|A|$ distinct elements listed in $pi = \left(a_1, a_2, \ldots, a_{|A|}\right)$, π is a permutation. ■

This proof shows something stronger than what we initially claimed. In effect, we can translate between permutations and bijections seamlessly, so that they are essentially different ways to look at the same kind of mathematical object.

Example 2.16. In a major company, the 12 department heads are to be re-assigned to the company's 12 departments. In how many ways can they be assigned?

Solution. We can imagine placing the 12 department heads into a line, and assigning them to a department, one by one. There are 12 possible departments for the first department head, 11 for the second department head, and so on, until there is only one choice for the 12th department head. The multiplication principle implies that there are 12! permutations of the department heads. ■

Theorem 2.17. *In general, there are $n!$ permutations for a set with n elements.*

Proof. Let A be a set with $|A| = n$. We will count the number of ways to construct a permutation, as a sequence. There are n choices for the element a_1, $n-1$ choices for the element a_2, and so on, until there is 1 choice for the a_n. The multiplication principle implies that there are $n(n-1)(n-2)\cdots 1$ ways to construct the sequence. ■

Definition 2.18. Let A be a finite set. A k-*permutation*, or a *permutation of* A *taken* k *at a time*, of a is an ordered listing of k elements of A.

Theorem 2.19. *Let* A *be a set with* $|A| = n$. *The number* $P(n, k)$ *of* k-*permutations of* A *is*

$$n \times (n-1) \times \cdots \times (n-k+1).$$

Proof. We can prove this directly by applying the multiplication principle, but there is a more fruitful way. Notice that a k-permutation on A is a sequence of k elements selected from A. Given a k-permutation, we can turn it into a permutation on A by arranging the remaining $(n-k)$ elements after the first k. There are $(n-k)!$ permutations of the $(n-k)$ elements. Since there are $n!$ permutations of A, and for each k-permutation there are $(n-k)!$ permutations of A that agree with it on the first k elements, there are

$$\frac{n!}{(n-k)!}$$

k-permutations of A. ∎

This proof illustrates the

Definition 2.20 (Division Principle)**.** If for each element of A there are k elements of B, then

$$|A| = \frac{|B|}{k}.$$

Definition 2.21. Let A be a finite set. A *combination* is an unordered listing of the elements of A.

The fact that a combination is an unordered listing means that, although we might make the listing in some order, the order in which we make it is irrelevant. Listings of the same elements are considered to be the same combination if they merely differ in their order. A combination of elements of A is naturally modeled as a subset of A, since sets the equality of sets only depends on their elements, not the order in which they are written.

Theorem 2.22. *Let A be a set with $|A| = n$. There are*

$$\frac{n!}{k!(n-k)!}$$

subsets of A with exactly k elements.

Proof. Consider that there are $P(n, k)$ k-permutations of A. Pick a k-permutation. Its elements define a combination. On the other hand, a rearrangement of the k-permutation results in a new k-permutation, but results in the same combination. In particular, for each combination, there are $k!$ equivalent k-permutations. The division principle implies that there are

$$\frac{P(n,k)}{k!} = \frac{n!}{k!(n-k)!}$$

combinations. ■

Definition 2.23. The quantity

$$\binom{n}{k} = \frac{n!}{k!(n-k)!}$$

is called a *binomial coefficient*.

Example 2.24. 100 senators will vote on an important bill. Assuming all outcomes occur with equal probability, what is the probability that exactly 51 of them will vote for the bill?

Solution. Each senator will choose to vote for or against. The multiplication principle implies that there are a total of 2^{100} ways in which the senators can cast their votes. On the other hand, the admissible outcomes are those when exactly 51 of the senators vote for the bill. We count these outcomes by counting the number of subsets with exactly 51 elements. The probability we seek is

$$\frac{\binom{100}{51}}{2^{100}} = 0.078.$$ ■

Example 2.25. In how many ways can a committee of 2 language professors, 2 science professors, and 2 art professors be selected if there are 8 language professors, 12 science professors, and 6 art professors?

Solution. We can choose the language professors in $\binom{8}{2}$ ways, the science professors in $\binom{12}{2}$ ways, and the art professors in $\binom{6}{2}$ ways. ■

Example 2.26. Suppose that a jar contains r red balls and b black balls. If we draw n balls without replacement, what is the probability p_k that we draw k red balls?

Solution. We can select n balls from the jar in

$$\binom{r+b}{n}$$

ways. Now we will count the admissible outcomes. There are $\binom{r}{k}$ ways to choose k red balls, and there are $\binom{b}{n-k}$ ways to choose the black balls. The multiplication principle implies that there are $\binom{r}{k}\binom{b}{n-k}$ to choose k red balls and $n-k$ black balls, so that

$$p_k = \frac{\binom{r}{k}\binom{b}{n-k}}{\binom{r+b}{n}}.$$ ■

The probabilities p_k define the *hypergeometric distribution*.

Example 2.27. Five cards are drawn from a standard deck of 52 cards. What is the probability of drawing exactly 4 hearts?

Solution. There are 13 hearts in a standard deck of cards, and 39 cards belong to other suits. We can choose 4 hearts from the 13 hearts in $\binom{13}{4}$ ways, and we can choose the last card in $\binom{39}{1}$ ways. Finally, we can draw 5 cards from a standard deck in $\binom{52}{5}$ ways, so that the probability we seek is

$$\frac{\binom{13}{4}\binom{39}{1}}{\binom{52}{5}} \approx 1.1\%.$$ ■

Example 2.28. Five cards are drawn from a standard deck of 52 cards. What is the probability that we draw at least one card from each suit?

Solution. Since there are 4 suits, and we are drawing 5 cards, there will be two cards from a certain suit and one card from each of the other suits in an admissible hand. We will call the suit with two cards in the hand 'special'. For concreteness, we assume that hearts is special. Then there are

$$\binom{13}{2}\binom{13}{1}^3$$

hands with 2 hearts and 1 of each of the other suits. By symmetry, this implies that there are

$$\binom{13}{2}\binom{13}{1}^3$$

admissible hands for each suit, since each suit can be special. In total, there are

$$4\binom{13}{2}\binom{13}{1}^3$$

admissible hands, so that the probability is

$$\frac{4\binom{13}{2}\binom{13}{1}^3}{\binom{52}{5}} \approx 0.2638. \qquad \blacksquare$$

So far, when we have considered permutations, we have treated the elements of A as *distinguishable.* This is to say that each element has an identity of its own, and if any pair of elements are interchanged, the resulting permutation is distinct from the original. The assumption that the objects are distinguishable makes sense, for example, when people are involved. Tom, Fred, and Jerry may get into a line in that order, but if there are only two prizes waiting for them, it certainly matters to Fred and Jerry who is second in line. On the other hand, consider counting the number of arrangements of red and black balls. If we interchange two red balls, and leave the others untouched, the arrangement of colored balls is the same as it was before the balls were moved.

We use the division principle to solve the

Example 2.29 (MISSISSIPPI Problem). In how many distinguishable ways can the letters of the word 'MISSISSIPPI' be rearranged?

The point of the example is that because some of the objects are indistinguishable, there are fewer distinguishable ways to arrange them. An arrangement of letters is distinguishable from another one when we can tell the difference between them. But, for example, the first S is indistinguishable from the third.

Solution. We see that the word MISSISSIPPI contains 11 letters, and that there are 11! permutations of the letters if we treat them as distinguishable. On the other hand, for each permutation of the 11 letters, since there are 4 S's, there are 4! permutations move that S's to S's, while leaving everything else fixed. Similarly, there are 4! permutations that move the I's to I's, while leaving everything else fixed, 2! permutations that move P's to P's, and 1 permutation that moves M to M. The division principle implies that there are

$$\frac{11!}{4!4!2!1!} = 34,650$$

distinguishable ways to rearrange the letters. ■

In general, if there are k kinds of indistinguishable objects, and the ith kind has r_i members, there are

$$\frac{(r_1 + r_2 + \cdots + r_k)!}{r_1!r_2!\cdots r_k!}$$

ways to arrange them.

Definition 2.30. The quantity

$$\binom{r_1 + r_2 + \cdots + r_k}{r_1, r_2, \cdots, r_k} = \frac{(r_1 + r_2 + \cdots r_k)!}{r_1!r_2!\cdots r_k!}$$

is called a *multinomial coefficient*.

We see that the binomial coefficient is a special case of the multinomial coefficient, and we can re-interpret the act of choosing elements in terms of distinguishable permutations. In particular, the choice of k elements from n elements is formally equivalent to assigning to each member one of k indistinguishable objects of one kind or $n-k$ indistinguishable objects of another. For example, we can choose k members for a committee from n people by assigning to each person one of k indistinguishable red balls or $n-k$ indistinguishable black balls.

We can also consider arrangements of objects around a circle, such as, for example, people around a circular table or beads on a necklace.

Definition 2.31. An arrangement of objects around a circle is called a *circular permutation*.

Because of the circular symmetry, we are not interested in the absolute positions of people or beads, but their relationships with each other. Given that there are n people to be seated in n seats, we seat them by choosing one of the n seats as our starting point. Given that we choose a starting point, we can arrange the n people in $n!$ ways. But arrangements that differ only in their starting point are considered equivalent. This implies that there are $(n-1)!$ circular arrangements of distinguishable objects. We have proved

Theorem 2.32. *There are* $(n-1)!$ *circular permutations of distinguishable objects.*

Similarly, we can count circular arrangements of indistinguishable objects. In general,

Theorem 2.33. *If there are* k *kinds of indistinguishable objects, and each kind has* r_i *objects, the objects can be arranged around a circle in*

$$\frac{(r_1 + r_2 + \cdots + r_k - 1)!}{r_1! \cdot r_2! \cdots r_k!}$$

ways.

Example 2.34. A jeweler has 8 diamonds, 10 emeralds, and 12 rubies. Each of these is mounted on a in such a way that they can only face one way. If all the stones must be used, in how many ways can they be arranged in a row on a necklace?

Solution. Because the stones can only face one way, the number of circular permutations is

$$\frac{29!}{12!10!8!}.$$

■

EXERCISES

1° A fair die is rolled twice. Given that the first roll is odd, what is the probability that the sum of the outcomes is 7?

2° Cards are drawn from a deck of cards until an ace is drawn. What is the probability that it takes more than 13 draws?

3° An unfair coin is tossed repeatedly. The probability that it lands heads is 0.55. What is the probability that the fifth head occurs on the eighth toss?

4° In a large company, 5 departments require 5 employees each. In how many ways can the 25 new hires be assigned to the five departments?

5° A box contains 8 green balls, 5 red balls, and 7 black balls. 3 balls are selected at random, without replacement. What is the probability that they are the same color?

6° Let $S_0 = \{1, 2, \ldots, 9\}$. Count the number of different sequences of sets $S_1, S_2, \ldots, S_5$ such that

$$S_5 \subset S_4 \subset S_3 \subset S_2 \subset S_1 \subset S_0.$$

7° An urn contains 24 red balls and 48 black balls. What is the probability that the first red ball drawn is the 8th ball drawn?

8° Six squares are chosen at random from a 5 by 5 grid of squares by throwing stones at the grid. What is the probability that exactly one column and one row contains two stones?

9° On an 8 by 8 chessboard, what is the probability that a randomly chosen rectangle is a square?

10° A fruit cart had 10 apples this morning, 2 of which have worms. When you arrive, 4 apples remain unsold. You select one at random. What is the probability that it has a worm?

11° 8 people, including one couple, are invited to a party. All of them will come, except for possibly one person, who will flip a coin to decide. At the party, everybody is seated around a circular table at random. What is the probability that the couple will sit together?

SOLUTIONS

1° Let A be the event that the first roll is odd. Then, we write A as

$$A = \{(x,y)\colon x \in \{1,3,5\}, y \in \{1,2,3,4,5,6\}\}$$

We see that, by the multiplication principle, $|A| = 18$. Let B be the event that the sum of the outcomes is 7. We write B as

$$B = \{(1,6),(2,5),(3,4),(4,3),(5,2),(6,1)\}.$$

Then

$$A \cap B = \{(1,6),(3,4),(5,2)\},$$

and $|A \cap B| = 3$. Finally, we see that

$$\mathbf{P}[B|A] = \frac{|A \cap B|}{|A|} = \frac{1}{6}.$$

2° A sequence of draws is admissible if no ace is drawn in the first 13 draws, so we will count the number of ways to draw 13 cards without drawing an ace. Since there are 4 aces, we can choose any 13 of 48 cards. This implies that there are $\binom{48}{13}$ admissible outcomes. On the other hand, there are $\binom{52}{13}$ ways to draw 13 cards from the deck. This implies the probability we seek is

$$\frac{\binom{48}{13}}{\binom{52}{13}} \approx 0.3038.$$

3° A sequence of tosses is admissible if the firth head occurs on the 8th toss. This implies that the 8th toss must be heads, an event that occurs with probability 0.55 independently of the other tosses. Since it is the fifth head to occur, we must calculate the probability that 4 heads occur in the first 7 tosses. We calculate that the probability that the first four tosses are heads and the last three are tails is $p^4(1-p)^3$. Since heads are indistinguishable, there are $\binom{7}{4}$ in distinguishable arrangements of the heads, each occurring with the same probability. This implies that the probability four heads occur in the first seven tosses is

$$\binom{7}{4} p^4(1-p)^3,$$

so that the probability that the fifth head occurs on the 8th toss is

$$\binom{7}{4} p^5(1-p)^3 = 0.1605.$$

4° Arrange the departments into a line into a line. This can be achieved in 5! ways. The first department's employees can be selected in $\binom{25}{5}$ ways. Given that this selection is made, the second department's employees can be selected in $\binom{20}{5}$ ways. Similarly, the third department's employees can be selected in $\binom{15}{5}$ ways and the fourth's department's employees can be selected in $\binom{10}{5}$ ways. The fifth department's employees are determined by the first four assignments. Since there are 5! ways to order the departments, the number of ways to assign employees to departments is

$$\frac{\binom{25}{5}\binom{20}{5}\binom{15}{5}\binom{10}{5}}{5!} = \frac{25!}{(5!)^6}.$$

5° The events that the balls are all the same colors are mutually exclusive, so we can add their probabilities. The probability is

$$\frac{\binom{8}{3}\binom{5}{0}\binom{7}{0}+\binom{5}{3}\binom{8}{0}\binom{7}{0}+\binom{7}{3}\binom{8}{0}\binom{5}{0}}{\binom{20}{3}}=\frac{\binom{8}{3}+\binom{5}{3}+\binom{7}{3}}{\binom{20}{3}},$$

which is approximately 0.0886.

6° Any increasing sequence of subsets can be constructed by starting with the sequence

$$\emptyset \subset \emptyset \subset \emptyset \subset \emptyset \subset \emptyset \subset S_0$$

and adding an element s to the last n_s subsets. As a result, for each element $s \in S_0$, we can choose n_s in 6 ways. The choice of n_s represents the smallest n subset in which s appears. There are 9 elements in S_0, so there answer is $6^9 = 10077696$.

7° Let $r = 24$ be the number of red balls and $b = 48$ be the number of black balls. We can interpret the experiment in terms of placing the $r + b$ balls in a random order, while treating the red balls as indistinguishable and the black balls as indistinguishable. The total number T of orders is

$$\frac{(b+r)!}{b!r!}=\binom{b+r}{r}.$$

The number A of ways of placing the balls so that the first k are black and the next one is red is the same as the number of ways of placing the red balls so that the first one is in position $(k+1)$ and the rest are in later positions. That number is

$$\binom{r+b-(k+1)}{r-1}.$$

We calculate the probability as the ratio $\frac{A}{T}$. We calculate the numerical value as 0.0185, being careful to set $k = 7$.

8° The event that exactly one column and one column and one row contain two stones is guaranteed to occur if, after the fifth row, no column or row contains more than one stone. We call such an arrangement admissible.

We calculate the probability by counting the admissible arrangements and dividing by the number of possible arrangements.

For an arrangement to be admissible, the first throw can land in any of the 25 squares. It determines a column and a row that the other throws may not land on. In particular, the next throw can land on any of 16 squares. In general, the k-th throw can land on any of $(6-k)^2$ squares. We see that there are $25 \times 16 \times 9 \times 4 \times 1 = 14400$ admissible arrangements.

On the other hand, we can count the total number of arrangements by noting that each stone may land in any of the 25 squares, so that there are 25^6 arrangements.

The probability of an admissible arrangement is approximately 0.00147.

9° We will calculate this probability using the usual technique of combinatorial probability: we count the squares and divide by the number of rectangles. The difficulty is finding the number of squares and rectangles.

We will begin by counting the squares. Consider a 1 by 1 square, placed at the top left corner. We can move it to other positions by shifting it downwards to any of 8 positions and rightwards to any of 8 positions, including leaving it where it is. This means there are 8^2 positions for the 1 by 1 square.

Similarly, consider a 2 by 2 square placed at the top left corner. We can move it to other positions by shifting it downwards to up to 7 squares and shifting it rightward by up to 7 squares, including leaving it where it is. This means there are 7^2 squares that can be placed in the top corner of the board by shifting.

In general, for a k by k square, there are $(9-k)^2$ positions in which it can be placed. Equivalently, there are $(9-k)^2$ squares that can be shifted to the top left corner of the board. This implies that there are

$$8^2 + 7^2 + 6^2 + 5^2 + 4^2 + 3^2 + 2^2 + 1^2 = 204$$

squares. We will now count the rectangles. A rectangle is determined by two dimensions. In particular, the choice of any two positions on the chessboard determines a rectangle, by determining a top left corner and a bottom right corner. There are $\binom{64}{1} = 64$ choices for the first square and, similarly, 64 choices for the second square, for a total of 64^2 rectangles. The probability of choosing a square is

$$\frac{204}{64^2} \approx 0.0498$$

10° Let S_k be the event that k apples with worms have sold before you arrive. Let W be the event that you buy an apple with a worm. By the law of total probability,

$$\mathbf{P}[W] = \mathbf{P}[W|S_0]\,\mathbf{P}[S_0] + \mathbf{P}[W|S_1]\,\mathbf{P}[S_1] + \mathbf{P}[W|S_2]\,\mathbf{P}[S_2]\,.$$

In general, the probability that k wormy apples are sold is

$$\mathbf{P}[S_k] = \frac{\binom{2}{k}\binom{8}{6-k}}{\binom{10}{6}}.$$

Similarly, given that k wormy apples are sold, the probability that you buy the wormy apple is

$$\mathbf{P}[W|S_k] = \frac{\binom{2-k}{1}\binom{2+k}{0}}{\binom{4}{1}} = \frac{2-k}{4}.$$

We substitute into our first equation, so that

$$\mathbf{P}[W] = \frac{1}{2}\frac{\binom{2}{0}\binom{8}{6}}{\binom{10}{6}} + \frac{1}{4}\frac{\binom{2}{1}\binom{8}{5}}{\binom{10}{6}} = \frac{1}{5}.$$

11° Given that n people go to the party, the number of arrangements of people around the circular table is $(n-1)!$. Without loss of generality, suppose that one member of the couple is invited to sit first, and that the second member of the couple is invited to sit next. The only admissible arrangements occur when the second member sits in one of two seats. The probability that the second member is assigned either is $2/(n-1)$.

Now we use the law of total probability to calculate the probability that the couple sits together. The conditional probability that the couple sits together, given that 8 people go to the party, is 2/7. 8 people will go to the party with probability 1/2. The conditional probability that the couple sits together, given that 7 people go to the party, is 2/6. The total probability is $(2/7)(1/2) + (2/6)(1/2) = 13/42$.

3

RANDOM VARIABLES

Random variables are a mathematical formulation of observations or measurements. Intuitively, a random variable is the result of an experiment. For example, suppose that we conduct an experiment consisting of drawing 5 cards of a standard deck. Then the hand we draw, which we call H, is a random variable. This is because H is determined by random chance, in the course of conducting the experiment. The theory of random variables allows us to say interesting things about H even before we conduct the experiment!

Definition 3.1. Let Ω be a sample space and let $\mathbf{P}$ be a probability measure on Ω. A *random variable* X is a function $X\colon \wp(\Omega) \to \mathbf{R}$. In particular, X is a function that maps events to numerical quantities.

Notice how this definition mirrors our intuitive explanation. Given that an event ω occurs, we would observe or measure $X(\omega)$. We typically suppress the argument ω unless we have a technical reason to talk about the random variable X in terms of a function. In other words, instead of referring to the observation as $X(\omega)$, we refer to it as X.

At the elementary level, random variables are typically taken to be numerical observations. So strictly speaking, the random variable H we discussed above is a *generalized random variable,* because we are observing a hand instead of a number. We can call H a random hand, if we were so inclined. Similarly, we can construct an experiment where we measure multiple numerical quantities. We can call the result of such an experiment a random vector. Also notice that we can frequently extract numerical information from generalized random variables. For example, we might want to know how many diamonds we drew in H. This is a function of the hand H. If we call this function d, we see that $d(H) = d(H(\omega)) = (d \circ H)(\omega)$ is a strict random variable–that is, a function that maps an event (a draw) to a number (the number of diamonds). We will focus on the strict definition of a random variable, but much of what we say here extends naturally to generalized random variables.

Part of the reason for our focus on number valued random variables is that there is so much that we can say about them. For example, because we can perform arithmetic on numbers, we can "lift" arithmetic up to the level of random numbers. In general, given a function $f\colon \mathbf{R} \to \mathbf{R}$ and a random variable X, $f(X)$ is a random variable too.

Example 3.2. A game consists of rolling a die. If we let N be the number thrown, the player wins $W = N^2 - N - 1$ dollars. What are the possible winnings W?

Solution. The die has six faces, numbered 1 to 6. We take $\Omega = \{1, 2, 3, 4, 5, 6\}$. The possible values for W are

N	1	2	3	4	5	6
W	−1	1	5	11	19	29

■

As we have seen, random variables are closely related to events, since they are formally functions on events. We can use this relationship to define events in terms of random variables. Formally, this requires us to calculate the preimage of the admissible values.

Example 3.3. A game consists of rolling a die. If the number N is rolled, the player wins $W = (N - 3.5)^2$. What is the probability that $W < 3$?

Solution. We begin by noting that the possible values for W are

N	1	2	3	4	5	6
W	6.25	2.25	0.25	0.25	2.25	6.25

We note that this listing is the *graph* of the function W. In particular, we can use this listing to find the admissible values of W, and then look up the values of N that lead to them. Since we asked for the probability that $W < 3$, the admissible values of W are those that are less than 3. We see that these are 2.25 and 0.25. We can express the event that $\left[W = 2.25\right]$ in terms of N as the event $\left[N \in \{2,5\}\right] = \left[\{2,5\}\right]$. Similarly, $\left[W = 0.25\right] = \left[N \in \{3,4\}\right] = \left[\{3,4\}\right]$. Finally, we can calculate

$$\mathbf{P}\left[N < 3\right] = \mathbf{P}\left[\{2,5\} \cup \{3,4\}\right] = \mathbf{P}\left[\{2,3,4,5\}\right] = 2/3. \qquad \blacksquare$$

Definition 3.4. Let A be an event, and define a random variable $\mathbb{1}_A$ by

$$\mathbb{1}_A = \begin{cases} 1, & \text{if } A \text{ occurs,} \\ 0, & \text{if } A' \text{ occurs.} \end{cases}$$

$\mathbb{1}_A$ is called the *indicator variable* for A.

Indicator variables are useful for a variety of reasons. If we have a sequence of events A_i, the sequence of indicator variables $\mathbb{1}_{A_i}$ can be used to count the number of events A_i that occur. For example,

Example 3.5. Let $\{A_i\}$ be a partition of the sample space. Then

$$1 = \sum_i \mathbb{1}_{A_i}.$$

We can prove this by noting that the outcome ω must be an element of some event A_k, and that $\mathbb{1}_{A_k} = 1$, but $\mathbb{1}_{A_i} = 0$ if $i \neq k$.

DISCRETE RANDOM VARIABLES

Definition 3.6. A random variable X is a *discretediscrete random variable* random variable if it is defined on a countable sample space.

When a random variable is discrete, it is possible to enumerate all the values it can assume.

Definition 3.7. For a discrete random variable X, its *probability mass function* is the function

$$f_X(k) = \mathbf{P}\left[X = k\right] \text{ for } k \in X.$$

Theorem 3.8. *Let* $\{x_1, x_2, \ldots\}$ *be an enumeration of the possible values of a discrete random variable* X. *Then*

$$f_X(x_k) \geq 0$$

and

$$\sum_{k=1}^{\infty} f_X(x_k) = 1$$

Proof. The first property follows trivially, since $f_X(x_k) = \mathbf{P}\left[X = x_k\right]$. Since the outcomes $X = x_k$ and $X = x_j$ are mutually exclusive if $j \neq k$, $\{x_1, x_2, \ldots\}$ is an enumeration of all possible values of X, the second property follows from the axioms of probability. ■

Definition 3.9. For a discrete random variable X, its *probability distribution function* is the function $F_X(k)$ defined by

$$F_X(k) = \sum_{x \leq k} f_X(x).$$

As we have seen, we have introduce two ways to specify the probabilities of involving discrete random variables. The probability mass function $f_X(k)$ gives us the probability that X assumes some value k, while the probability density function $F_X(k)$ gives us the probability that X assumes some value less than or equal to k. In an important sense, both of these functions encode the same information, since, in principle, given one, we can recover the other.

Theorem 3.10. *Let the random variable* X *take on values in* $\mathbf{N}$. *Then*

$$f_X(k) = F_X(k) - F_X(k-1).$$

Proof. Note that

$$F_X(k) = f_X(1) + f_X(2) + \cdots + f_X(k-1) + f_X(k)$$

and

$$F_X(k-1) = f_X(1) + f_X(2) + \cdots + f_X(k-1).$$

We obtain the result by subtracting the second equation from the first. ∎

CONTINUOUS RANDOM VARIABLES

Definition 3.11. X is a *continuous random variable* if there exists a non-negative function f such that

$$\mathbf{P}[X \in A] = \int_A f_X(x)\,dx$$

for any event A. The function f_X is called the *probability density function* for X. The set of points

$$\{x\colon f_X(x) \neq 0\}$$

is called the *support* of f.

The probability density function does not give us probabilities directly. In order to get a probability from a density function, we must integrate the function on an event.[1]

1 Compare this to the physical situation, such as when we have a function that describes the density of a gas at each point in a balloon. To calculate the mass of the gas in the balloon, we subdivide the balloon's interior into small regions. For each region, we estimate the mass of the gas in it by multiplying the density at a point in the region by the region's volume. We then add up the estimated masses in each region. This procedure becomes more precise as the number of subregions increases. By taking the limit as the number of regions increases, we see that this procedure is the same as integrating the density function for the entire interior of the balloon. Following this analogy, the probability that an event occurs is a mass, and we find the probability mass for the event by integrating the probability density function on the event.

Example 3.12. A random variable X has the density function

$$f_X(x) = \frac{5}{x^2} \text{ with support } x \geq 5.$$

What is the probability that $X > 8$?

Solution. We see that we seek the probability

$$\mathbf{P}[X > 8] = \mathbf{P}[(8, \infty)] = \int_8^\infty \frac{5}{x^2}\,dx = \left(-\frac{5}{x}\bigg|_{x=8}^{\infty} \right) = \frac{5}{8}. \qquad \blacksquare$$

Since $X \in \mathbf{R}$, f_X must satisfy

$$\mathbf{P}[X \in \mathbf{R}] = \int_{\mathbf{R}} f_X(x)\,dx = 1.$$

Example 3.13. Let X be a continuous random variable with density function

$$f_X(x) = c(x^3 + x), \text{ for } 0 < x < 1.$$

What is c?

Solution. Since f_X is a density function,

$$1 = \int_0^1 f_X(x)\,dx = \int_0^1 c(x^3 + x)\,dx = c\left(\frac{x^4}{4} + \frac{x^2}{2}\bigg|_0^1 \right) = c\left(\frac{1}{4} + \frac{1}{2}\right)$$

which implies that $c = 4/3$. ■

In general, to calculate the probability that X lies in some interval $[a, b]$, we calculate

$$\mathbf{P}[a \leq X \leq b] = \int_a^b f_X(x)\,dx.$$

We can use this to show that, for any real number a, $\mathbf{P}[X = a] = 0$. In particular, we write

$$\mathbf{P}[X = a] = \mathbf{P}[a \leq X \leq a] = \int_a^a f_X(x)\,dx = 0,$$

by the fundamental theorem of calculus. We might find this result counter-intuitive. After all, a random variable must land on *some* number. There are at least two ways to understand this apparent incongruity.[2] First, an event A is not impossible merely because $\mathbf{P}[A] = 0$. In order for the event A to be impossible, $A \cap \Omega$ must be empty. Second, we must consider that a random variable is the numeric outcome of an idealized experiment or a measurement. If we experimentally find that the circumference of a circle is 3.14 with some probability, we do so by measuring the circumference, and there are limits to its precision. The experimental result of 3.14 is *not* the same kind of number as $3.14\overline{0}$, and saying that the result is 3.14 is not equivalent to the claim that the result is $3.14\overline{0}$. On the idealized side of random variables, any number in the interval $(3.14 - \epsilon, 3.14 + \epsilon')$ can result in an observed measurement of 3.14.

Because $\mathbf{P}[X = a]$ is 0 for any real number a, we see that

$$\mathbf{P}[X \in (a,b)] = \mathbf{P}[X \in [a,b)] = \mathbf{P}[X \in (a,b]] = \mathbf{P}[X \in [a,b]].$$

Definition 3.14. Let X be a continuous random variable. Its *probability distribution function* is

$$F_X(x) = \mathbf{P}[X < x] = \int_{-\infty}^{x} f_X(x)\,dx$$

and its *survival function* is

$$S_X(x) = \mathbf{P}[X > x] = 1 - F_X(x) = \int_{x}^{\infty} f_X(x)\,dx.$$

Example 3.15. Suppose that a random variable X has the density function

$$f_X(x) = e^{-x} \text{ for } x > 0.$$

What is its survival function?

Solution. We will solve this problem by way of calculating the distribution function for X. We see

$$F_X(x) = \int_{0}^{\infty} e^{-x}\,dx = \left(-e^{-x}\big|_{0}^{\infty}\right) = 1 - e^{-x},$$

2 It is important to note that these are *not* competing points of view.

which implies

$$S_X(x) = 1 - (1 - e^{-x}) = e^{-x}. \qquad \blacksquare$$

Example 3.16. Let X be the age when a person dies, and suppose X has the density function

$$f_X(x) = \frac{5 \cdot 55^2}{x^6}, \text{ for } x > 55.$$

Find the probability that the person dies before age 80, given that they survive to 65.

Solution. We must find the probability

$$\mathbf{P}[X < 80 | X > 65] = \frac{\mathbf{P}[65 < X < 80]}{\mathbf{P}[X > 65]} = \frac{S_X(65) - S_X(80)}{S_X(65)}.$$

We calculate the distribution function

$$F_X(x) = \int_{55}^{x} \frac{5 \cdot 55^2}{x^6} = 1 - \left(\frac{55}{x}\right)^5,$$

so that

$$S_X(x) = \left(\frac{55}{x}\right)^5.$$

The probability we seek is

$$\frac{S_X(65) - S_X(80)}{S_X(65)} \approx 0.6459. \qquad \blacksquare$$

By the fundamental theorem of calculus, we have

Theorem 3.17. *For a random variable* X,

$$f_X(x) = \frac{d}{dx} F_X(x).$$

Let $x < y$ and consider the events $[X < x]$ and $[X < y]$. Clearly, $[X < x] \subset [X < y]$. The axioms of probability imply that

$$F_X(x) = \mathbf{P}[X < x] < \mathbf{P}[X < y] = F_X(y).$$

This establishes

Theorem 3.18. *For any random variable* X, $F_X(x)$ *is a non-decreasing function of* x.

Similarly, by definition,

Theorem 3.19. *For a random variable* X,

$$\lim_{x \to -\infty} F_X(x) = 0$$

and

$$\lim_{x \to \infty} F_X(x) = 1.$$

We can define some other interesting properties of continuous random variables and their distributions.

Definition 3.20. The *mode* of a random variable X is the value of X with maximum density. In particular, it is the value m which satisfies

$$f_X(m) = \max_{x \in \mathbf{R}} f_X(x).$$

In analogy to the discrete case, we can intuitively think of the mode for a random variable as the 'likeliest value' for X. But this must remain an informal understanding, since a density is note the same thing as a probability. In the case that the density function $f(x)$ is differentiable, we can find the mode using the usual techniques of calculus:

i. Find the first derivative $f'(x)$.

ii. Set the first derivative of $f'(x)$ equal to 0 and solve for x.

iii. For each solution x, check that the second derivative at x is negative.

iv. For each solution x with a negative second derivative, calculate $f(x)$ and compare the results.

v. Compare these results with the values of f at the endpoints of its domain.

Example 3.21. A random variable X has the probability density function

$$f_X(x) = e^{-\lambda x}, \text{ for } x > 0.$$

What is the mode of X?

Solution. We calculate the derivative of f_X as

$$f_X'(x) = -\lambda e^{-\lambda x}.$$

We see that $e^{-\lambda x}$ is always positive, so the derivative is always negative. In other words, $f_X'(x) = 0$ does not have a solution in x. This implies that the maximum of f_X must occur either at 0 or 'at' ∞. We see that

$$\lim_{x \to 0} f_X(x) = 1 \quad \text{and} \quad \lim_{x \to \infty} f_X(x) = 0.$$

so that the mode is $x = 0$. ■

Definition 3.22. Let X be a random variable and let p be a percentage, normalized so that $p \in [0, 1]$. The pth *percentile* for X is the smallest value of x such that

$$\mathbf{P}[X \le x] \le p \quad \text{and} \quad \mathbf{P}[X > x] \le (1 - p).$$

The pth percentile has a natural interpretation. If x is the pth percentile for the random variable X, then a fraction p of the probability mass is concentrated on values below x and a fraction $(1 - p)$ is concentrated on values greater than x. Of particular importance is

Definition 3.23. The *median* for a random variable X is its 50th percentile.

If a random variable X has median x, then $\mathbf{P}[X < x] = \mathbf{P}[X > x] = 1/2$.

Example 3.24. Let X be a random variable with probability density function

$$f_X(x) = c\left(x + \frac{1}{2}\right) \text{ for } 0 < x < 1.$$

What is the difference between the median and the 80th percentile?

Solution. Calculate

$$F_X(x) = c\int_0^x x + \frac{1}{2}\,dx = c\left(\frac{x^2}{2} + \frac{x}{2}\Big|_0^x\right).$$

Since F_X is a distribution function, $F_X(1) = 1$, which implies $c = 1$. We seek the difference between the 80th percentile and the median. So we calculate the 80th percentile by solving for x_{80} in

$$F_X(x_{80}) = 0.8 = \frac{1}{2}x_{80}^2 + \frac{1}{2}x_{80},$$

so that the 80th percentile is $x_{80} \approx 0.949$. We find the median x_{50} by solving for it in

$$F_X(x_{50}) = 0.5 = \frac{1}{2}x_{50}^2 + \frac{1}{2}x_{50},$$

so that the median is 0.618. The difference is $x_{80} - x_{50} = 0.3311$. ■

JOINTLY DISTRIBUTED RANDOM VARIABLES

Joint probability distributions arise when an experiment has random vectors as outcomes. For example, we might be interested in measuring both a person's height and weight. In this case, the outcomes we are interested are random vectors (H, W). The joint probability distribution is strictly more informative than the distributions of H and W. With knowledge of the distribution of (H, W), we can extract information about the relationships between height and weight which would be lost merely by knowing the distributions of H and W alone.

Example 3.25. Let X be the number of heads that land in two coin tosses, and define $Y = 1 - X$. Y clearly has the same probability distribution as X, but the only possible values of (X, Y) are $(1, 0)$ and $(0, 1)$.

Definition 3.26. For random variables X and Y, the *joint probability distribution function* is the function

$$F_{X,Y}(x, y) = \mathbf{P}\big[\,[X \leq x] \wedge [Y \leq y]\,\big].$$

The definition for the joint cumulative distribution function applies equally well to any combination of discrete and continuous random variables X and Y.

Example 3.27. Let X be the number of heads that land in two coin tosses, and define $Y = 1 - X$. What is the joint distribution function for X and Y?

Solution. Since $(X, Y) \in \{(1, 0), (0, 1)\}$, we see

$$F_{X,Y}(x, y) = \begin{cases} 0, & \text{if } x \leq 0 \text{ and } y \leq 0 \\ \frac{1}{2}, & \text{if } x \leq 1 \text{ and } y \leq 0 \\ \frac{1}{2}, & \text{if } x \leq 0 \text{ and } y \leq 1 \\ 1, & \text{if } x \leq 1 \text{ and } y \leq 1. \end{cases} \quad \blacksquare$$

Joint probability distribution functions are awkward to work with, so we will soon introduce joint probability mass and density functions. Before then, we introduce an important theorem for calculating probabilities with joint probability distribution functions. It is similar to our result

$$\mathbf{P}\big[a < X < b\big] = F_X(b) - F_X(a)$$

for one-dimensional probability distributions.

Theorem 3.28. *For jointly distributed random variables X and Y,*

$$\begin{aligned} \mathbf{P}\big[a < X < b, c < Y < d\big] = F_{X,Y}(b, d) + F_{X,Y}(a, c) \\ - F_{X,Y}(a, d) - F_{X,Y}(b, c). \end{aligned}$$

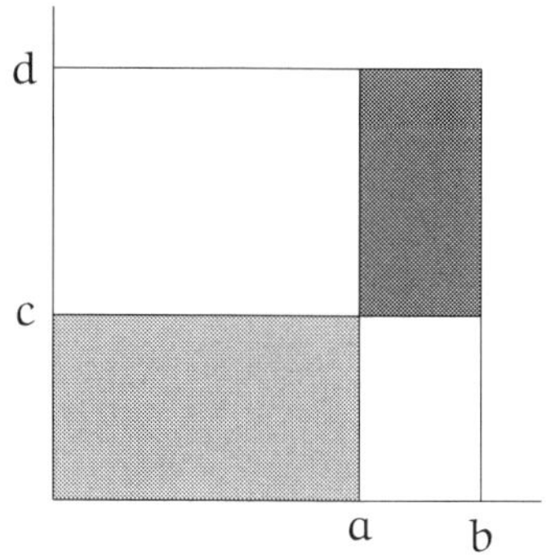

Figure 5: Calculating the probability that $a < X < b$ and $c < Y < d$.

Proof. Refer to figure 5. We seek the probability that element belongs in the dark gray rectangle. We take the probability for the rectangle with top-right corner (b, d), and subtract the probability for the rectangle with top-right corner (b, c). Similarly, we subtract the probability for the rectangle with top-right corner (a, d). But this is an under-estimate since we subtracted the probability for the rectangle with top-right corner (a, c) twice. We add this probability to obtain the result. ■

Definition 3.29. Let X and Y be jointly distributed discrete random variables. The *joint probability mass function* for X and Y is

$$f_{X,Y}(x, y) = \mathbf{P}\left[X = x, Y = y\right].$$

Definition 3.30. Let X and Y be jointly distributed continuous random variables with the differentiable joint distribution function $F_{X,Y}$. The *joint probability density function* for X and Y is

$$f_{X,Y}(x, y) = \frac{\partial^2}{\partial x \partial y} F_{X,Y}(x, y).$$

We can use the joint probability density function to calculate probabilities, as in

Theorem 3.31. *For jointly distributed continuous random variables* X *and* Y, *then* $\mathbf{P}\left[a < X < b, c < Y < d\right]$ *is*

$$\mathbf{P}\left[a < X < b, c < Y < d\right] = \int_a^b \int_c^d f_{X,Y}(x, y)\, dy dx.$$

Given the joint probability mass or density function for the random variables X and Y, we can recover the probability density or mass function for X or Y by applying the addition rule for probabilities. This is called *marginalization*.

Definition 3.32. Let X and Y be jointly distributed discrete random variables with joint probability mass function $f_{X,Y}$. Then the *marginal density function* for X is

$$f_X(x) = \sum_{y \in Y} f_{X,Y}(x, y).$$

The intuition behind these definitions is that since our outcomes are the pairs (X, Y), and distinct pairs are mutually exclusive, the probability that $\mathbf{P}\left[X = x\right]$ is

$$\begin{aligned}
\mathbf{P}\left[X = x\right] &= \mathbf{P}\left[X = x, Y = y_1\right] + \mathbf{P}\left[X = x, Y = y_2\right] + \cdots. \\
&= \sum_{y \in Y} \mathbf{P}\left[X = x, Y = y\right] \\
&= \sum_{y \in Y} f_{X,Y}(x, y).
\end{aligned}$$

Similarly, the continuous analog is

Definition 3.33. Let X and Y be jointly distributed continuous random variables with probability mass function $f_{X,Y}$. Then the *marginal mass function* for X has the density function

$$f_X(x) = \int_{\mathbf{R}} f_{X,Y}(x, y)\, dy.$$

We can also extend this definition to distribution functions.

Definition 3.34. Let X and Y be jointly distributed random variables. The *marginal distribution function* for X is

$$F_X(x) = \lim_{y \to \infty} F_{X,Y}(x, y).$$

Example 3.35. Let X and Y be jointly distributed with joint probability distribution function

$$F_{X,Y}(x,y) = xy^2, \text{ for } 0 \leq x \leq 1, 0 \leq y \leq 1.$$

What is the marginal density for Y?

Solution. We calculate the marginal distribution function for Y as

$$F_Y(y) = \lim_{x \to 1} F_{X,Y}(x,y) = F_{X,Y}(1,y) = y^2,$$

which implies that

$$f_Y(y) = 2y.$$ ■

We can extend the notion of condition probabilities to probability mass and density functions for joint random variables. We begin with

Definition 3.36. Let X and Y be jointly distributed random variables. The conditional probability distribution function of X given Y is

$$F_{X|Y}(x,y) = \frac{F_{X,Y}(x,y)}{F_Y(y)} = \frac{\mathbf{P}[X < x, Y < y]}{\mathbf{P}[Y < y]}.$$

where $F_Y(y)$ is the marginal distribution of Y. In other words, we see this is exactly the conditional probability for $X < x$, given that $Y < y$.

For probability mass functions, we define

Definition 3.37. Let X and Y be jointly distributed continuous random variables. The conditional probability mass function for X given that $Y = y$ is

$$f_{X|Y}(x|y) = \frac{f_{X,Y}(x,y)}{f_Y(y)} = \frac{\mathbf{P}[X = x, Y = y]}{\mathbf{P}[Y = y]} = \mathbf{P}[X = x | Y = y].$$

Finally, we define the conditional probability density function for X given $Y = y$ as

Definition 3.38. Let X and Y be jointly distributed continuous random variables. The conditional probability density function for X given that $Y = y$ is

$$f_{X|Y}(x|y) = \frac{f_{X,Y}(x,y)}{f_Y(y)}.$$

Example 3.39. Let (X, Y) have the joint density function

$$f_{X,Y}(x,y) = ke^{-(x+y)} \text{ for } 0 < x < 1, 0 < y < \infty.$$

Calculate the conditional density function for Y given X.

Solution. We begin by calculating the marginal density of X as

$$f_X(x) = \int_0^\infty ke^{-(x+y)}\,dy = ke^{-x}\int_0^\infty e^{-y}\,dy = ke^{-x}.$$

This implies that

$$f_{Y|X}(y|x) = \frac{f_{X,Y}(x,y)}{f_X(x)} = \frac{ke^{-(x+y)}}{ke^{-x}} = e^{-y}.$$ ■

We can find the probability density function for the sum of jointly distributed random variables X and Y as follows. Since for any z, $X + Y = z$ implies that $Y = z - X$, we write

$$\begin{aligned} F_{X+Y}(z) &= \int_{\mathbf{R}}\int_{-\infty}^{z-x} f_{X,Y}(x,y)\,dydx \\ &= \int_{\mathbf{R}}\int_{-\infty}^{z} f_{X,Y}(x,v-x)\,dvdx \\ &= \int_{-\infty}^{z}\int_{\mathbf{R}} f(x,v-x)\,dvdx. \end{aligned}$$

We differentiate so that

$$f_{X+Y}(z) = \int_{\mathbf{R}} f_{X,Y}(x,z-x)dx.$$

If X and Y are independent

$$f_{X+Y}(z) = \int_{\mathbf{R}} f_X(x)f_Y(z-x)dx.$$

We call this integral the *convolution* of f_X and f_Y.

TRANSFORMATIONS OF RANDOM VARIABLES

As we have seen, if we are given a continuous random variable X, and apply a function g to it, the resulting value $g(X)$ is a random variable as well. If g is an invertible differentiable function, we can recover the density function for $g(X)$ in terms of the density function for X. To motivate this, we begin with a simple theorem.

Theorem 3.40. *Let X be a continuous random variable and g be a strictly increasing function. Then*

$$\mathbf{P}\left[g(X) < x\right] = \mathbf{P}\left[X < g^{-1}(x)\right],$$

where g^{-1} is the inverse of g.

The main idea behind this theorem is that $\left[g(X) < x\right]$ is the same event as $\left[X < g^{-1}(x)\right]$. A proof of the theorem merely expresses this fact formally.

Example 3.41. Let X be a positive random variable, and let $g(X) = X^2$. Then

$$\mathbf{P}\left[g(X) < 9\right] = \mathbf{P}\left[X^2 < 9\right] = \mathbf{P}\left[X < 3\right].$$

Theorem 3.42. *Let g be an increasing differentiable function. Let X be a continuous random variable with density function f_X. Then $Y = g(X)$ has the density function*

$$f_Y(y) = \frac{f_X(g^{-1}(y))}{\left|g'(g^{-1}(y))\right|}.$$

Proof. Note that

$$F_Y(y) = \mathbf{P}\left[Y < y\right] = \mathbf{P}\left[g(X) < y\right] = \mathbf{P}\left[X < g^{-1}(y)\right] = F_X(g^{-1}(y)).$$

We take the derivative to calculate

$$f_Y(y) = \frac{d}{dy}F_X(g^{-1}(y)) = f'_X(g^{-1}(y))\frac{d}{dy}g^{-1}(y).$$

The inverse function theorem from calculus implies that this is

$$= \frac{f_X(g^{-1}(y))}{\left|g'(g^{-1}(y))\right|}. \qquad \blacksquare$$

Example 3.43. Let X be a random variable with probability density function $f_X(x) = e^{-x}$, with $x > 0$, and let $Y = X^2$. What is $f_Y(y)$?

Solution. Since $Y = g(X) = X^2$, $g^{-1}(Y) = \sqrt{Y}$. We calculate

$$g'(y) = 2y$$

so that

$$f_Y(y) = \frac{f_X(g^{-1}(y))}{\left|g'(g^{-1}(y))\right|} = \frac{1}{2}y^{-\frac{1}{2}}e^{-\sqrt{y}}. \qquad \blacksquare$$

In the author's experience, it is typically easier to do this kind of problem directly, using the reasoning we used to prove theorem 3.42 on the preceding page, which is sometimes called the *distribution function method*, and we recommend this method when convenient. There is less room for confusion if we don't directly apply the inverse function theorem. On the other hand, understanding how to apply the theorem is necessary as well, since exam problems may give us a density function instead of a distribution function. Moreover, there is no straight-forward analog for the reasoning we used to prove theorem 3.42 in the multi-variable case. In that setting, we must rely on a formally similar formula. Consider the next example, in which we are given a distribution function for X, and so use the distribution function method.

Example 3.44. Let X be a continuous random variable with distribution function

$$F_X(x) = 1 - e^{-\lambda x} \text{ for } x > 0.$$

and define $Y = X^\alpha$ for $\alpha \neq 0$. Find the density for Y.

Solution. We calculate

$$\mathbf{P}[Y < y] = \mathbf{P}[X^\alpha < y] = \mathbf{P}\left[X < y^{\frac{1}{\alpha}}\right] = F_X\left(y^{\frac{1}{\alpha}}\right).$$

We take the derivative, so that

$$f_Y(y) = \frac{d}{dy}F_X\left(y^{\frac{1}{\alpha}}\right) = \frac{\lambda}{\alpha}\left(y^{\frac{1}{\alpha}-1}\right)e^{-\lambda y^{\frac{1}{\alpha}}}. \qquad \blacksquare$$

We can compare this result with the previous example, by setting $\alpha = 2$ and $\lambda = 1$.

Suppose that we have jointly distributed random variables (X, Y) and an invertible function $f\colon \mathbf{R}^2 \to \mathbf{R}^2$. We can use the tools of the multi-variable calculus to generalize our previous result. First, we recall an important definition from the multi-variable calculus.

Definition 3.45. Let the function f be defined by

$$f(x, y) = (f_1(x, y), f_2(x, y)),$$

where f_1 and f_2 are differentiable functions of x and y. The *Jacobian* of f is the determinant

$$J_f = \begin{vmatrix} \frac{\partial f_1}{\partial x_1} & \frac{\partial f_2}{\partial x_1} \\ \frac{\partial f_1}{\partial x_2} & \frac{\partial f_2}{\partial x_2} \end{vmatrix} = \left| \frac{\partial f_1}{\partial x_1}\frac{\partial f_2}{\partial x_2} - \frac{\partial f_2}{\partial x_1}\frac{\partial f_1}{\partial x_2} \right|.$$

Theorem 3.46. *Let (X, Y) jointly distributed random variables, and let f be an invertible function such that both f and f^{-1} are differentiable. Then the joint density function for $(U, V) = f(X, Y)$ is*

$$f_{(U,V)}(u, v) = \frac{f_{X,Y}(f^{-1}(u, v))}{|J_f|},$$

where $|J_f|$ is the Jacobian of f.

As a practical matter, we prefer to use a variant of this formula. Instead of calculating the Jacobian of f and evaluating it at $f^{-1}(u, v)$, we prefer to calculate f^{-1} and its Jacobian. In this case, the formula is

$$f_{(U,V)}(u, v) = f_{X,Y}(f^{-1}(u, v)) \cdot |J_{f^{-1}}|.$$

ORDER STATISTICS

Since random variables are numeric outcomes for experiments, there is a natural notion of order for random variables. In particular, we can compare the random variables X and Y by their sizes, and consider events of the form $[X < Y]$. Given that the random variables $X_1, X_2, \dots, X_n$ are identically distributed and independent, they can be placed in order of increasing size. We define

Definition 3.47. Let $\{X_i\}$ be a sequence of n independent identically distributed random variables, and let $(X_{(1)}, X_{(2)}, \dots, X_{(n)})$ be an arrangement of the $\{X_i\}$ in increasing order. Then $X_{(i)}$ is the ith *order statistic*.

We might sometimes use the notation $X_{(i)}$ for the ith variable in an ordered sequence of random variables, even if they are not identically distributed. However, we reserve the term 'order statistic' for the case when the various variables are identically distributed, because certain useful formulas for the probability distributions and densities are possible. Before we derive these formulas, we will examine the behavior of the min and max functions. Intuitively, $\max A$ is the largest element in A, while $\min A$ is the smallest element in A. We formalize this notion in

Definition 3.48. Let $A = \{x_1, x_2, \dots, x_n\}$ be a finite set of real numbers. Then $\min A$ is the element $x \in A$ such that if $y \in A$ and $y \leq x$, then $x = y$. $\max A$ is the element $x \in A$ such that if $y \in A$ and $x \geq y$, then $x = y$.

Based on the formal definition, we see that if $\min A < z$, then at least one element $x \in A$ is satisfies $x < z$. On the other hand, if $\max A < z$, then *every* element of A is less than z.

Theorem 3.49. *Let* $A = \{X_1, X_2, \dots, X_n\}$ *be a set of independent random variables. The probability distribution function for* $X_{(1)} = \min A$ *is*

$$F_{X_{(1)}}(x) = 1 - \prod_{i=0}^{n} 1 - F_{X_i}(x),$$

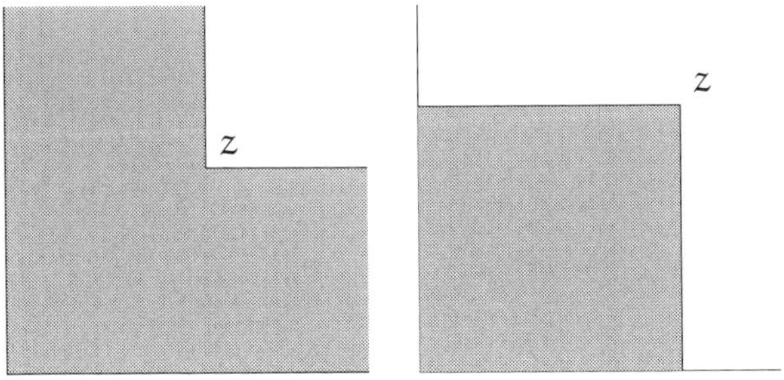

Figure 6: On the left, the shaded region corresponds to the event $\min\{X, Y\} < z$. On the right, the shaded region corresponds to the event $\max\{X, Y\} < z$.

and if the random variables are identically distributed, the distribution function for $X_{(1)}$ is

$$F_{X_{(1)}}(x) = 1 - (1 - F_{X_i}(x))^n.$$

Proof. The result is a straight-forward calculation.

$$\begin{aligned}
\mathbf{P}\left[X_{(1)} < z\right] &= \mathbf{P}\left[\min\left\{X_1, X_2, \ldots, X_n\right\} < z\right] \\
&= 1 - \mathbf{P}\left[\min\left\{X_1, X_2, \ldots, X_n\right\} > z\right] \\
&= 1 - \mathbf{P}\left[X_1 > z, X_2 > z, \ldots, X_n > z\right] \\
&= 1 - \mathbf{P}\left[X_1 > z\right] \mathbf{P}\left[X_2 > z\right] \cdots \mathbf{P}\left[X_n > z\right] \\
&= 1 - (1 - F_{X_1}(x))(1 - F_{X_2}(x)) \cdots (1 - F_{X_n}(x)),
\end{aligned}$$

and if the random variables are identically distributed,

$$= 1 - (1 - F_{X_i}(x))^n \qquad \blacksquare$$

Theorem 3.50. *Let $A = \left\{X_1, X_2, \ldots, X_n\right\}$ be a set of independent random variables. The probability distribution function for $X_{(n)} = \max A$ is*

$$F_{X_{(n)}}(x) = \prod_{i=0}^{n} F_{X_i}(x),$$

and if the random variables are identically distributed, the distribution function for $X_{(n)}$ is

$$F_{X_{(n)}}(x) = F_{X_i}(x)^n.$$

Proof. The result follows from the calculation

$$\begin{aligned}\mathbf{P}[X_{(n)} < z] &= \mathbf{P}[X_1 < z, X_2 < z, \ldots, X_n < z] \\ &= \mathbf{P}[X_1 < z]\,\mathbf{P}[X_2 < z] \cdots \mathbf{P}[X_n < z] \\ &= \prod_{i=0}^{n} F_{X_i}(x),\end{aligned}$$

and if the random variables are identically distributed,

$$= F_{X_i}(x)^n.$$

■

Example 3.51. let X_1, X_2, and X_3 have the probability density function

$$f_X(x) = cx^3 \text{ for } 0 < x < 1.$$

What is the probability density function for $\min\{X_1, X_2, X_3\}$?

Solution. We begin by calculating the probability distribution function

$$F_X(x) = \int_0^x cx^3\,dx = c\left(\frac{x^4}{4}\bigg|_0^x\right) = x^4,$$

since c must be 4. This implies that

$$F_{X_{(1)}}(x) = 1 - (1 - x^4)^3.$$

We differentiate to find

$$f_{X_{(1)}}(x) = 12x^3(1 - x^4)^2.$$

■

EXERCISES

1° Let X be a random variable with the probability density function

$$f_X(x) = c(1 - x)x^2, \text{ for } 0 < x < 1.$$

Find the probability that $X > \frac{1}{2}$.

2° Let X be a random variable with the density function

$$f_X(x) = \begin{cases} 0, & \text{if } x < 0 \text{ or } x > 10 \\ \frac{x}{25}, & \text{if } 0 \leq x \leq 5 \\ \frac{10-x}{25}, & \text{if } 5 \leq x \leq 10. \end{cases}$$

Calculate the probability $\mathbf{P}\left[X^2 - 9X + 18 > 0\right]$.

3° Let X be a random variable with the probability density function

$$f_X(x) = \frac{1}{2} + \frac{3}{8}x, \text{ for } -1 < x < 1.$$

Calculate the probability that $X > 0$, given that $X < 1/2$.

4° The random variable X has the density

$$f(x) = c(x^3 + x^2) \text{ on } 0 < x < 10.$$

Find the probability that X is between 5 and 7, given that X is less than 8.

5° The random variable X has probability density function

$$f_X(x) = \begin{cases} cx, & \text{for } 0 \leq x \leq 3, \\ c(6-x), & \text{for } 3 < x \leq 6, \\ 0, & \text{otherwise.} \end{cases}$$

Calculate $\mathbf{P}\left[2 < X < 5\right]$

6° A random variable has the probability distribution function

$$F(x) = 1 - e^{-\left(\frac{x}{2}\right)^2}.$$

Calculate the median of X.

7° A random variable X has the density function

$$f_X(x) = c(\alpha^2 - x^2) \text{ on } 0 \le x \le 1,$$

and its median is 2/5. What is α?

8° Let X and Y have the joint density function

$$f_{X,Y}(x, y) = 1, \text{ for } 0 < x < 1, 0 < y < 1.$$

What is the probability that $XY \le 1/2$.

9° The random variables X and Y have the joint density function

$$f_{X,Y}(x, y) = c(x + y) \text{ on the region } 0 < x < 1, x^2 < y < x^{\frac{1}{2}}.$$

Find the probability that $X < \frac{1}{2}$.

10° Let X and Y be jointly distributed with density

$$f_{X,Y}(x, y) = \frac{x^2 + y}{4}, \text{ for } 0 < x < y < 2.$$

Find the conditional density of Y given X.

11° Let X and Y be jointly distributed with joint density function

$$f_{X,Y}(x, y) = \frac{1}{4}e^{-(x+y)}(x^2 + y^2) \text{ on } 0 < x, 0 < y.$$

Find the probability that $X < \frac{4}{3}$, given that $Y = 3$.

12° Let T_1 and T_2 be independent random variables with joint density function

$$f_{T_1,T_2}(t_1, t_2) = 1 \text{ for } 0 < t_1, t_2 < 1.$$

Calculate the probability that $T_1 + 2T_2$ is less than 1.

13° Let X have density

$$f_X(x) = e^{-x}, \text{ for } x > 0,$$

and let $Y = X^5$. Find the density for Y.

14° Let X have the density function

$$f_X(x) = \frac{1}{3}, \text{ on } 0 < x < 3,$$

and let $Y = X^2$. What is the density f_Y?

15° Let X have the density function

$$f_X(x) = \frac{1}{2\sqrt{\pi}}e^{-\frac{1}{2}x^2},$$

and define $Y = \sqrt{|X|}$. Find the density of Y.

16° An actuary models the damage due to strong hurricanes with the random variable $Y = e^{-\frac{X^2}{2}}$, where

$$f_X(x) = e^{-x}.$$

What is the density function for Y?

17° Let X and Y be jointly distributed with joint density

$$f_{X,Y}(x,y) = \frac{1}{y} e^{-\frac{x}{y}} e^{-x}, \text{ where } x, y > 0.$$

Calculate $\mathbf{E}[X]$.

18° Let X and Y be exponential random variables with mean 1. Find the variance of $\frac{X}{X+Y}$.

19° Let $\{X_i\}$ be independent random variables with densities

$$f_{X_i}(x) = c(i+1)x^i, \text{ for } 0 \leq x < 1,$$

and let

$$X = \max\{X_1, X_2, X_3, X_4, X_5\}.$$

Find the 5th percentile of X.

20° Messages are transmitted over a noisy network. Each node, in black, flips a bit with probability $p = 0.01$, independently of the other nodes and the other bits in the message. By 'flipping a bit', we mean that a 1 is erroneously turned into a 0, and a 0 is turned into a 1. Messages are sent on the shortest operational path. A node can fail independently with probability $p_f = 0.03$, and we assume failure can never occur during the transmission of a message. If A, in gray, sends an 8 bit long message, what is the probability that B, in gray, receives the same sequence of bits?

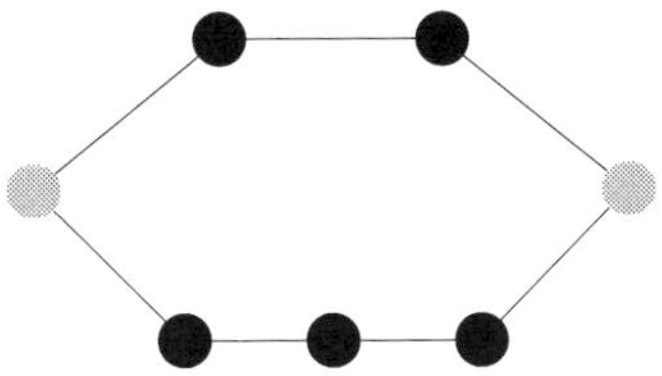

SOLUTIONS

1° We calculate the distribution function for X as

$$F_X(x) = c\int_0^x x^2 - x^3\,dx = c\left(\frac{x^3}{3} - \frac{x^4}{4}\right).$$

Since F is a probability distribution function, $F(1) = 1$. This implies that $c = 12$. Finally, we calculate

$$\mathbf{P}\left[X > \frac{1}{2}\right] = 1 - \mathbf{P}\left[X < \frac{1}{2}\right] = 1 - F_X\left(\frac{1}{2}\right) = \frac{11}{16}.$$

2° We calculate

$$\begin{aligned}
\mathbf{P}\left[X^2 - 9X + 18 > 0\right] &= \mathbf{P}\left[(X-3)(X-6) > 0\right] \\
&= \mathbf{P}\left[X < 3\right] + \mathbf{P}\left[X > 6\right] \\
&= \int_0^3 \frac{x}{25}dx + \int_6^{10} \frac{10-x}{25}dx \\
&= \left.\frac{x^2}{50}\right|_0^3 + \left.\frac{(10-x)^2}{50}\right|_6^{10} \\
&= \frac{9}{50} + \frac{16}{50} \\
&= \frac{1}{2}.
\end{aligned}$$

3° We can calculate the distribution function as

$$F_X(x) = \int_{-1}^{x} \frac{1}{2} + \frac{3}{8}y\,dy = \left.\frac{1}{2}y + \frac{3}{16}y^2\right|_{-1}^{x} = \frac{1}{2}(x+1) + \frac{3}{16}(x^2 - 1).$$

We seek the probability

$$\mathbf{P}\left[X > 0 | X < \frac{1}{2}\right] = \frac{\mathbf{P}\left[0 < X < \frac{1}{2}\right]}{\mathbf{P}\left[X < \frac{1}{2}\right]} = \frac{F\left(\frac{1}{2}\right) - F(0)}{F\left(\frac{1}{2}\right)} = 0.4872.$$

4° We seek $\mathbf{P}\left[5 < X < 7 | X < 8\right]$:

$$\begin{aligned}
\mathbf{P}\left[5 < X < 7 | X < 8\right] &= \frac{\mathbf{P}\left[5 < X < 7, X < 8\right]}{\mathbf{P}\left[X < 8\right]} \\
&= \frac{\mathbf{P}\left[5 < X < 7\right]}{\mathbf{P}\left[X < 8\right]} \\
&= \frac{c \int_5^7 x^3 + x^2 \, dx}{c \int_0^8 x^3 + x^2 \, dx} \\
&= \frac{\frac{x^4}{4} + \frac{x^3}{3} \Big|_5^7}{\frac{x^4}{4} + \frac{x^3}{3} \Big|_0^8} \\
&\approx 0.43.
\end{aligned}$$

Typically, for problems where a parameter like c is unknown, we would have to solve for the parameter before proceeding to calculate specific probabilities. However, because we are calculating a conditional probability, the c term is canceled.

5° We can express the probability distribution function as

$$\begin{aligned}
F_X(x) &= c \int_0^{\min(x,3)} x \, dx + c \int_3^{\max(3,x)} (6 - x) \, dx \\
&= c \left(\frac{x^2}{2} \Big|_0^{\min(3,x)} \right) + c \left(6x - \frac{x^2}{2} \Big|_3^{\max(3,x)} \right),
\end{aligned}$$

so that

$$\begin{aligned}
1 = F_X(6) &= c \left(\frac{x^2}{2} \Big|_0^3 \right) + c \left(6x - \frac{x^2}{2} \Big|_3^6 \right) \\
&= c \left(\frac{9}{2} + 36 - 18 - 18 + \frac{9}{2} \right) \\
&= 9c,
\end{aligned}$$

which implies that $c = 1/9$. Since

$$\begin{aligned}\mathbf{P}\left[2 < X < 5\right] &= F_X(5) - F_X(2) \\ &= \frac{1}{9}\left(\frac{9}{2} + 30 - \frac{25}{2} - 18 + \frac{9}{2}\right) - \frac{1}{9}\left(\frac{4}{2}\right) \\ &= \frac{13}{18}.\end{aligned}$$

6° By definition, the median is the value x which satisfies

$$\begin{aligned}\frac{1}{2} &= 1 - e^{-\left(\frac{x}{2}\right)^2} \\ &= e^{-\left(\frac{x}{2}\right)^2}\end{aligned}$$

so that

$$\log \frac{1}{2} = -\left(\frac{x^2}{4}\right)$$

and

$$\begin{aligned}x &= \sqrt{-4 \log \frac{1}{2}} \\ &\approx 1.67.\end{aligned}$$

7° We calculate the probability distribution function as

$$F_X(x) = c\left(\alpha^2 x - \frac{x^3}{3}\right).$$

Since F_X is a probability distribution function,

$$1 = c\left(\alpha^2 - \frac{1}{3}\right).$$

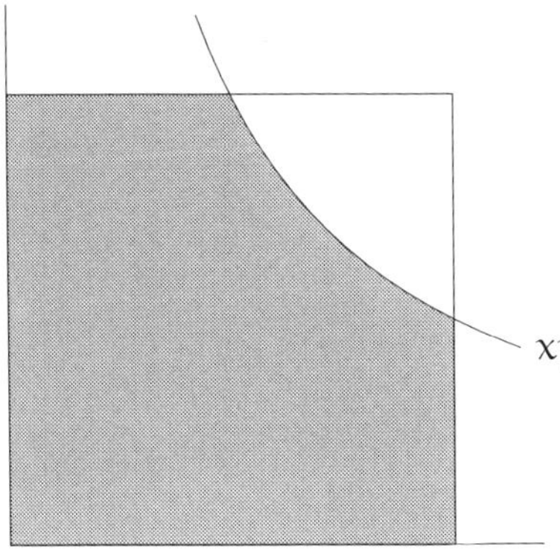

Figure 7: We must integrate over the region in gray.

And since the median is 2/5,

$$\frac{1}{2} = c\left(\frac{2}{5}\alpha^2 - \frac{8}{375}\right).$$

This implies that

$$2c\left(\frac{2}{5}\alpha^2 - \frac{8}{375}\right) = c\left(\alpha^2 - \frac{1}{3}\right).$$

We solve for $\alpha \approx 1.21$.

8° We see that

$$\left[XY \leq \frac{1}{2}\right] = \left[X \leq \frac{1}{2Y}\right].$$

We have drawn the region in figure 7 on the previous page. We can calculate the probability by integrating over the event. But this integral is complicated, so we instead calculate

$$\begin{aligned}
\mathbf{P}\left[XY \leq \frac{1}{2}\right] &= 1 - \mathbf{P}\left[XY > \frac{1}{2}\right] = 1 - \int_{\frac{1}{2}}^{1}\int_{\frac{1}{2y}}^{1} dxdy \\
&= 1 - \int_{\frac{1}{2}}^{1}\left(x\Big|_{\frac{1}{2y}}^{1}\right) dy = 1 - \int_{\frac{1}{2}}^{1}\left(1 - \frac{1}{2y}\right) dy \\
&= 1 - \left[\left(\int_{\frac{1}{2}}^{1} dy\right) - \frac{1}{2}\left(\int_{\frac{1}{2}}^{1} \frac{1}{y} dy\right)\right] \\
&= 1 - \left(y\Big|_{\frac{1}{2}}^{1}\right) + \left(\frac{1}{2}\log y\Big|_{\frac{1}{2}}^{1}\right) \\
&= 1 - \frac{1}{2} + \frac{1}{2}\log\frac{1}{2} \\
&\approx 0.85
\end{aligned}$$

We could have instead proceeded by inspecting the region in figure 7 on the preceding page, and noting that the event has probability

$$\frac{1}{2} + \int_{\frac{1}{2}}^{1} \frac{1}{2x}\, dx.$$

9° We begin by calculating $F_X(x)$

$$\begin{aligned}
F_X(x) &= c\int_0^x \int_{x^2}^{x^{\frac{1}{2}}} x + y\, dydx \\
&= c\int_0^x \left(xy + \frac{1}{2}y^2\Big|_{x^2}^{x^{\frac{1}{2}}} \right) dx \\
&= c\int_0^x x^{\frac{3}{2}} + \frac{1}{2}x - x^3 - \frac{1}{2}x^4\, dx \\
&= c\left(\frac{2}{5}x^{\frac{5}{2}} + \frac{1}{4}x^2 - \frac{1}{4}x^4 - \frac{1}{10}x^5\right).
\end{aligned}$$

Now, we can solve for c by noting that F_X is continuous, so that $\lim_{x\to 1} F_X(x)$ exists and is 1 since F_X is a distribution function. We solve for c in

$$1 = F_X(1) = c\left(\frac{2}{5}x^{\frac{5}{2}} + \frac{1}{4}x^2 - \frac{1}{4}x^4 - \frac{1}{10}x^5\right),$$

so that $c = \frac{10}{3}$. Now we have a complete expression of F_X:

$$F_X(x) = \frac{10}{3}\left(\frac{2}{5}x^{\frac{5}{2}} + \frac{1}{4}x^2 - \frac{1}{4}x^4 - \frac{1}{10}x^5\right).$$

Finally, we calculate $\mathbf{P}\left[X < \frac{1}{2}\right] = F_X(\frac{1}{2}) \approx 0.38$.

10° We begin by calculating the marginal distribution of X as

$$f_X(x) = \frac{1}{4}\int_x^2 x^2 + y\,dy = \frac{1}{4}\left(x^2y + \frac{1}{2}y^2\Big|_x^2\right) = \frac{1}{4}\left(\frac{3}{2}x^2 + 2 - x^3\right),$$

so that

$$f_{Y|X}(y|x) = \frac{f_{X,Y}(x,y)}{f_X(x)} = \frac{2(x^2+y)}{3x^2 - 2x^3 + 4}.$$

11° We must calculate the conditional distribution function for X given Y. To that end, we calculate the marginal density for Y and then the conditional density for (X|Y).

$$\begin{aligned} f_Y(y) &= \int_0^\infty \frac{1}{4}e^{-x}e^{-y}(x^2+y^2)\,dx \\ &= \frac{1}{4}e^{-y}\int_0^\infty e^{-x}(x^2+y^2)\,dx \\ &= \frac{1}{4}e^{-y}\left[(-e^{-y})\left(x^2+y^2+2x+2\right)\Big|_0^\infty\right] \\ &= \frac{1}{4}e^{-y}[y^2+2]. \end{aligned}$$

With the joint and marginal densities, we can calculate the conditional density

$$\begin{aligned} f(x|y) &= \frac{f_{X,Y}(x,y)}{f_Y(y)} \\ &= \frac{\frac{1}{4}e^{-(x+y)}(x^2+y^2)}{\frac{1}{4}e^{-y}[y^2+2]} \\ &= e^{-x}\frac{x^2+y^2}{2+y^2}. \end{aligned}$$

We are now in a position to calculate the marginal distribution function by integrating the marginal density function.

$$\begin{aligned} F(x|y) &= \int_0^x e^{-x}\frac{x^2+y^2}{2+y^2}\,dx \\ &= \frac{1}{2+y^2}\int_0^x x^2e^{-x}+y^2e^{-x}\,dx \\ &= \frac{y^2}{2+y^2}(1-e^{-x}) + \left[\frac{1}{2+y^2}(-e^{-x})(x^2+2x+2)\Big|_0^x\right] \\ &= \frac{y^2(1-e^{-x})+2-e^{-x}(x^2+2x+2)}{2+y^2} \end{aligned}$$

We use the conditional distribution to calculate

$$\mathbf{P}\left[X < \frac{4}{3}\,\middle|\, Y=3\right] = F_{(X|Y)}\left(\frac{4}{3}\,\middle|\, 3\right) = 0.63.$$

12° We draw the diagram in figure 8 on the next page to figure out the limits of integration. The event $[T_1 + 2T_2 < 1]$ is equivalent to $[T_1 < 1 + 2T_2]$. We calculate

$$\begin{aligned} \mathbf{P}[T_1 < 1+2T_2] &= \int_0^{\frac{1}{2}}\int_0^{1-2t_2} 1\,dt_1dt_2 = \int_0^{\frac{1}{2}}\left(t_1\Big|_0^{1-2t_2}\right) \\ &= \int_0^{\frac{1}{2}} 1-2t_2\,dt_2 = \left(t_2 - t_2^2\Big|_0^{\frac{1}{2}}\right) \\ &= \frac{1}{4}. \end{aligned}$$

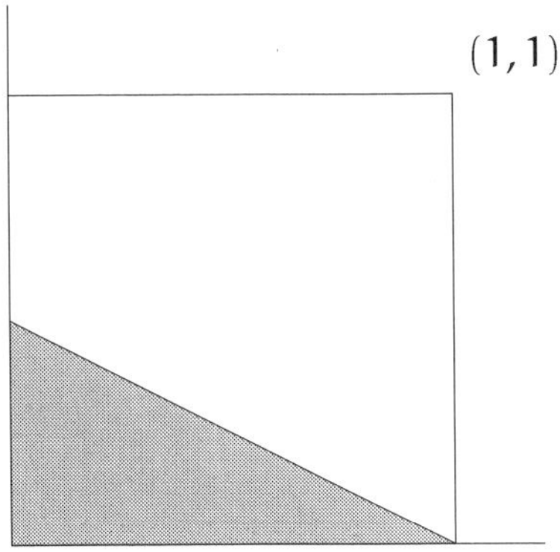

Figure 8: We must integrate over the region in gray.

13° Since $Y = X^5$, we can write $X = Y^{\frac{1}{5}}$. This implies that

$$\frac{dX}{dY} = \frac{1}{5}Y^{-\frac{4}{5}}.$$

The density for Y is

$$f_Y(y) = f_X(y^{\frac{1}{5}}) \cdot \left|\frac{dX}{dY}\right| = \frac{1}{5}y^{-\frac{4}{5}} \exp\left\{-y^{\frac{1}{5}}\right\}.$$

14° Since $Y = X^2$, $X = Y^{\frac{1}{2}}$. This implies that

$$\frac{dX}{dY} = \frac{1}{2}Y^{-\frac{1}{2}}.$$

The density function is

$$f_Y(y) = f_X(y^{\frac{1}{2}}) \left|\frac{dX}{dY}\right| = \frac{1}{6}y^{-\frac{1}{2}}.$$

15° Define $g(x) = \sqrt{|x|}$. Of course, $Y = g(X)$. Note that g is a 2-to-1 function, since $g(x) = g(-x)$. In particular, it does not have a true inverse. However, we define $g^{-1}(y) = y^2$ for $y > 0$. Because of the symmetry $g(x) = g(-x)$, we can calculate

$$\begin{aligned} f_Y(y) &= 2\left(f_X \circ g^{-1}\right)(y) \cdot \left|\frac{\partial}{\partial y} g^{-1}(y)\right| \\ &= \frac{4y}{\sqrt{2\pi}} e^{-\frac{y^4}{2}}. \end{aligned}$$

16° We calculate

$$\begin{aligned} \mathbf{P}\left[Y < y\right] = \mathbf{P}\left[e^{-\frac{X^2}{2}} < y\right] &= \mathbf{P}\left[-\frac{X^2}{2} < \log y\right] = \mathbf{P}\left[X^2 > -2\log y\right] \\ &= \mathbf{P}\left[X > \sqrt{-2\log y}\right] = S_X(\sqrt{-2\log y}), \end{aligned}$$

where $S_X(x)$ is $1 - F_X(x)$. We calculate

$$F_X(x) = \int_0^x e^{-x}\,dx = 1 - e^{-x},$$

so that $S_X(x) = e^{-x}$, and

$$f_Y(y) = \frac{\partial}{\partial y} F_Y(y) = \frac{\partial}{\partial y} S_X(\sqrt{-2\log y}) = \frac{\sqrt{2}}{2y} \cdot \frac{e^{-\sqrt{2}\sqrt{-\log y}}}{\sqrt{-\log y}}$$

by the chain rule.

17° We would typically solve this type of problem by finding the marginal distribution for X and calculating the expectation from there. However, this problem requires an alternative approach.

Let $W = \frac{X}{Y}$ and $Z = Y$. Solve for X and Y so that $Y = Z$ and $X = WZ$. We calculate the Jacobian

$$J = \left|\frac{\partial W, Z}{\partial X, Y}\right| = \begin{vmatrix} z & 0 \\ w & 1 \end{vmatrix} = |z|,$$

so that

$$\begin{aligned} f_{W,Z}(w,z) &= f_{X,Y}(wz,z) \cdot |z| \\ &= \left(\frac{1}{z}e^{-\frac{wz}{z}}\right)(ze^{-z}) \\ &= (e^{-w})(e^{-z}). \end{aligned}$$

This shows that $W = \frac{X}{Y}$ and $Z = Y$ are independent exponential random variables. We conclude that $\mathbf{C}\left[\frac{X}{Y}, Y\right] = \mathbf{E}\left[\frac{X}{Y} \cdot Y\right] - \mathbf{E}\left[\frac{X}{Y}\right]\mathbf{E}\left[Y\right] = 0$. We find, by inspection, that $\mathbf{E}\left[\frac{X}{Y}\right]$ and $\mathbf{E}\left[Y\right]$ are both 1, so that $\mathbf{E}\left[X\right] = 1$.

18° Put $U = \frac{X}{X+Y}$ and $V = X + Y$. Solve for X and Y in this system to find that $X = UV$ and $Y = V(1-U)$. We calculate the Jacobian for this transformation:

$$J = \begin{vmatrix} \frac{\partial U}{\partial X} & \frac{\partial V}{\partial X} \\ \frac{\partial U}{\partial Y} & \frac{\partial V}{\partial Y} \end{vmatrix} = \begin{vmatrix} V & U \\ -V & 1-U \end{vmatrix} = V$$

We find the joint density function for U and V is

$$\begin{aligned} f_{U,V}(u,v) &= f_{X,Y}(x,y)|J| \\ &= f_{X,Y}\left(uv, v(1-u)\right) \\ &= e^{-uv}e^{v+uv} \cdot |v| \\ &= ve^{-v} \end{aligned}$$

for $0 < u < 1$ and $v > 0$. This means that $U = \frac{X}{X+Y}$ is uniformly distributed over the unit interval, so that $\mathbf{V}\left[\frac{X}{X+Y}\right] = \frac{1}{12}$.

19° We calculate that X_i has the distribution function

$$F_{X_i}(x) = \int_0^x c(1+i)x^i \, dx = cx^{i+1},$$

which implies that $c = 1$. We seek the value of x such that $\mathbf{P}[X < x] = 0.05$. Because

$$X = \max\{X_1, X_2, X_3, X_4, X_5\},$$

we find that $X < x$ only when all the $X_i < x$. We calculate

$$\begin{aligned}\mathbf{P}[X < x] &= \mathbf{P}[\max\{X_1, X_2, X_3, X_4, X_5\} < x] \\ &= \mathbf{P}[X_1 < x]\,\mathbf{P}[X_2 < x]\,\mathbf{P}[X_3 < x]\,\mathbf{P}[X_4 < x]\,\mathbf{P}[X_5 < x] \\ &= x^2 \cdot x^3 \cdot x^4 \cdot x^5 \cdot x^6 \\ &= x^{20}\end{aligned}$$

We find the 5th percentile of X by solving for x in $0.05 = x^{20}$, so that $x \approx 0.86$.

20° Let $[A = B]$ denote the event that B receives the same 1 bit message that A sends. Let P_u be the event that the message travels over the upper path and P_d be D'_u. We want to calculate $\mathbf{P}[A = B]$. By the law of total probability, it is

$$\mathbf{P}[A = B] = \mathbf{P}[A = B|P_u]\,\mathbf{P}[P_u] + \mathbf{P}[A = B|P_d]\,\mathbf{P}[P_d].$$

Since the message is sent over the shortest operational path, the probability that it is sent via P_u is $(1 - p_f)^2 \approx 0.9409$. This represents the probability that neither node in the path has failed. The message is sent over the lower path only in the event that at least one node in the upper path has failed but all three in the lower path remain operational. This implies that the probability that the message is sent via P_d is

$$\left(\binom{2}{1} p_f(1 - p_f) + \binom{2}{2} p_f^2\right) p_f^2 = 0.0591.$$

Suppose that the message is sent via the upper path P_u. There are two events where a 1 bit message can be transmitted via P_u and arrive exactly as sent. Either neither node flips the bit, which occurs with probability $(1-p)^2 = 0.99^2$; or both nodes flip the bit, which occurs with probability $p^2 = 0.01^2$. This implies that

$$\mathbf{P}\left[A = B | P_u\right] \mathbf{P}\left[P_u\right] = \left(0.99^2 + 0.01^2\right)(0.9409) \approx 0.9223.$$

Similarly, if the message is sent via the lower node, there are two cases in which a 1 bit message can arrive as it was sent. Either no node flips the bit, which occurs with probability 0.99^3, or two nodes flip the bit, which occurs with probability $\binom{3}{2}0.01^2 0.99$. We find that

$$\mathbf{P}\left[A = B | P_d\right] \mathbf{P}\left[P_d\right] = \left(0.99^2 + \binom{3}{2} 0.01^2 \times 0.99\right) \times 0.0591 \approx 0.0574.$$

This implies that the probability that a single bit message is transmitted correctly is $\mathbf{P}\left[A = B\right] = 0.97963$. Since the message contains 8 bits, the probability we seek is $\mathbf{P}\left[A = B\right]^8 \approx 0.8482$.

4

MOMENTS

In an important sense, all of the problem solving methods for probability theory we have learned and will learn allow us to extract 'information' from a probability model. We have already seen a way to specify a probability model–in general, as a function which maps an event to the probability that it occurs. For example, a probability mass function or probability density function 'contains' all of the information required to uniquely specify a probability model. In this chapter, we will introduce *moment generating functions*, which allow an alternative way to represent a probability model. Moment generating functions can be very convenient for problem solving, since they can transform hard calculations about a probability measure into easier calculations about the moment generating function. Before then, we will introduce the first few *moments* of random variables.

EXPECTATION

The expectation of a random variable can intuitively be thought of as the location of the random variable's center. As we have seen, a probability distribution for a discrete random variable X lets us calculate $\mathbf{P}[X = x]$ at each point x. If we treat this as a function of x, we recover the probability mass function $f_X(x) = \mathbf{P}[X = x]$. The probability mass function tells us how much 'mass' there is at the point x, and the expectation tells us the *center of mass*—the balance point for the random variable.

Definition 4.1. For a discrete random variable X, we define the *expectation* $\mathbf{E}[X]$ by

$$\mathbf{E}[X] = \sum_{x \in X} x \cdot \mathbf{P}[X = x],$$

provided that the series is absolutely convergent.

Notice that we are abusing our notation here, but in a very natural way. We allow the index of summation x to vary among all the possible values that X can take. We weigh each of these values x by the probability that $X = x$, and then sum. In other words, the expectation is a probability-weighted average of the values of X. We can make a similar definition for continuous random variables. The condition that the sum is absolutely convergent is a technical condition that allows us to rearrange the series without affecting the expectation. But this technical condition does imply that some random variables might not have an expectation. For example, the series may either diverge, or converge, but not absolutely.

Definition 4.2. For a continuous random variable X, we define the *expectation* $\mathbf{E}[X]$ by

$$\mathbf{E}[X] = \int_{-\infty}^{\infty} x f_X(x)\, dx,$$

where f_X is the probability density function for X.

If a random variable X is constant, $\mathbf{E}[X] = X$. On the other hand, we can construct a random variable X_c for any real number c, by declaring that $X_c = c$. We can conclude

Theorem 4.3. *For any real number* c, $\mathbf{E}[c] = c$.

Example 4.4. A die is rolled twice. What is the expected sum of the outcomes?

Solution. Let N be the sum of the outcomes. We previously calculated the probability mass function for N, in example 2.8 on page 29, as

$$f_N(k) = \begin{cases} \frac{k-1}{6} & \text{if } k \leq 7 \\ \frac{13-k}{6} & \text{otherwise.} \end{cases}$$

We can calculate

$$\begin{aligned}\mathbf{E}[N] &= 2\cdot\frac{1}{36}+3\cdot\frac{2}{36}+4\cdot\frac{3}{36}+5\cdot\frac{4}{36}+6\cdot\frac{5}{36}+7\frac{6}{36}\\ &\quad+8\cdot\frac{5}{36}+9\cdot\frac{4}{36}+10\cdot\frac{3}{36}+11\cdot\frac{2}{36}+12\cdot\frac{1}{36}\\ &=7.\end{aligned}$$

■

We can see that calculating expectations for discrete random variables directly, from the basic definition, can be tedious. As we have seen, it requires calculating the probability $\mathbf{P}[X = x]$ for each $x \in X$. We will soon develop an important property for calculating expectations.

Example 4.5. Let X be a positive random variable with a probability mass function given by

$$f_X(k) = e^{-\lambda}\frac{\lambda^k}{k!}, \text{ for } k \geq 0.$$

What is $\mathbf{E}[X]$?

Solution. We will calculate this expectation directly, by evaluating the sum

$$\mathbf{E}[X] = \sum_{k=0}^{\infty} ke^{-\lambda}\frac{\lambda^k}{k!}.$$

We can re-index this series, since if $k = 0$, it contributes no value to the series. This means we don't have to include this case in the sum.

$$\begin{aligned}&= \sum_{k=1}^{\infty} ke^{-\lambda}\frac{\lambda^k}{k!}\\ &= e^{-\lambda}\sum_{k=1}^{\infty} k\frac{\lambda^k}{k!}\\ &= e^{-\lambda}\sum_{k=1}^{\infty}\frac{\lambda^k}{(k-1)!}\\ &= \lambda e^{-\lambda}\sum_{k=1}^{\infty}\frac{\lambda^{k-1}}{(k-1)!}\end{aligned}$$

We re-index the series again, so that

$$= \lambda e^{-\lambda} \sum_{k=0}^{\infty} \frac{\lambda^k}{k!}.$$

We recognize that the series equals e^{λ}, so that

$$\mathbf{E}[X] = \lambda. \qquad \blacksquare$$

Perhaps the most important steps to understand are the re-indexing steps. Re-indexing a sum or series to make it easier to compute is an essential exam skill.

Example 4.6. Let X be a positive random variable with a probability mass function given by

$$f_X(k) = q^{k-1}p,$$

where $p \in (0, 1)$ and $q = 1 - p$. What is $\mathbf{E}[X]$?

Solution. X is a geometric random variable. We will discuss this probability distribution in detail later, but will calculate its expectation here. We will do so using a neat trick from calculus. We begin with

$$\begin{aligned} \mathbf{E}[X] &= \sum_{k=1}^{\infty} kpq^{k-1} \\ &= p(1 + 2q + 3q^2 + \cdots). \end{aligned}$$

We recognize that the sum in parentheses is the derivative of the geometric series on q. Recall that we can write the geometric series as

$$1 + q + q^2 + \cdots = \frac{1}{1-q}.$$

We find that the derivative of the geometric series is $(1-q)^{-2} = p^{-2}$, so that $\mathbf{E}[X] = p^{-1}$. $\blacksquare$

It is important to note that the expectation of X is a function of X, but it is not a random variable. In particular, the expectation function **E** is an *operator*, that is, a function which maps functions–in this case random variables–to numbers. We can write the signature of the expectation operator **E** as $\mathbf{E}\colon (\Omega \to \mathbf{R}) \to \mathbf{R}$. We have seen examples of operators in previous courses, such as calculus. Notice that the definite integral is an operator that maps a function f to a number

$$I(f) = \int_a^b f(x)\,dx.$$

We are focusing on treating the expectation as an operator to abstract away the differences between the expectation of a discrete random variable and a continuous random variable, or even a mixture variable. In all cases, we have the following

Theorem 4.7. *The expectation operator is a* linear operator, *which means that for jointly distributed random variables* X *and* Y *and constants* α *and* β*,*

$$\mathbf{E}\left[\alpha X + \beta Y\right] = \alpha \mathbf{E}\left[X\right] + \beta \mathbf{E}\left[Y\right].$$

Proof. We will prove this in the discrete case now. We write

$$\mathbf{E}\left[X + Y\right] = \sum_{x \in X} \sum_{y \in Y} (x + y) f(x, y)$$

We can expand this sum as

$$\left(\sum_{x \in X} \sum_{y \in Y} x f(x, y) \right) + \left(\sum_{x \in X} \sum_{y \in Y} y f(x, y) \right).$$

We can rearrange the right hand summation to

$$\left(\sum_{x \in X} \sum_{y \in Y} x f(x, y) \right) + \left(\sum_{y \in Y} \sum_{x \in X} y f(x, y) \right).$$

Now, focus on the sum

$$\sum_{y \in Y} x f(x, y).$$

Since x does not depend on y, we can factor it out of the sum, writing it as

$$x \sum_{y \in Y} f(x, y).$$

We recognize that

$$\sum_{y \in Y} f(x, y)$$

is the marginal probability mass function for X. In other words, we can write

$$x \sum_{y \in Y} f(x, y) = x f_X(x)$$

We can apply the same argument to the other sum, so that

$$\mathbf{E}[X + Y] = \left(\sum_{x \in X} x f_X(x) \right) + \left(\sum_{y \in Y} y f_Y(y) \right)$$

which is clearly equal to $\mathbf{E}[X] + \mathbf{E}[Y]$. ■

The linearity property of expectation is perhaps the most useful property for solving practical problems involving expectations. The linearity property can greatly simplify the calculation of expectations.

Example 4.8. A die is rolled three times. What is the expected sum of the outcomes?

Solution. It is certainly possible to calculate this expectation directly, but describing the sample space and finding the probability mass function is very tedious. Instead, we can use the linearity of expectation. We let S be the sum, and let S_1, S_2, and S_3 be the outcomes of the first, second, and third rolls respectively. Then, $S = S_1 + S_2 + S_3$, and by the linearity of expectation,

$$\mathbf{E}[S] = \mathbf{E}[S_1] + \mathbf{E}[S_2] + \mathbf{E}[S_3] .$$

We can calculate these easily, using the direct definition, since

$$\mathbf{E}[S_1] = \frac{1+2+3+4+5+6}{6} = 3.5.$$

The outcomes of the other throws have the same distribution, so that $\mathbf{E}[S] = 3 \times 3.5 = 10.5$. ■

Example 4.9. An unfair coin is known to land heads with probability $p = 3/5$, independently of other flips. It is flipped 100 times. What is the expected number of heads obtained?

Solution. Let N be the number of heads obtained. N is a binomial random variable, which we will discuss fully in section 5.2 on page 136. For now, we will assume that we have derived the probability mass function for the distribution. Then the expectation $\mathbf{E}[N]$ is given by

$$\mathbf{E}[N] = \sum_{n=1}^{100} n \binom{100}{n} p^n (1-p)^{n-1}.$$

This sum can be evaluated by hand, but it requires insight and is time consuming. Instead, we will use the linearity of expectation. To that end, we define random variables $N_1, N_2, \ldots N_{100}$, where

$$N_i = \begin{cases} 1 & \text{if the } i^{\text{th}} \text{ coin flip is heads,} \\ 0 & \text{otherwise.} \end{cases}$$

We can calculate the expectation for N_i easily, since

$$\mathbf{E}[N_i] = (1 \times p) + (0 \times (1-p)) = p = \frac{3}{5}.$$

By the linearity of expectation, we can write

$$\begin{aligned} \mathbf{E}[N] &= \mathbf{E}[N_1] + \mathbf{E}[N_2] + \cdots + \mathbf{E}[N_{100}] \\ &= 100 \times \frac{3}{5} \\ &= 60. \end{aligned}$$

■

CONDITIONAL EXPECTATION

In actuarial applications, we often want to calculate expectations with respect to some condition. For example, we might be interested in knowing the average loss due to car accidents caused by high risk drivers, as opposed to the average loss taken over all car accidents. This can make intuitive sense. We might expect that high risk drivers are riskier because they drive faster. High speed driving increases the severity of damage caused by an accident, so we might expect that a high risk drivers would cause more damage per accident than a low risk driver. We will cover this and other examples later. We begin by extending the notation for the expectation.

Definition 4.10. Let A be an event, and let X be a discrete random variable. We define the *conditional expectation of* X *given* A as

$$\mathbf{E}[X|A] = \sum_{x \in X} x f_X(x|A),$$

where $f_X(x|A)$ is the probability mass function for X given that A occurred. If X is a continuous random variable, we define

$$\mathbf{E}[X|A] = \int_{-\infty}^{\infty} x f_X(x|A)\, dx.$$

The following theorem lets us calculate unconditional expectations, given that we can calculate conditional expectations given disjoint events. This is perhaps too abstract, so will return to our original example. An insurance company categorizes its drivers as high risk and low risk. The company estimates that the average loss due to accidents by high risk drivers is $\mathbf{E}[X|H]$, and the average loss due to accidents by low risk drivers is $\mathbf{E}[X|H']$. How can the company estimate $\mathbf{E}[X]$, the average loss due to all drivers? The law of total expectation helps us answer this question.

Theorem 4.11 (Law of Total Expectation). *Let $\{E_i\}$ be a countable partition of the sample space, and let X be a random variable. Then the* law of total expectation,

$$\mathbf{E}[X] = \sum_{i=1}^{\infty} \mathbf{E}[X|E_i]\, \mathbf{P}[E_i]$$

holds.

Proof. The law of total expectation is very closely related to the law of total probability, which we learned about in theorem 1.35 on page 12 and we will in fact appeal to the law of total probability to prove this theorem for the discrete case. We begin by considering the sum

$$\sum_{i=1}^{\infty} \mathbf{E}[X|E_i]\, \mathbf{P}[E_i] = \sum_{i=1}^{\infty} \left(\sum_{x \in X} x\mathbf{P}[X = x|E_i] \right) \mathbf{P}[E_i] .$$

We can distribute the $\mathbf{P}[E_i]$ term over the inner series and change the order of summation, so that we have the quantity

$$\sum_{x \in X} \sum_{i=1}^{\infty} x\mathbf{P}[X = x|E_i]\, \mathbf{P}[E_i] .$$

Since x does not depend on i, we can factor it out of the inner sum so that we have

$$\sum_{x \in X} x \left(\sum_{i=1}^{\infty} \mathbf{P}[X = x|E_i]\, \mathbf{P}[E_i] \right) .$$

We apply the law of total probability to the inner sum, to find that this quantity is

$$\sum_{x \in X} x\mathbf{P}[X = x] = \mathbf{E}[X] .$$ ■

The law of total expectation is especially powerful when combined with recursion. Generally speaking, recursion is a mathematical technique that models situations where an event can recur. In recursion, a function is defined in terms of itself, such as how the factorial function ! is defined by

$$n! = \begin{cases} n \times (n-1)!, & \text{if } n > 0, \\ 1, & \text{if } n = 0. \end{cases}$$

Recursion is a complement to mathematical induction. We can use recursion to define mathematical structures and induction to prove things about recursively defined mathematical structures. Recursion and induction are very powerful techniques, and their full applicability is outside of the scope of this book. However, we will note that recursion can often be applied to model situations where 'starting over' is allowed.

Example 4.12. A student works on a complicated math problem. If he does not make any mistakes, it takes him 30 minutes to complete it. If he does make a mistake, it takes him 15 minutes to notice the mistake, and then he must start over. The probability that he makes a mistake is 4/5. What is the expected length of time until the student finishes the problem?

Solution. Let X be the time, and let M be the event that the student makes a mistake. The law of total probability implies that

$$\mathbf{E}[X] = \mathbf{E}[X|M']\,\mathbf{P}[M'] + \mathbf{E}[X|M]\,\mathbf{P}[M]$$

Since it takes the student 15 minutes to find a mistake, and then the student must start over, $\mathbf{E}[X|M] = 15 + \mathbf{E}[X]$, so that

$$\begin{aligned} \mathbf{E}[X] &= \mathbf{E}[X|M']\,\mathbf{P}[M'] + (15 + \mathbf{E}[X])\,\mathbf{P}[M] \\ &= 18 + \frac{4}{5}\mathbf{E}[X] \end{aligned}$$

We solve for $\mathbf{E}[X] = 90$. ■

Now consider a situation where we have jointly distributed random variables X and Y. Given a fixed y, we can consider the event $[Y = y]$, so that we can calculate $\mathbf{E}[X|Y = y]$, using definition 4.10 on page 94. Since we have chosen a fixed y, $\mathbf{E}[X|Y = y]$ is *not* a random variable. But notice that we can define a function $f(y) = \mathbf{E}[X|Y = y]$, which we can alternatively express as $f(Y) = \mathbf{E}[X|Y]$. f is a real-valued function of the random variable Y, so that $f(Y) = \mathbf{E}[X|Y]$ is a random variable.

Definition 4.13. Let X and Y be random variables. Let $f(y) = \mathbf{E}[X|Y = y]$. The *conditional expectation of* X *given* Y is the random variable

$$\mathbf{E}[X|Y] = f(Y).$$

If the outcome for a random variable X does not depend on the outcome for a random variable Y, then knowing Y cannot yield information about X. In the context of conditional expectations, this means that

Theorem 4.14. *For independent random variables* X *and* Y,

$$\mathbf{E}[X|Y] = \mathbf{E}[X].$$

Proof. Since X and Y are independent, $\mathbf{P}[X = x|Y = y] = \mathbf{P}[X = x]$. Then, it follows that

$$\mathbf{E}[X|Y] = \sum_{x \in X} x\mathbf{P}[X = x|Y = y] = \sum_{x \in X} x\mathbf{P}[X = x] = \mathbf{E}[X]. \qquad \blacksquare$$

Example 4.15. In a certain game, a player rolls a red die and black die. We let R and B be the outcomes for the red and black dice respectively. The total prize won is given by RB. What is $\mathbf{E}[RB|B]$?

Solution. We are asked to calculate the expected prize, conditional on B. We will do this directly. Note that if $B = b$, the total prize is

$$g(b) = \mathbf{E}[Rb|B = b] = b\mathbf{E}[R].$$

Substituting B for b, we find

$$\mathbf{E}[RB|B] = B\mathbf{E}[R] = 3.5B. \qquad \blacksquare$$

Pay particular attention to the structure of this argument. In the context of calculating the conditional expectation given B, we treated B as a constant. Conditioning, in general, lets us model the *consequences of having knowledge*, even if we don't have that knowledge yet. Conditional on B, we 'know' what B is. In an absolute sense, B is still random. And that is why the conditional expectation is a random variable–because we are assuming that we know what B is, and we calculate the conditional expectation under that assumption. This argument is, essentially, the intuition for

Theorem 4.16 (Factoring a known quantity). *Let X and Y be random variables. Then*

$$\mathbf{E}[XY|Y] = Y\mathbf{E}[X] .$$

VARIANCE

As we saw in section section 4.1 on page 87, the expectation tells us the center of mass for a random variable. The variance is a similar measure. Intuitively, it tells us how spread out the random variable is around the center of mass.

Consider the quantity $(X - \mathbf{E}[X])$ for a moment. It is obviously the difference between X and its expectation, so that $\mathbf{E}[\,(X - \mathbf{E}[X])\,]$ is the average difference between X and $\mathbf{E}[X]$. This is somewhat close to what we want from a measure of spread-out-ness, but it ignores the possibility of cancellation.

Example 4.17. Let X take on the values -1 and 1 with equal probability, and let $Y = 100X$. Calculate $\mathbf{E}[X - \mathbf{E}[X]\,]$ and $\mathbf{E}[Y - \mathbf{E}[Y]\,]$.

Solution. We can see that $\mathbf{E}[X] = 0$. This means that the difference $X - \mathbf{E}[X]$ has the same distribution as X. In particular, $\mathbf{E}[X - \mathbf{E}[X]\,] = \mathbf{E}[X] = 0$. Similarly, $\mathbf{E}[Y] = 0$, so that $Y - \mathbf{E}[Y]$ has the same distribution as Y and $\mathbf{E}[Y - \mathbf{E}[Y]\,] = \mathbf{E}[Y] = 0$. ■

This example shows us that $\mathbf{E}[X - \mathbf{E}[X]\,]$ is not a suitable measure of spread-out-ness, since Y is intuitively much more spread out than X. The problem is that we are taking the average *difference* between X and $\mathbf{E}[X]$, which can be negative. What we really want to consider is the average *distance* between X and $\mathbf{E}[X]$. The distance between two points is always positive, which means that we can't run into our problem with cancellation.

Example 4.18. Let X take on the values -1 and 1 with equal probability, and let $Y = 100X$. Calculate $\mathbf{E}[|X - \mathbf{E}[X]|]$ and $\mathbf{E}[|Y - \mathbf{E}[Y]|]$.

Solution. We can see that $\mathbf{E}[X]$ and $\mathbf{E}[Y]$ are both 0. This means that

$$\mathbf{E}[|X - \mathbf{E}[X]|] = \mathbf{E}[|X|] = 1.$$

Similarly,

$$\mathbf{E}[|Y - \mathbf{E}[Y]|] = \mathbf{E}[|Y|] = 100.$$ ■

This is certainly a plausible measure of spread-out-ness. The problem with using $\mathbf{E}[|X - \mathbf{E}[X]|]$ is that it is surprisingly difficult to work with. There are not many algebraic identities that let us calculate this quantity quickly and easily. So instead of using the absolute value function, we square the distance, and define

Definition 4.19. The variance of the random variable X is

$$\mathbf{V}[X] = \mathbf{E}\left[(X - \mathbf{E}[X])^2\right].$$

One minor inconvenience with the variance as a measure of spread-out-ness is that it grows faster than we might expect. To correct that, we define

Definition 4.20. The *standard deviation* of the random variable X is

$$\sigma_X = \sqrt{\mathbf{V}[X]}$$

We motivated our definition of the variance on the grounds that it allows easy calculations. We will now derive an important tool for calculating the variance.

Theorem 4.21. *For a random variable* X,

$$\mathbf{V}[X] = \mathbf{E}\left[X^2\right] - \mathbf{E}[X]^2.$$

Proof. The proof is a straight-forward calculation.

$$\begin{aligned}\mathbf{V}[X] &= \mathbf{E}\left[(X - \mathbf{E}[X])^2\right] \\ &= \mathbf{E}\left[X^2 - 2X\mathbf{E}[X] + \mathbf{E}[X]^2\right] \\ &= \mathbf{E}\left[X^2\right] - 2\mathbf{E}[X]^2 + \mathbf{E}[X]^2 \\ &= \mathbf{E}\left[X^2\right] - \mathbf{E}[X]^2.\end{aligned}$$

■

Example 4.22. Four cards are drawn from a standard deck, with replacement. Let H be the number of hearts drawn, and calculate the standard deviation σ_H.

Solution. We break down this calculation into two steps. First, we calculate $\mathbf{E}[H]$. Then we calculate $\mathbf{E}[H^2]$, and finally, we calculate σ_H. We recognize that H is a binomial random variable, so we can calculate $\mathbf{E}[H] = 4 \times (13/52) = 1$. Let $p = 13/52$, and calculate

$$\begin{aligned}\mathbf{E}\left[H^2\right] &= 1\binom{4}{1}p^1(1-p)^3 + 2^2\binom{4}{2}p^2(1-p)^2 \\ &\quad + 3^2\binom{4}{3}p^3(1-p)^1 + 4^2\binom{4}{4}p^4(1-p)^0 \\ &= 1.75.\end{aligned}$$

From this, we can conclude that $\mathbf{V}[H] = 0.75$, and $\sigma_H = 0.86603$. We will find a formula for the variance of a binomially distributed random variable in section 5.2 on page 136. ■

We will prove several important basic properties of the variance. Since the variance is the expected squared distance from the expectation, the variance is a constant property of a random variable. In other words, the variance is not a random variable. The variance is not a linear function, either. Indeed, we can prove that

Theorem 4.23. *For a random variable* X, *if* $\mathbf{V}[X]$ *exists,*

$$\mathbf{V}[X + c] = \mathbf{V}[X]$$

for any real number c.

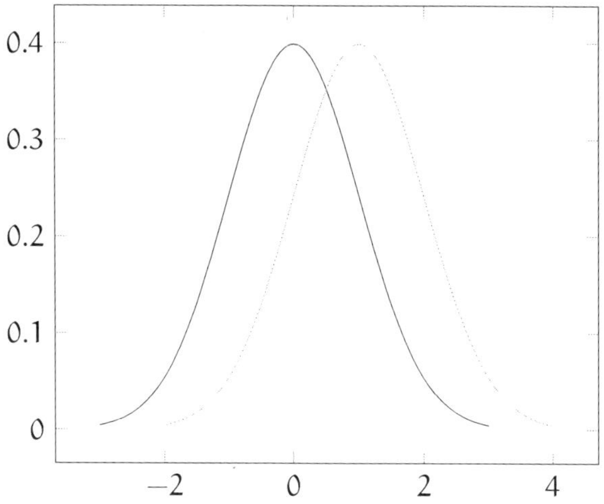

Figure 9: The variance of X and $X + c$ is the same. We see that shifting a random variable by c moves the probability function for it, but does not make it more spread out.

Proof. This is a purely computational proof:

$$\begin{aligned}
\mathbf{V}[X+c] &= \mathbf{E}\left[(X+c)^2\right] - \mathbf{E}[X+c]^2 \\
&= \mathbf{E}\left[X^2 + 2cX + c^2\right] - \left[\mathbf{E}[X]^2 + 2c\mathbf{E}[X] + c^2\right] \\
&= \mathbf{E}\left[X^2\right] - \mathbf{E}[X]^2 \\
&= \mathbf{V}[X]\,.
\end{aligned}$$

■

Intuitively, this theorem means that shifting a random variable by a constant amount does not affect how spread out the random variable is. Refer to figure 9. Similarly, we can prove

Theorem 4.24. *For a random variable X, if* $\mathbf{V}[X]$ *exists, then*

$$\mathbf{V}[cX] = c^2\mathbf{V}[X]\,.$$

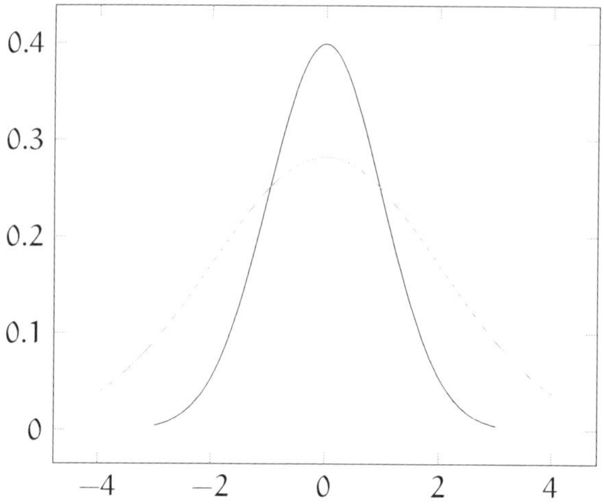

Figure 10: The probability density function for the random variable X is plotted in black, and the probability density function for the random variable 2X is plotted in gray. We see that 2X is much more spread out than X.

Proof. This is another straight forward computation.

$$\begin{aligned}
\mathbf{V}[cX] &= \mathbf{E}\left[(cX)^2\right] - \mathbf{E}[cX]^2 \\
&= \mathbf{E}\left[c^2X^2\right] - (c\mathbf{E}[X])^2 \\
&= c^2\mathbf{E}\left[X^2\right] - c^2\mathbf{E}[X]^2 \\
&= c^2\left(\mathbf{E}\left[X^2\right] - \mathbf{E}[X]^2\right) \\
&= c^2\mathbf{V}[X]\,.
\end{aligned}$$

■

This scaling property for the variance is the reason why we introduce the standard deviation. Since the standard deviation for X is $\sigma = \sqrt{\mathbf{V}[X]}$, the standard deviation for 2X is $\sqrt{4\mathbf{V}[X]} = 2\sigma$. Refer to figure figure 10.

Example 4.25. A recent study has shown that each household spent an average of 8910 on health care last year, with a variance of 12257000. Projections estimate that health care costs will increase by 7% in the next year. What will be the standard deviation of health care costs next year?

Solution. Let X be the cost of health care. We are given that $\mathbf{V}[X] = 12557000$, and we must find

$$\sqrt{\mathbf{V}[1.07X]} = \sqrt{1.07^2\mathbf{V}[X]} = 1.07\sqrt{\mathbf{V}[X]} \approx 3746.$$

■

We can also show that the variance of a constant number is 0. This should make intuitive sense, since the value constant random variable takes does not depend on an experiment's outcome. In particular, the probability mass for it is all concentrated at the one point the random variable takes. Intuitively, it's spread-out-ness is as small as a random variable's spread-out-ness can be.

The calculation of variances of sums of random variables is not as simple as the calculation of expectations of sums of random variables. Because the variance operator lacks the linearity property, calculating the variance of a sum of random variables requires more information that just the variances of each random variable. We require

Definition 4.26. The *covariance* of the random variables X and Y is

$$\mathbf{C}[X, Y] = \mathbf{E}[XY] - \mathbf{E}[X]\,\mathbf{E}[Y]\,.$$

The *correlation* between X and Y is given by

$$\rho = \frac{\mathbf{C}[X, Y]}{\sigma_X \sigma_Y}.$$

As saw in section 4.1, if X and Y are independent, then $\mathbf{E}[XY] = \mathbf{E}[X]\,\mathbf{E}[Y]$. We can see that the covariance, then, is a measure of the dependence between X and Y. But, much like the variance, the measure grows faster than we would expect. This is why we introduce the correlation coefficient ρ, which normalizes the covariance in the same way as the standard deviation normalizes the covariance. Indeed, $\mathbf{C}[X, X] = \mathbf{E}[X^2] - \mathbf{E}[X]^2 = \mathbf{V}[X]$.

We can intuitively see why the variance of $X+Y$ depends on the covariance between X and Y. If X and Y tend to vary in opposite ways, so that if X increases when Y decreases, then the sum of their values will tend to be smaller than if they were independent, and the cancellation would tend to make $X+Y$ less spread out. If they vary together, then the sum will tend to be larger than if they were independent. This effect would tend to make the sum $X+Y$ more spread out. Consider these extreme examples: if $Y=-X$ then $X+Y$ is constantly 0, and has a variance of 0. On the other hand, if $X=Y$, then $X+Y=2X$, and $X+Y$ is twice as spread out as X.

Theorem 4.27. *Let X and Y be jointly distributed random variables with finite variances. Then*

$$\mathbf{V}[X+Y]=\mathbf{V}[X]+\mathbf{V}[Y]+2\mathbf{C}[X,Y].$$

Proof. The proof is a straight-forward computation. We write the variance of $\mathbf{V}[X+Y]$ as

$$\begin{aligned}
&\mathbf{E}\left[(X+Y)^2\right]-\mathbf{E}[X+Y]^2\\
&\quad=\mathbf{E}\left[X^2+2XY+Y^2\right]-(\mathbf{E}[X]+\mathbf{E}[Y])^2\\
&\quad=\mathbf{E}\left[X^2\right]+2\mathbf{E}[XY]+\mathbf{E}\left[Y^2\right]-\mathbf{E}[X]^2-2\mathbf{E}[X]\,\mathbf{E}[Y]-\mathbf{E}[Y]^2\\
&\quad=\mathbf{V}[X]+\mathbf{V}[Y]+2\mathbf{C}[X,Y].
\end{aligned}$$

■

This theorem extends naturally to sums of more than two random variables.

Theorem 4.28. *Let $X_1,\ldots,X_n$ be random variables with finite variances and $X=X_1+\cdots X_n$. Then*

$$\mathbf{V}[N]=\sum_{i=1}^{n}\mathbf{V}[X_i]+2\sum_{j,k}\mathbf{C}[X_j,X_k],$$

where j and k vary over the $\binom{n}{2}$ pairs (j,k) with $j<k$. In this way, we account for the covariance between each pair of variables, once. We can also express the variance of N as

$$\mathbf{V}[N]=\sum_{j=1}^{n}\sum_{k=1}^{j}\mathbf{C}[X_j,X_k].$$

Example 4.29. A deck of cards with the numbers 1 to n are put into a random order so that each of the $n!$ orders is equally likely. Let N be the number of cards that were not moved by the reordering. What is the variance of N?

Solution. Let X_k be an indicator variable for the event that the card numbered k is at the kth position in the new order. Then $N = X_1 + \cdots + X_n$. Each card has probability $\frac{1}{n}$ to appear at the kth place, so that $\mathbf{E}[X_k] = \frac{1}{n}$ and $\mathbf{E}[N] = 1$. Similarly, the $\mathbf{E}[N^2] = \frac{1}{n}$, so that

$$\mathbf{V}[N] = \frac{1}{n} - \frac{1}{n^2} = \frac{n-1}{n^2}.$$

Now we calculate $\mathbf{E}[X_j X_k]$. The product $X_j X_k$ is either 0 or 1, and it is only 1 if both the card numbered j and the card numbered k both appear in their admissible places. The probability for that event is $\frac{1}{n(n-1)}$. This implies that

$$\mathbf{E}[X_j X_k] = \frac{1}{n(n-1)}$$

and

$$\mathbf{C}[X_j, X_k] = \frac{1}{n(n-1)} - \frac{1}{n^2} = \frac{1}{n^2(n-1)}$$

We calculate the variance of N as

$$\mathbf{V}[N] = \frac{n(n-1)}{n^2} + 2\binom{n}{2}\frac{1}{n^2(n-1)} = 1. \qquad \blacksquare$$

We also introduce the coefficient of variation to allow us to compare the variability of random variables. Consider, for example, a random variable X that measures a quantity in miles and another random variable Y that measures the same quantity in feet. Numerically, the standard deviation of X will be much smaller than the standard deviation of Y. But each 'unit' of the standard deviation of X represents a much larger deviation in real terms. The coefficient of variation attempts to normalize these unit-driven differences in the measurement of spread-out-ness by creating a unitless measure.

Definition 4.30. The *coefficient of variation* for a random variable X is

$$\frac{\sigma_X}{\mu_X}.$$

COVARIANCE AND CORRELATION

We previously discussed the covariance in relation to the sum of random variables. When calculating the variance of the sum $X+Y$, we must take care to account for how the variables relate to each other. We briefly discussed that the covariance is a measure of the dependence of the random variables. Strictly speaking, the covariance is a measure of *linear dependence*, and is not a measure of dependence in general. If the random vector (X, Y) tends to lie along a line with positive slope, the covariance will be positive. If (X, Y) tends to lie a long a line with negative slope, the covariance will be negative. Interpreting the size of the correlation is somewhat difficult, the correlation coefficient ρ is introduced.[1]

As we said, the covariance measures the linear dependence between vectors, and is not a general measure of dependence. In particular, while the covariance between independent random variables is 0, it is not generally the case that $\mathbf{C}[X, Y] = 0$ implies independence.

Example 4.31. Let X be uniformly distributed on $[-1, 1]$, and let $Y = X^2$. X and Y are clearly dependent, but

$$\mathbf{C}\left[X, X^2\right] = \mathbf{E}\left[X^3\right] - \mathbf{E}[X]\,\mathbf{E}\left[X^2\right] = 0 - \left(0 \times \mathbf{E}\left[X^2\right]\right) = 0.$$

We can prove various algebraic properties about the covariance. For example, since multiplication of real numbers is commutative,

Theorem 4.32. *For random variables* X *and* Y, $\mathbf{C}[X, Y] = \mathbf{C}[Y, X]$.

1 The covariance can be interpreted as an L^2 inner product of real valued functions. The correlation coefficient, then, is the cosine of the angle between the real-valued functions, as defined by the covariance inner product. Unfortunately, making this explanation rigorous requires graduate-level real analysis to, for example, define the L^2 space of real functions.

Proof. This is a straight-forward computation.

$$\mathbf{C}[X,Y] = \mathbf{E}[XY] - \mathbf{E}[X]\,\mathbf{E}[Y] = \mathbf{E}[YX] - \mathbf{E}[Y]\,\mathbf{E}[X] = \mathbf{C}[Y,X]\,.$$

∎

Theorem 4.33. *For a real number* a *and random variables* X *and* Y,

$$a\mathbf{C}[X,Y] = \mathbf{C}[aX,Y] = \mathbf{C}[X,aY]\,.$$

Proof. To begin with, note that

$$a\mathbf{C}[X,Y] = a\mathbf{E}[XY] - a\mathbf{E}[X]\,\mathbf{E}[Y]$$

but we also have

$$\begin{aligned}\mathbf{C}[X,aY] &= \mathbf{E}[aXY] - \mathbf{E}[X]\,\mathbf{E}[aY]\\ &= a\mathbf{E}[XY] - a\mathbf{E}[X]\,\mathbf{E}[Y]\\ &= \mathbf{E}[aXY] - \mathbf{E}[aX]\,\mathbf{E}[Y]\\ &= \mathbf{C}[aX,Y]\,.\end{aligned}$$

∎

Theorem 4.34. *For random variables* X *and* Y, *and real numbers* a *and* b,

$$\mathbf{C}[a+X,b+Y] = \mathbf{C}[X,Y]\,.$$

Proof. This is another straight-forward calculation.

$$\begin{aligned}\mathbf{C}[a+X,b+Y] &= \mathbf{E}[(a+X)(b+Y)] - \mathbf{E}[a+X]\,\mathbf{E}[b+Y]\\ &= \mathbf{E}[ab+aY+bX+XY] - (a+\mathbf{E}[X])\,(b+\mathbf{E}[Y])\\ &= ab + a\mathbf{E}[Y] + b\mathbf{E}[X] + \mathbf{E}[XY]\\ &\quad - (ab + a\mathbf{E}[Y] + b\mathbf{E}[X] + \mathbf{E}[X]\,\mathbf{E}[Y])\\ &= \mathbf{E}[XY] - \mathbf{E}[X]\,\mathbf{E}[Y]\\ &= \mathbf{C}[X,Y]\,.\end{aligned}$$

∎

Theorem 4.35. *For random variables* X, Y, V, *and* W, *and real numbers* a, b, c, *and* d,

$$\begin{aligned}\mathbf{C}[aX+bY,cW+dV] &= ac\mathbf{C}[X,W] + ad\mathbf{C}[X,V]\\ &\quad + bc\mathbf{C}[Y,W] + bd\mathbf{C}[Y,V]\,.\end{aligned}$$

The proof of this theorem is another straight-forward calculation. It is good practice, and important for the exam, so we leave it as an exercise for the reader.

CONDITIONAL VARIANCE

Just as we defined the conditional expectations, we can define conditional variances. The conditional variance of a random variable X is a measure of how 'spread out' the random variable is, given that some condition holds. For example, consider the case of high and low risk drivers again. A low risk driver has fewer and less severe accidents than a high risk driver. Intuitively, it seems plausible that the damage due to accidents from low risk drivers has a lower variance than the damage due to accidents by high risk drivers.

Definition 4.36. Let X and Y be jointly distributed random variables and let C be an event. We define the variance of X given C by

$$\mathbf{V}[X|C] = \mathbf{E}\left[(X - \mathbf{E}[X|C])^2 \right].$$

We define the *conditional variance* of X given Y as

$$\mathbf{V}[X|Y] = \mathbf{E}\left[(X - \mathbf{E}[X|Y])^2 \right].$$

From the definition, we can easily show that

$$\mathbf{V}[X|C] = \mathbf{E}\left[X^2|C\right] - \mathbf{E}[X|C]^2$$

and

$$\mathbf{V}[X|Y] = \mathbf{E}\left[X^2|Y\right] - \mathbf{E}[X|Y]^2$$

using essentially the same arguments we used to show that $\mathbf{V}[X] = \mathbf{E}[X^2] - \mathbf{E}[X]^2$.

The conditional variance of X given Y is a real-valued function of the value Y, and so it is a random variable. This is similar to the situation with the conditional expectation $\mathbf{E}[X|Y]$. Indeed, we have a result analogous to the law of total expectation, for conditional variances.

Theorem 4.37 (Law of total variance). *For random variables* X *and* Y *with finite variance,*

$$\mathbf{V}[X] = \mathbf{V}[\mathbf{E}[X|Y]] + \mathbf{E}[\mathbf{V}[X|Y]].$$

Proof. The proof is a straight-forward computation. On the one hand, we have

$$\mathbf{V}[\mathbf{E}[X|Y]] = \mathbf{E}[\mathbf{E}[X|Y]]^2 - \mathbf{E}[\mathbf{E}[X|Y]]^2 = \mathbf{E}[\mathbf{E}[X|Y]]^2 - \mathbf{E}[X]^2.$$

On the other hand, we have

$$\begin{aligned}\mathbf{E}[\mathbf{V}[X|Y]] &= \mathbf{E}\left[\mathbf{E}\left[X^2|Y\right] - \mathbf{E}[X|Y]^2\right]\\ &= \mathbf{E}\left[\mathbf{E}\left[X^2|Y\right]\right] - \mathbf{E}\left[\mathbf{E}[X|Y]^2\right]\\ &= \mathbf{E}\left[X^2\right] - \mathbf{E}\left[\mathbf{E}[X|Y]^2\right].\end{aligned}$$

Adding these together, we find

$$\mathbf{V}[X] = \mathbf{V}[\mathbf{E}[X|Y]] + \mathbf{E}[\mathbf{V}[X|Y]]. \qquad \blacksquare$$

We have seen that the first two moments, $\mathbf{E}[X]$ and $\mathbf{E}[X^2]$, can be used to describe properties of a random variable, such as where its center is, and how spread out it is. Strictly speaking, these are properties about the probability mass and density functions, and they give us rough quantitative information about the shape of the probability density function. Since the probability density function contains the information necessary to determine the probability that an event occurs, even rough information about its shape can lead to information about the probabilities of some events. As we have seen, a small variance indicates that large deviations from the mean are unlikely, a statement made precise in

Theorem 4.38 (Chebyshev's Inequality). *For a random variable* X *with mean* μ *and variance* σ^2*,*

$$\mathbf{P}[|X - \mu| > k] \leq \frac{\sigma^2}{k^2}.$$

MOMENT GENERATING FUNCTIONS

As we have seen, random variables model numerical outcomes of experiments. Each time an experiment is performed, some outcome ω occurs, and the random variable X corresponds to the image $X(\omega)$. But as we have seen in this chapter, a random variable's properties are encoded in how the random variable is distributed. Its probability function assigns weights to the various outcomes the random variable can take. If we step back and treat the random variable X as a function again, we see that it is a mathematical object in its own right, distinct from the notion of the result of an experiment, just as the function $f(x) = x^2$ is distinct from the pair $(5, 25)$. In these terms, we can think of a random variable as a *collection* of possibilities—a sample space in its own right.[2]

In this chapter, we have committed a common abuse of language in probability theory. We have been saying that moments like $\mathbf{E}[X]$ and $\mathbf{E}[X^2]$ are properties of a random variable. But it is perhaps fairer to say that they are properties of probability functions. In order for a random variable to have a 'center' or 'width', it must be a 'geometrical' object. In order for us to think of a random variable in this way, we must think about it as a collection of possible outcomes, weighted by the probabilities that they occur. This is precisely the information that the probability function f_X encodes.

We have made this brief digression in order to motivate moment generating functions. Students familiar with calculus or real and complex analysis will be familiar with the idea that some kinds of functions can be represented as a sequence of simpler objects. For example, a continuously differentiable function can be written as a Taylor series, and the original function can be recovered from the Taylor series. But each Taylor series is uniquely determined by its coefficients. In other words, the Taylor series construction determines a 'transform' that maps a function f to a sequence of coefficients $\{c_k\}$, and vice versa.

2 Technically, we say that a random variable *induces* a sample space.

Similarly, the Fourier series construction determines the Fourier transform, which maps a continuous periodic function to a sequence of coefficients representing the amplitudes of waves that add up to the original function. In general, these alternative encodings for a function are useful because they turn problems about a function into algebraic or combinatorial problems.

Definition 4.39. The *moment generating function* for a random variable X is

$$M_X(t) = \mathbf{E}\left[e^{Xt}\right]$$

Since the moment generating function is defined by an expectation, it might not exist. But if it does, it implies that all moments of X exist. We call M_X the moment generating function because the coefficients of its Taylor series are the moments of X. Because of this property, we see that if a moment generating function exists, the sequence of moments for the random variable X determines the distribution of X.

Example 4.40. Let X have the probability density function $f(x) = \lambda e^{-\lambda x}$ for $x > 0$. What is its moment generating function?

Solution. The moment generating function is given by

$$\begin{aligned} M_X(t) &= \mathbf{E}\left[e^{tX}\right] = \int_0^\infty e^{tx}\lambda e^{-\lambda x}\,dx = \int_0^\infty e^{-(\lambda-t)x}\,dx \\ &= \frac{\lambda}{\lambda-t}\left(-e^{-(\lambda-t)x}\Big|_0^\infty\right) = \frac{\lambda}{\lambda-t}. \end{aligned}$$

■

Theorem 4.41. *If the moment generating function* $M_X(t)$ *exists, the* k^{th} *derivative of* M_X *evaluated at* $t = 0$ *equals the* k^{th} *moment of* X.

Proof. We write the Taylor series for e^{Xt} as

$$e^{Xt} = 1 + \sum_{n=1}^{\infty} \frac{t^n X^n}{n!}.$$

The series converges uniformly, which implies that we can take the expectation termwise

$$M_X(t) = \mathbf{E}\left[e^{Xt}\right] = 1 + \sum_{n=1} \mathbf{E}\left[\frac{t^n X^n}{n!}\right] = 1 + \sum_{n=1} \frac{t^n}{n!}\mathbf{E}\left[X^n\right].$$

Similarly, the uniform convergence implies that we can differentiate the series termwise. This implies that the nth derivative is

$$M_X^{(n)}(t) = \mathbf{E}\left[X^n\right] + \sum_{k=1} \frac{n!t^k}{(n+k)!}\mathbf{E}\left[X^{n+k}\right],$$

which approaches $\mathbf{E}\left[X^n\right]$ as t approaches 0. ■

Much of the usefulness of moment generating functions is a result of the following theorem.

Theorem 4.42. *Let* $X_1, X_2, \ldots, X_n$ *be independent random variables with moment generating functions* M_{X_i}. *Then the moment generating function for* $X = X_1 + X_2 + \cdots + X_n$ *is*

$$M_X(t) = \left(M_{X_1}(t)\right)\left(M_{X_2}(t)\right)\cdots\left(M_{X_n}(t)\right).$$

Proof. We write

$$\begin{aligned} M_X(t) &= \mathbf{E}\left[e^{tX}\right] = \mathbf{E}\left[e^{t(X_1+X_2+\cdots+X_n)}\right] = \mathbf{E}\left[e^{tX_1}e^{tX_2}\cdots e^{tX_n}\right] \\ &= \mathbf{E}\left[e^{tX_1}\right]\mathbf{E}\left[e^{tX_2}\right]\cdots\mathbf{E}\left[e^{tX_n}\right] \\ &= \left(M_{X_1}(t)\right)\left(M_{X_2}(t)\right)\cdots\left(M_{X_n}(t)\right). \end{aligned}$$

■

Many interesting random variables can be expressed as sums of simpler random variables, and this property makes calculating their moments as easy as calculating a product and its derivatives. We have a similar result for random variables of the form $aX + b$.

Theorem 4.43. *Let* X *be a random variable with moment generating function* M_X. *Then, for constants* $a, b \in \mathbf{R}$,

$$M_{aX+b}(t) = e^{bt}M_X(at).$$

We leave the proof as an exercise for the reader, since it is good practice for working with moment generating functions.

Definition 4.44. For jointly distributed random variables X and Y, the *joint moment generating function* is

$$M_{X,Y}(s,t) = \mathbf{E}\left[e^{sX+tY}\right].$$

Similar theorems apply for joint moment generating functions as for regular moment generating functions. In particular, we can calculate the moments of X by taking derivatives with respect to s and we can calculate moments of Y by taking derivatives of t. Perhaps more interestingly, we can calculate moments of the form $\mathbf{E}\left[X^j Y^k\right]$ as

$$\mathbf{E}\left[X^j Y^k\right] = \frac{\partial^{j+k}}{\partial s^j \partial t^k} M_{X,Y}\Big|_{(s,t)\to(0,0)}.$$

EXERCISES

1° Let X and Y be continuous random variables and prove that

$$\mathbf{E}\left[X+Y\right] = \mathbf{E}\left[X\right] + \mathbf{E}\left[Y\right].$$

2° A discrete random variable X has the probability mass function

$$f_X(x) = k(3x-2), \text{ for } x \in \left\{1,2,3,4,5,6\right\}.$$

Calculate $\mathbf{E}\left[X\right]$.

3° A random variable X has a probability mass function given by

X	p_X
10	0.05
15	0.15
20	0.30
25	0.25
30	0.10
35	0.10
40	0.05

Calculate the probability that X is farther than one standard deviation away from the mode.

4° A raffle ticket costs \$1, and the first ticket drawn wins \$1000, the second ticket drawn wins \$500, and the next 5 tickets drawn each win \$100. What is the expected gain for a person who buys one ticket? out of 5000 tickets

5° A random variable X has the distribution function

$$F_X(x) = c\left(\alpha x^{\beta} - \beta x^{\alpha}\right), \text{ for } 0 < x < 1.$$

Calculate the kth moment of X.

6° Let X be a random variable with distribution function

$$F_X(x) = \frac{2\alpha x}{\alpha^2 + x^2}, \text{ for } 0 < \alpha \text{ and } 0 < x < \alpha.$$

Calculate $\mathbf{E}[X]$.

7° A special die is labeled 1, 3, 5, 7, 9, and 11. A coin is flipped, and if it lands heads, this special die is thrown. If the coin lands tails, a normal die is thrown. Find the variance of the number thrown.

8° Light bulbs have a lifetime with mean 1000, unless they are defective, in which case the mean lifetime is 100. A large number of bulbs is tested, and the mean lifetime of the tested bulbs is 950 hours. What is the probability that a bulb is defective?

9° A hand of 4 cards is drawn from a standard deck of 52 cards. What is the expected number of hearts drawn?

10° Dave and Sara sit in the same row at a theater. The row has 8 seats. If the row is full, and each arrangement of patrons is equally likely, what is the average number of people between them?

11° The random variable X has the density

$$f(x) = c(x^3 + x^2) \text{ on } 0 < x < 10.$$

Find $\mathbf{E}\left[X|5 < X < 7\right]$.

12° A student is preparing for a computer based test, and knows that the problems are randomly selected from a bank of questions. Each question is multiple choice, with 5 choices.

The basic questions make up 20% of the bank. Questions about random variables make up 45% of the bank. Questions about expectations make up 25% percent of the bank. The remaining questions are about insurance.

The student has kept track of his practice results, and has found that the probability that he knows the answer to a basic question is 0.8, the probability that he knows the answer to a question about random variables is 0.85, the probability he knows the answer to a question about expectations is 0.95, and the probability he knows the answer to a question about insurance is 0.75.

If the test consists of 30 problems, what is the coefficient of variation on the number of correct answers?

13° What is the expected number of times a fair coin must be flipped until you get 8 consecutive heads in a row?

14° Let X be uniformly distributed on $[-1, 1]$ and let $Y = \max\{X, X^2\}$. What is the expected value of Y?

15° The random variables X and Y have the joint density function

$$f_{X,Y}(x, y) = c(x + y) \text{ on the region } 0 < x < 1, x^2 < y < x^{\frac{1}{2}}.$$

Find the expected value $\mathbf{E}[X]$.

16° Let X and Y have the joint probability density function

$$f(x, y) = \frac{3}{2}(x^2 + y^2), \text{ for } 0 < x < 1 \text{ and } 0 < y < 1.$$

Calculate $\mathbf{E}[X^2 + Y^2]$.

17° Let X and Y be jointly distributed random variables such that

i. $\mathbf{E}[X] = 6$

ii. $\mathbf{E}[Y] = 8$

iii. $\mathbf{C}[4X, 6Y] = 864$.

What is $\mathbf{E}[XY]$?

18° Let (X, Y) be uniformly distributed on the region $0 < y < 2$, $\frac{1}{2}y < x < \sqrt{y}$. What is the covariance of X and Y?

19° Let X and Y be random variables with $\mathbf{V}[X] = 3$, $\mathbf{V}[Y] = 4$, and $\rho_{X,Y} = 0.35$. Find the real number α which minimizes the variance of $X + \alpha Y$.

20° Let X and Y be independent samples from the distribution with a probability mass function

$$f = \begin{cases} 1, & \text{with probability } \frac{3}{4} \\ 0, & \text{with probability } \frac{1}{4}. \end{cases}$$

What is the moment generating function for $XY + X + Y$?

21° Let X be a random variable with moment generating function

$$M_X(t) = \frac{1}{(1-3t)^2}.$$

What is the standard deviation of X?

22° A random variable X has the moment generating function

$$M_X(t) = \left(\frac{2}{5} - p\right) + \frac{3}{5}e^t + pe^{2t}.$$

Find the value of p which maximizes the variance of X.

23° Suppose that a random variable X has the distribution function

$$F_X(x) = \begin{cases} 0, & \text{for } x < 0 \\ \frac{1}{5} + \frac{3}{10}x, & \text{for } 0 < x < 2, \\ 1, & \text{for } x > 2. \end{cases}$$

Let $Y = 2^X$. Calculate the standard deviation of Y.

24° The random variables X and Y have the joint moment generating function

$$M_{X,Y}(s,t) = 0.3\left(e^{s+t} + e^{2(s+t)}\right) + 0.25e^{2s+t} + 0.15e^{s+2t}.$$

Calculate $\mathbf{E}\left[X^2 + 2XY + Y^2\right]$.

25° The random variables X and Y have the joint moment generating function

$$M_{X,Y}(s,t) = 0.3e^{s+t} + 0.2e^{2s+t} + 0.17e^{s+2t} + 0.08e^{s+3t} + 0.1e^{2s+3t}.$$

Calculate $\mathbf{V}\left[Y^2 | X + Y = 3\right]$.

SOLUTIONS

1° We begin by writing the expectation as

$$\mathbf{E}\left[X+Y\right] = \int_{-\infty}^{\infty}\int_{-\infty}^{\infty} (x+y) f(x,y)\, dx\, dy.$$

We can expand this integral as

$$\left(\int_{-\infty}^{\infty}\int_{-\infty}^{\infty} x f(x,y)\, dx\, dy\right) + \left(\int_{-\infty}^{\infty}\int_{-\infty}^{\infty} y f(x,y)\, dx\, dy\right).$$

We can apply Fubini theorem to change the order of integration in the left-most term

$$\left(\int_{-\infty}^{\infty}\int_{-\infty}^{\infty} x f(x,y)\, dy\, dx\right) + \left(\int_{-\infty}^{\infty}\int_{-\infty}^{\infty} y f(x,y)\, dx\, dy\right).$$

Now, because x does not depend on the variable of integration, we can factor it. Similarly, we can factor y out of the inner integral on the right, to write

$$\int_{-\infty}^{\infty} x \left(\int_{-\infty}^{\infty} f(x,y)\, dy\right) dx + \int_{-\infty}^{\infty} y \left(\int_{-\infty}^{\infty} f(x,y)\, dx\right) dy.$$

We recognize the inner integrals as the marginal probability densities for y and x respectively, and write

$$\left(\int_{-\infty}^{\infty} x f_X(x)\, dx\right) + \left(\int_{-\infty}^{\infty} y f_Y(y)\, dy\right)$$

which is clearly equal to $\mathbf{E}[X] + \mathbf{E}[Y]$.

2° Since f_X is a probability mass function, we have

$$\begin{aligned}
1 &= \sum_{x=1}^{6} f_X(x) \\
&= \sum_{x=1}^{6} k(3x-2) \\
&= k\left(\sum_{x=1}^{6}(3x-2)\right) \\
&= k\left[\left(\sum_{x=1}^{6} 3x\right) - 12\right] \\
&= k\left[3\left(\sum_{x=1}^{6} x\right) - 12\right] \\
&= k\left(3\frac{6\times 7}{2} - 12\right) \\
&= 51k,
\end{aligned}$$

so that $k = 1/51$. We calculate the expectation as

$$\mathbf{E}[X] = \frac{1 + (2\times 4) + (3\times 7) + (4\times 10) + (5\times 13) + (6\times 16)}{51} = 4.53.$$

3° This problem is most easily solved using your calculator's statistics functions. However, we will do this problem by hand. We see that

$$\begin{aligned} \mathbf{E}[X] &= (10 \times 0.05) + (15 \times 0.15) + (20 \times 0.3) + (25 \times 0.25) \\ &\quad + (30 \times 0.1) + (35 \times 0.1) + (40 \times 0.05) \\ &= 23.5 \end{aligned}$$

Similarly,

$$\begin{aligned} \mathbf{E}\left[X^2\right] &= (10^2 \times 0.05) + (15^2 \times 0.15) + (20^2 \times 0.3) + (25^2 \times 0.25) \\ &\quad + (30^2 \times 0.1) + (35^2 \times 0.1) + (40^2 \times 0.05) \\ &= 607.5. \end{aligned}$$

We calculate $\sigma_X = \sqrt{\mathbf{E}[X^2] - \mathbf{E}[X]^2} = 7.433$. Now, recall that the mode is the value m such that $p_X(m)$ is maximal. By inspection, we see that the mode is $m = 20$. We see that the values outside of one standard deviation of the mode are 10, 30, 35, and 40, so that the probability that X is more than one standard deviation outside of the mode is 0.3.

4° Let W be the amount won. W is distributed as

$$W = \begin{cases} 1000 & \text{with probability } \frac{1}{5000} \\ 500 & \text{with probability } \frac{1}{5000} \\ 100 & \text{with probability } \frac{5}{5000} \end{cases}$$

We calculate the expected winnings as

$$\mathbf{E}[W] = 1000\frac{1}{5000} + 500\frac{1}{5000} + 100\frac{5}{5000} = 0.4,$$

so that the expected gain is $\mathbf{E}[W - 1] = -0.6$.

5° Since F_X is a distribution function, $F_X(1) = 1$, which implies that $c = (\alpha - \beta)^{-1}$. We calculate the density function by taking the derivative of F_X.

$$f_X(x) = F_X'(x) = c\left(\alpha\beta x^{\beta-1} - \alpha\beta x^{\alpha-1}\right) = \frac{\alpha\beta}{\alpha-\beta}\left(x^{\beta-1} - x^{\alpha-1}\right).$$

We use this expression for f_X to calculate

$$\begin{aligned}
\mathbf{E}\left[X^k\right] &= \frac{\alpha\beta}{\alpha-\beta}\int_0^1 x^k\left(x^{\beta-1} - x^{\alpha-1}\right)\,dx \\
&= \frac{\alpha\beta}{\alpha-\beta}\int_0^1 \left(x^{\beta+k-1} - x^{\alpha+k-1}\right)\,dx \\
&= \frac{\alpha\beta}{\alpha-\beta}\left(\frac{x^{\beta+k}}{\beta+k} - \frac{x^{\alpha+k}}{\alpha+k}\bigg|_0^1\right) \\
&= \frac{\alpha\beta}{\alpha-\beta}\left(\frac{1}{\beta+k} - \frac{1}{\alpha+k}\right) \\
&= \frac{\alpha\beta}{(\alpha+k)(\beta+k)}.
\end{aligned}$$

6° We see that the survival function for X is

$$S_X(x) = 1 - \frac{2\alpha x}{\alpha^2 + x^2}.$$

We can calculate

$$\begin{aligned}
\mathbf{E}[X] &= \int_0^\alpha 1 - \frac{2\alpha x}{\alpha^2+x^2}\,dx \\
&= \int_0^\alpha 1\,dx - \int_0^\alpha \frac{2\alpha x}{\alpha^2+x^2}\,dx \\
&= \left(x\big|_0^\alpha\right) - \left(\alpha\log(\alpha^2+x^2)\big|_0^\alpha\right) \\
&= \alpha(1 - \log 2\alpha^2 + \log\alpha^2) \\
&= \alpha(1 - \log 2).
\end{aligned}$$

7° Let X be the outcome of the roll, and let H and T represent heads or tails, respectively. We begin by calculating $\mathbf{E}[X]$ as

$$\begin{aligned}\mathbf{E}[X] &= \mathbf{E}[X|H]\,\mathbf{P}[H] + \mathbf{E}[X|T]\,\mathbf{P}[T] \\ &= \frac{1}{2}\frac{1}{6}(1+3+5+7+9+11) + \frac{1}{2}\frac{1}{6}(1+2+3+4+5+6) \\ &= 4.75.\end{aligned}$$

Similarly,

$$\begin{aligned}\mathbf{E}\left[X^2\right] &= \mathbf{E}\left[X^2|H\right]\mathbf{P}[H] + \mathbf{E}\left[X^2|T\right]\mathbf{P}[T] \\ &= \frac{1}{2}\frac{1}{6}(1^2+3^2+5^2+7^2+9^2+11^2) \\ &\quad + \frac{1}{2}\frac{1}{6}(1^2+2^2+3^2+4^2+5^2+6^2) \\ &\approx 31.417.\end{aligned}$$

This implies that $\mathbf{V}[X] = \mathbf{E}[X^2] - \mathbf{E}[X]^2 \approx 8.9$.

8° Let X be the lifetime of a bulb, and let D denote the event that it is defective. We use the law of total expectation to estimate that

$$\begin{aligned}950 = \mathbf{E}[X] &= \mathbf{E}[X|D]\,\mathbf{P}[D] + \mathbf{E}[X|D']\,\mathbf{P}[D'] \\ &= 100\mathbf{P}[D] + 1000\mathbf{P}[D'] \\ &= 100\mathbf{P}[D] + 1000\,(1-\mathbf{P}[D]) \\ &= 1000 - 900\mathbf{P}[D],\end{aligned}$$

so that $\mathbf{P}[D] = 0.056$.

9° Let H be the number of hearts drawn. We recognize that H has a hypergeometric distribution, so we can calculate

$$\mathbf{E}[H] = 0\frac{\binom{13}{0}\binom{39}{4}}{\binom{52}{4}} + 1\frac{\binom{13}{1}\binom{39}{3}}{\binom{52}{4}} + 2\frac{\binom{13}{2}\binom{39}{2}}{\binom{52}{4}} + 3\frac{\binom{13}{3}\binom{39}{1}}{\binom{52}{4}} + 4\frac{\binom{13}{4}\binom{39}{0}}{\binom{52}{4}},$$

so that $\mathbf{E}[H] = 1$.

This is a reasonable approach for calculating this expectation, since the number of card draws is fairly small. However, we can use a formula to calculate $\mathbf{E}[H]$. In general, if there are r admissible objects and b inadmissible objects, and objects are drawn without replacement, the expected number of admissible objects drawn is

$$\frac{r}{r+b}.$$

10° Let $n = 8$ be the number of seats, and let K be the number of seats between them. We will calculate the probability mass function for K, by constructing an admissible arrangement and counting the admissible permutations of it. Imagine that Dave and Sara's seats are specially marked. For for concreteness, we assume that $K = 2$, and draw their seats as filled circles at the left side of the row.

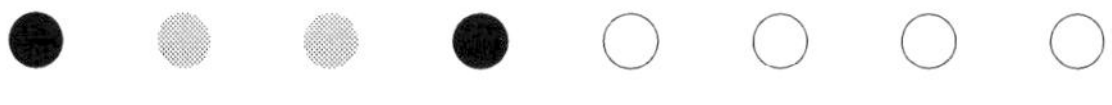

We treat the $K+2$ seats–the marked seats and the K between them–as a unit. We can, for example, move the entire unit one seat to the right. We can imagine that the unit is a bench with $K+2$ seats, while the other seats are indistinguishable chairs. And using this analogy, we can place the bench in any of $n-K-1$ places relative to the indistinguishable chairs.

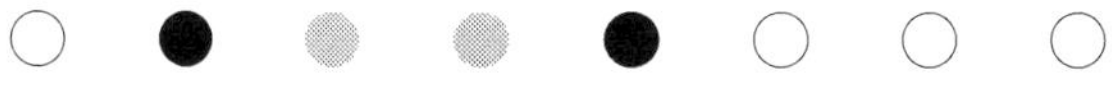

Given that the furniture is arranged, and seats for Dave and Sara are marked, Dave and Sara can sit in 2! ways. The other $n-2$ patrons can sit in $(n-2)!$ ways. Of course, there are $n!$ arrangements of the patrons in total. This implies that the probability that there are K seats between Sara and David is

$$f_K(k) = \frac{2(n-k-1)}{n(n-1)} = \frac{2(7-k)}{56}.$$

We use the probability mass function to calculate

$$\mathbf{E}[K] = 0\frac{1}{4} + 1\frac{3}{14} + 2\frac{5}{28} + 3\frac{1}{7} + 4\frac{3}{28} + 5\frac{1}{14} + 6\frac{1}{28} = 2.$$

11° We seek $\mathbf{E}[X|5 < X < y]$. We use the formula

$$\begin{aligned}
\mathbf{E}[X|5 < X < 7] &= \frac{c\int_5^7 xf(x)\,dx}{c\int_5^7 f(x)\,dx} \\
&= \frac{\int_5^7 x^4 + x^3\,dx}{\int_5^7 x^3 + x^2\,dx} \\
&= \frac{\left.\frac{x^5}{5} + \frac{x^4}{4}\right|_5^7}{\left.\frac{x^4}{4} + \frac{x^3}{3}\right|_5^7} \\
&\approx 6.15.
\end{aligned}$$

12° Let B represent a basic question, R represent a question about random variables, E represent a question about expectations, and I represent a question about insurance.

Let K_n be an indicator variable meaning that the student knows the correct answer to the nth question. Because it is an indicator variable, $\mathbf{E}[K_n] = \mathbf{P}[K_n]$, which by the law of total probability is

$$\begin{aligned}
\mathbf{P}[K_n] &= \mathbf{P}[K_n|B]\,\mathbf{P}[B] + \mathbf{P}[K_n|R]\,\mathbf{P}[R] \\
&\quad + \mathbf{P}[K_n|E]\,\mathbf{P}[E] + \mathbf{P}[K_n|I]\,\mathbf{P}[I] \\
&= 0.855.
\end{aligned}$$

Now, let C_n be the indicator variable for the event that the nth question was answered correctly, and let G_n be the indicator for the event that a guess on the nth question is correct. We write

$$\begin{aligned} \mathbf{E}[C_n] &= \mathbf{E}[C_n|K_n]\,\mathbf{P}[K_n] + \mathbf{E}[G_n|K_n']\,\mathbf{P}[K_n'] \\ &= \mathbf{P}[K_n] + \mathbf{E}[G_n|K_n']\,\mathbf{P}[K_n'] \\ &= 0.884 \end{aligned}$$

Because C_n is an indicator variable $\mathbf{E}[C_n^2] = \mathbf{E}[C_n]$, so that $\mathbf{V}[C_n] = 0.102544$. Let $C = C_1 + \cdots + C_{30}$ be the total number of correct answers. Then

$$\mathbf{E}[C] = \mathbf{E}[C_1 + \cdots C_{30}] = \mathbf{E}[C_1] + \cdots + \mathbf{E}[C_{30}] = 30\mathbf{E}[C_n] \approx 26.52$$

Similarly, since the C_n's are independent,

$$\mathbf{V}[C] = 30\mathbf{V}[C_n] \approx 3.07632.$$

We calculate $\sigma_C \approx 1.75$, so that the coefficient of variation is $\frac{\sigma_C}{\mu_C} \approx 6.6\%$.

13° We will proceed slightly more generally. Let p be the probability of flipping a head. Then the probability of being successful immediately is p^8. However, we might instead flip a tail immediately. In that case, the number of flips we need is $1 + \mathbf{E}[X]$, since 1 flip has been used, and we require 8 consecutive heads. Similarly, we might flip a head and then a tail. In this case, the number of flips we need is $2 + \mathbf{E}[X]$, since we used 2 flips but still require 8 consecutive heads. Similar reasoning applies for the cases up to 7 consecutive heads followed by a tail. In this case, we would have used 8 flips and require 8 consecutive heads. We put this all together to find

$$\begin{aligned}
\mathbf{E}[X] &= 8p^8 + (1-p)\left(\mathbf{E}[X]+1\right) + (1-p)p\left(\mathbf{E}[X]+2\right) + \cdots \\
&\quad +(1-p)p^7\left(\mathbf{E}[X]+8\right) \\
&= 8p^8 + (1-p)\sum_{i=0}^{i=7} p^i\left(\mathbf{E}[X]+i+1\right) \\
&= (1-p^8)\mathbf{E}[X] + \sum_{i=0}^{i=7} p^i \\
&= (1-p^8)\mathbf{E}[X] + \frac{1-p^8}{1-p} \\
&= \frac{1-p^8}{p^8(1-p)} \\
&= 510.
\end{aligned}$$

14° Perhaps the easiest way to solve this problem is to draw the graph of Y as a function of X. In doing so, we see that $X < X^2$ in the region $[-1, 0)$, and $X > X^2$ in the region $(0, 1]$. This implies that we can define Y as

$$Y = \begin{cases} X^2, & \text{for } X \in [-1, 0] \\ X, & \text{for } X \in (0, 1]. \end{cases}$$

We use the law of total expectation to calculate

$$\begin{aligned}
\mathbf{E}[Y] &= \mathbf{E}[X|X \le 0]\,\mathbf{P}[X \le 0] + \mathbf{E}[X|X > 0]\,\mathbf{P}[X > 0] \\
&= \frac{1}{2}\left(\mathbf{E}[X|X \le 0] + \mathbf{E}[X|X > 0]\right) \\
&= \frac{1}{2}\left(\frac{\int_{-1}^{0} x^2 f_X(x)\,dx}{\int_{-1}^{0} f_X(x)\,dx} + \frac{\int_{0}^{1} x f_X(x)\,dx}{\int_{0}^{1} f_X(x)\,dx}\right) \\
&= \frac{1}{2}\left(\left(\frac{x^3}{3}\Big|_{-1}^{0}\right) + \left(\frac{x^2}{2}\Big|_{0}^{1}\right)\right) \\
&= \frac{1}{2}\left(\frac{1}{3} + \frac{1}{2}\right) \\
&= \frac{5}{12}.
\end{aligned}$$

15° We begin by calculating $F_X(x)$

$$\begin{aligned}
F_X(x) &= c\int_0^x \int_{x^2}^{x^{\frac{1}{2}}} x + y\,dydx \\
&= c\int_0^x \left(xy + \frac{1}{2}y^2\Big|_{x^2}^{x^{\frac{1}{2}}}\right) dx \\
&= c\int_0^x x^{\frac{3}{2}} + \frac{1}{2}x - x^3 - \frac{1}{2}x^4\,dx \\
&= c\left(\frac{2}{5}x^{\frac{5}{2}} + \frac{1}{4}x^2 - \frac{1}{4}x^4 - \frac{1}{10}x^5\right).
\end{aligned}$$

Now, we can solve for c by noting that F_X is continuous, so that $\lim_{x\to 1} F_X(x)$ exists and is 1 since F_X is a distribution function. We solve for c in

$$1 = F_X(1) = c\left(\frac{2}{5}x^{\frac{5}{2}} + \frac{1}{4}x^2 - \frac{1}{4}x^4 - \frac{1}{10}x^5\right),$$

so that $c = \frac{10}{3}$. Now we have a complete expression of F_X

$$F_X(x) = \frac{10}{3}\left(\frac{2}{5}x^{\frac{5}{2}} + \frac{1}{4}x^2 - \frac{1}{4}x^4 - \frac{1}{10}x^5\right).$$

Finally, we calculate

$$\begin{aligned}
\mathbf{E}[X] &= \int_0^1 1 - F_X(x)\,dx \\
&= \int_0^1 1 - \frac{10}{3}\left[\frac{2}{5}x^{\frac{5}{2}} + \frac{1}{4}x^2 - \frac{1}{4}x^4 - \frac{1}{10}x^5\right] dx \\
&= x - \frac{10}{3}\left[\frac{4}{35}x^{\frac{7}{2}} + \frac{1}{12}x^3 - \frac{1}{20}x^5 - \frac{1}{60}x^6\right]\Bigg|_0^1 \\
&= 1 - \frac{10}{3}\left[\frac{4}{35} + \frac{1}{12} - \frac{1}{20} - \frac{1}{60}\right] \\
&\approx 0.56.
\end{aligned}$$

16° We calculate the expectation as

$$\begin{aligned}
\mathbf{E}\left[X^2 + Y^2\right] &= \int_{\mathbf{R}}\int_{\mathbf{R}} (x^2 + y^2) \cdot \frac{3}{2}(x^2 + y^2)\,dy dx \\
&= \frac{3}{2}\int_0^1\int_0^1 x^4 + 2x^2y^2 + y^4\,dy dx \\
&= \frac{3}{2}\int_0^1 \left(yx^4 + \frac{2}{3}x^2y^3 + \frac{1}{5}y^5\,dx\Bigg|_0^1\right) \\
&= \frac{3}{2}\int_0^1 x^4 + \frac{2}{3}x^2 + \frac{1}{5}dx \\
&= \frac{3}{2}\left(\frac{1}{5}x^5 + \frac{2}{9}x^3 + \frac{1}{5}x\Bigg|_0^1\right) \\
&= \frac{3}{2}\left(\frac{1}{5} + \frac{2}{9} + \frac{1}{5}\right) \\
&= \frac{14}{15}.
\end{aligned}$$

17° Since

$$\mathbf{C}\left[4X, 6Y\right] = 24\mathbf{C}\left[X, Y\right] = 864,$$

we can write

$$\mathbf{C}\left[X, Y\right] = \mathbf{E}\left[XY\right] - \mathbf{E}\left[X\right]\mathbf{E}\left[Y\right] = 36,$$

so that

$$\mathbf{E}\left[XY\right] = 84.$$

18° The joint density is constant in the region, so we integrate to find the constant c in

$$\begin{aligned} \frac{1}{c} &= \int_0^2 \int_{\frac{y}{2}}^{\sqrt{y}} 1 \, dy dx = \int_0^2 \left(x \Big|_{\frac{y}{2}}^{\sqrt{y}} \right) dy \\ &= \int_0^2 y^{\frac{1}{2}} - \frac{1}{2} y \, dy = \frac{2}{3} y^{\frac{3}{2}} - \frac{1}{4} y^2 \Big|_0^2 \\ &\approx 0.89. \end{aligned}$$

This implies that $c \approx 1.29$. We calculate a sequence of expectations.

$$\begin{aligned} \mathbf{E}\left[X\right] &= c \int_0^2 \int_{\frac{y}{2}}^{\sqrt{y}} x \, dx dy = c \int_0^2 \left(\frac{1}{2} x^2 \Big|_{\frac{y}{2}}^{\sqrt{y}} \right) dy \\ &= c \int_0^2 \frac{1}{2} y - \frac{1}{8} y^2 \, dy = c \left(\frac{1}{4} y^2 - \frac{1}{24} y^3 \Big|_0^2 \right) \\ &= \frac{2}{3} c. \end{aligned}$$

$$\begin{aligned}
\mathbf{E}[Y] &= c\int_0^2\int_{\frac{y}{2}}^{\sqrt{y}} y\,dxdy = c\int_0^2 y\left(x\Big|_{\frac{y}{2}}^{\sqrt{y}}\right)dy \\
&= c\int_0^2 y\left(y^{\frac{1}{2}} - \frac{1}{2}y\right)dy = c\int_0^2 y^{\frac{3}{2}} - \frac{1}{2}y^2\,dy \\
&= c\left(\frac{2}{5}y^{\frac{5}{2}} - \frac{1}{6}y^3\Big|_0^2\right) \\
&\approx 0.93c.
\end{aligned}$$

$$\begin{aligned}
\mathbf{E}[XY] &= c\int_0^2\int_{\frac{y}{2}}^{\sqrt{y}} xy\,dxdy = c\int_0^2 y\left(\frac{1}{2}x^2\Big|_{\frac{y}{2}}^{\sqrt{y}}\right)dy \\
&= c\int_0^2 y\left(\frac{y}{2} - \frac{y^2}{8}\right)dy = c\int_0^2 \frac{y^2}{2} - \frac{y^3}{7}\,dy \\
&= c\left(\frac{y^3}{6} - \frac{y^4}{32}\Big|_0^2\right) \\
&= \frac{5}{6}c
\end{aligned}$$

Now, $\mathbf{C}[X,Y] = \mathbf{E}[XY] - \mathbf{E}[X]\,\mathbf{E}[Y] \approx \frac{5}{6}c - \frac{2}{3}c^2(0.93) \approx 0.15$.

19° We must calculate the covariance of X and Y, by solving for it in

$$\rho_{X,Y} = 0.35 = \frac{\mathbf{C}[X,Y]}{\sigma_X\sigma_Y},$$

so that

$$\mathbf{C}[X,Y] = \rho_{X,Y}\sigma_X\sigma_Y \approx 1.21.$$

We can now calculate

$$\mathbf{V}[X+\alpha Y] = \mathbf{V}[X] + \alpha^2\mathbf{V}[Y] + 2\alpha\mathbf{C}[X,Y].$$

We take the derivative of $\mathbf{V}\left[X+\alpha Y\right]$ with respect to α and set the expression equal to zero.

$$\frac{\partial}{\partial\alpha}\mathbf{V}\left[X+\alpha Y\right] = 2\alpha\mathbf{V}\left[Y\right] + 2\mathbf{C}\left[X,Y\right] = 0$$

We solve for α, so that

$$\alpha = -\frac{\mathbf{C}\left[X,Y\right]}{\mathbf{V}\left[Y\right]} \approx -0.30.$$

20° Let $Z = XY + X + Y$. With some work, we see that Z has mass

$$f_Z = \begin{cases} 0, & \text{with } p = \frac{1}{16} \\ 1, & \text{with } p = \frac{6}{16} \\ 2, & \text{with } p = 0 \\ 3, & \text{with } p = \frac{9}{16}. \end{cases}$$

Since this is a discrete random variable, we can read off the moment generating function from the probability mass function as

$$M_Z(t) = \frac{1}{16} + \frac{6}{16}e^t + \frac{9}{16}e^{3t}.$$

21° We calculate the central moments $\mathbf{E}\left[X^k\right]$ by differentiating the moment generating function. In particular,

$$\mathbf{E}\left[X\right] = M_X'(0) = \left.\frac{6}{(1-3t)^3}\right|_{t=0} = 6$$

$$\mathbf{E}\left[X^2\right] = M_X''(0) = \left.\frac{54}{(1-3t)^4}\right|_{t=0} = 54$$

so that $\mathbf{V}\left[X\right] = \mathbf{E}\left[X^2\right] - \mathbf{E}\left[X\right]^2 = 18$ and $\sigma_X = \sqrt{\mathbf{V}\left[X\right]} = 3\sqrt{2} \approx 4.2$.

22° Since the coefficients of the moment generating function are probabilities, we see that $0 \le p \le \frac{2}{5}$. We calculate the variance of X by taking derivatives and using evaluating them at 0 to find the moments of X.

$$M'_X(t) = \frac{3}{5}e^t + 2pe^{2t} \qquad \mathbf{E}[X] = \frac{3}{5} + 2p$$
$$M''_X(t) = \frac{3}{5}e^t + 4pe^{2t} \qquad \mathbf{E}\left[X^2\right] = \frac{3}{5} + 4p$$

We calculate the variance as

$$\begin{aligned}\mathbf{V}[X] &= \mathbf{E}\left[X^2\right] - \mathbf{E}[X]^2 = \frac{3}{5} + 4p - \left(\frac{3}{5} + 2p\right)^2 \\ &= \frac{3}{5} + 4p - \frac{9}{25} - \frac{12}{5}p - 4p^2 = \frac{6}{25} + \frac{8}{5}p - 4p^2.\end{aligned}$$

We see that, as a function of p, the variance is a quadratic function with a maximum value. We take the derivative of $\mathbf{V}[X]$ as a function of p

$$\frac{\partial}{\partial p}\mathbf{V}[X] = \frac{8}{5} - 8p,$$

which equals 0 when $p = \frac{1}{5}$.

23° Note that this is a mixture distribution, with density

$$f_X(x) = \begin{cases} \frac{1}{5}, & \text{for } x = 0 \\ \frac{3}{10}, & \text{for } 0 < x < 2 \\ \frac{1}{5}, & \text{for } x = 2 \end{cases}$$

In particular, $\mathbf{P}[X = 0] = \mathbf{P}[X = 2] = \frac{1}{5}$. We calculate the moment generating function

$$\begin{aligned}M_X(t) &= \mathbf{E}\left[e^{Xt}\right] \\ &= \mathbf{P}[X = 0]\, e^{0\cdot t} + \mathbf{P}[X = 2]\, e^{2\cdot t} + \int_0^2 \frac{3}{10}e^{tx}\, dx \\ &= \frac{1}{5}\left(1 + e^{2t}\right) + \frac{3}{10t}\left(e^{2t} - 1\right).\end{aligned}$$

Now, we note that

$$\begin{aligned}
\mathbf{E}[Y] &= \mathbf{E}\left[2^X\right] \\
&= \mathbf{E}\left[e^{X \log 2}\right] \\
&= M_X(\log 2) \\
&= \frac{1}{5}\left(1 + e^{2\log 2}\right) + \frac{3}{10\log 2}\left(e^{2\log 2} - 1\right) \\
&\approx 2.3
\end{aligned}$$

Similarly,

$$\begin{aligned}
\mathbf{E}\left[Y^2\right] &= M_X(\log 4) \\
&= \frac{1}{5}\left(1 + e^{2\log 4}\right) + \frac{3}{10\log 4}\left(e^{2\log 4} - 1\right) \\
&\approx 6.65
\end{aligned}$$

so that $\mathbf{V}[Y] = \mathbf{E}[Y^2] - \mathbf{E}[Y]^2 \approx 1.36$ and $\sigma_Y = \sqrt{\mathbf{V}[Y]} \approx 1.17$.

24° First, note that $X^2 + 2XY + Y^2 = (X+Y)^2$, so that the expectation we seek is the second moment of $(X+Y)$.

We collect the terms in the original moment generating function to find the moment generating function of $X+Y$. We can think of this process as formally substituting t for s in the original moment generating function and simplifying, so that

$$M_{X+Y}(t) = 0.3e^{2t} + 0.4e^{3t} + 0.3e^{4t}.$$

We calculate derivatives:

$$\begin{aligned}
M'_{X,Y}(t) &= 0.6e^{2t} + 1.2e^{3t} + 1.2e^{4t} \\
M''_{X,Y}(t) &= 1.2e^{2t} + 3.6e^{3t} + 4.8e^{4t}.
\end{aligned}$$

Recall that $\mathbf{E}\left[(X+Y)^2\right] = M''_{X+Y}(t)\big|_{t=0}$, so that $\mathbf{E}\left[(X+Y)^2\right] = 9.6$.

25° We can find the probability that $X + Y = 3$ by reading off from the moment generating function. In particular, $\mathbf{P}[X + Y = 3] = 0.2 + 0.17 = 0.37$. Notice that these are the coefficients of e^{2s+t} and e^{s+2t}. We can calculate expectations using a similar method. Specifically, we write

$$\mathbf{E}[Y|X+Y=3] = \frac{(1 \times 0.12) + (2 \times 0.17)}{0.37} \approx 1.24$$

and

$$\mathbf{E}\left[Y^2|X+Y=3\right] = \frac{1^2 \times 0.12 + 2^2 \times 0.17}{0.37} \approx 2.16,$$

so that

$$\mathbf{V}\left[Y^2|X+Y=3\right] = \mathbf{E}\left[Y^2|X+Y=3\right] - \mathbf{E}[Y|X+Y=3]^2 \approx 0.90.$$

Notice that, in principle, we could have taken derivatives of the moment generating function to find these moments, but that since we were able to read off the probabilities from the moment generating function, this method was faster.

5

COMMON DISTRIBUTIONS

In this chapter, we discuss commonly used probability distributions. We strongly recommend memorizing the formulas we derive in this chapter. These formulas are commonly used and found on Exam P—often 'embedded' in other problems—and are easy to memorize. Knowing these formulas can make time consuming problems significantly easier.

BERNOULLI TRIALS

Definition 5.1. A *Bernoulli trial* models an experiment with two possible outcomes, typically called 'success' and 'failure', which occur with probabilities p and $q = 1 - p$.

Example 5.2. A game consists of flipping a coin. You win a dollar if the coin lands heads. If we equate heads with success, a round of the game is a Bernoulli trial.

Definition 5.3. A random variable X follows the Bernoulli distribution when it has the probability law

$$X = \begin{cases} 1, & \text{with probability } p, \\ 0, & \text{otherwise.} \end{cases}$$

Theorem 5.4. *If X follows the Bernoulli distribution, $\mathbf{E}[X^k] = p$ for any $k \neq 0$. This implies that $\mathbf{E}[X] = p$ and $\mathbf{V}[X] = pq$.*

Proof. Since X is 1 with probability p and 0 otherwise, $\mathbf{E}[X] = (1 \times p) + (0 \times q) = p$. Similarly, if $k \neq 0$, X^k is 1 with probability p. ∎

Theorem 5.5. *If* X *follows the Bernoulli distribution, the moment generating function for* X *is*

$$M_X(t) = q + pe^t.$$

Definition 5.6. A *Bernoulli process* is a sequence of independent Bernoulli trials.

Bernoulli trials are important because they serve as a very simple building block as a model for random events. Many useful distributions are random variables on the space of Bernoulli processes. These include the binomial, geometric, and negative binomial distributions, which we will discuss shortly. On the other hand, it is often the case that complex random events can have outcomes we might call success and failure. By calculating the probability that these complex experiments succeed, we can apply the 'compound Bernoulli' distributions, such as the binomial distribution, to answer questions about the distribution of experiment successes.

BINOMIAL DISTRIBUTION

Definition 5.7. Consider a sequence of n independent Bernoulli trials. We are interested in the number of successes N. N is said to follow the *binomial distribution*.

We can derive a probability mass function for N. Suppose that the first k Bernoulli trials result in success, and that the remaining $n-k$ result in failure. Because the Bernoulli trials are independent, the probability of this sequence occurring is $p^k q^{n-k}$. Also by independence, sequences of Bernoulli trials that differ only in the order of successes and failures have the same probability. There are $\binom{n}{k}$ equally probable sequences. This implies

Theorem 5.8. *For a binomial random variable* N,

$$\mathbf{P}[N = k] = \binom{n}{k} p^k q^{n-k}.$$

Since we are considering the number of successes in n independent Bernoulli trials, we can write N as the sum of n Bernoulli random variables. The linearity of expectation implies that

Theorem 5.9. *For a binomial random variable* N, $\mathbf{E}[N] = np$ *and* $\mathbf{V}[N] = npq$.

Similarly, since N is the sum of n independent Bernoulli random variables, we can conclude that

Theorem 5.10. *The moment generating function for a binomial random variable* N *is*

$$M_N(t) = \left(q + pe^t\right)^n.$$

Example 5.11. Let M be a binomial random variable with parameters m and p, and let N be a binomial random variable with parameters n and p. Find the probability distribution for $M + N$.

Solution. Since a binomial random variable counts the number of successes in a sequence of identically distributed Bernoulli trials, we might intuitively expect that $M + N$ has a binomial distribution with parameters $m + n$ and p. We show that this is true, using the moment generating functions for M and N.

$$M_{M+N}(t) = M_M(t)M_N(t) = \left(q + pe^t\right)^m \left(q + pe^t\right)^n = \left(q + pe^t\right)^{m+n}.$$

■

GEOMETRIC DISTRIBUTION

We have seen that calculating probabilities for sequences of Bernoulli trials has a combinatorial flavor. We calculate the probability of an event that is convenient to express, and then count the number of equivalent events. The geometric distribution is another probability distribution of this kind.

Definition 5.12. Consider a sequence of Bernoulli trials, and let N be the number of trials until the first success occurs. Then N has a *geometric distribution*.

Theorem 5.13. *Let* N *be a geometric random variable. Then the probability mass function for* N *is*

$$f_N(n) = (1-p)^{n-1}p.$$

Proof. We see that there is only one admissible sequence of outcomes. If the first success occurs on the Nth trial, then the first $N-1$ trials must be failures. The probability that the first $N-1$ trials are failures is $(1-p)^{n-1}$, and the probability that the Nth trial is a success is p. These events are independent, so the product rule implies that the probability for this event is $(1-p)^{N-1}p$. ■

Theorem 5.14. *For a geometric random variable* N,

$$\mathbf{P}\left[N \leq k\right] = \frac{1-(1-p)^{k+1}}{1-p}.$$

Proof. This is a straight-forward calculation. We take advantage of the fact that

$$\sum_{i=0}^{k} r^i = \frac{1-r^{n+1}}{1-r}.$$

We write

$$\mathbf{P}\left[X \leq k\right] = \sum_{i=0}^{k} p(1-p)^{i-1} = \frac{p}{1-p}\sum_{i=0}^{k}(1-p)^i = \frac{1-(1-p)^{k+1}}{1-p}.$$

■

We calculated the expectation for the geometric random variable N in example 4.6 on page 90. We will soon use a different technique to calculate the second moment for N, and ultimately its variance. Before then, we will calculate the moment generating function for N.

Theorem 5.15. *The moment generating function for a geometrically distributed random variable* N *is*

$$M_N(t) = \frac{pe^t}{1-qe^t}.$$

Proof. Define a random variable X by the probability mass function

$$f_X(k) = q^k p.$$

We see that N has the same distribution as $X + 1$. Because of this, we can see that the moment generating function for N is the same as the moment generating function for X multiplied by the moment generating function for the constant 1. So we shall calculate $M_X(t)$ as

$$M_X(t) = \mathbf{E}\left[e^{tX}\right] = \sum_{n=0}^{\infty} e^{tn} q^n p = p \sum_{n=0}^{\infty} \left(e^t q\right)^n = \frac{p}{1 - qe^t}$$

On the other hand, the moment generating function for the constant random variable 1 is

$$M_1(t) = \mathbf{E}\left[e^t\right] = e^t \times 1 = e^t.$$

This implies that

$$M_{X+1}(t) = M_N(t) = \frac{pe^t}{1 - qe^t}. \qquad \blacksquare$$

The random variable X we introduced here is sometimes also called the geometric random variable. It counts the number of failures before the first success, instead of the number of trials until the first success. Familiarity with the distribution for X is useful for the exam, but on the exam, *the geometric distribution always refers to the number of trials until the first success.*

Since we have calculated the moment generating function for N, we can calculate the moments for the geometric distribution with ease. We will now find its variance.

Theorem 5.16. *The variance of a geometric random variable* N *is*

$$\mathbf{V}[N] = \frac{1 - p}{p^2}.$$

Proof. We calculate the derivatives of the moment generating function for N. In particular,

$$M_N'(t) = \frac{\left(1 - qe^t\right) pe^t + pe^t \left(qe^t\right)}{\left(1 - qe^t\right)^2} = \frac{pe^t}{\left(1 - qe^t\right)^2}$$

so that the second derivative is

$$M_N''(t) = \frac{(1-qe^t)^2 pe^t + 2pe^t(1-qe^t)qe^t}{(1-qe^t)^4}.$$

This expression is complicated, but we can simplify it significantly since we are calculating the second moment of N. In particular, $\mathbf{E}[N^2] = M_N''(0)$, so that

$$\mathbf{E}\left[N^2\right] = \frac{(1-q)^2 p + 2p(1-q)q}{1-q^4} = \frac{p^3+2p^2q}{p^4} = \frac{p+2q}{p^2} = \frac{2-p}{p^2}.$$

Since $\mathbf{E}[N] = p^{-1}$,

$$\mathbf{V}[N] = \mathbf{E}\left[N^2\right] - \mathbf{E}[N]^2 = \frac{2-p}{p^2} - \frac{1}{p^2} = \frac{1-p}{p^2}.$$

■

The geometric distribution is *memoryless*.

Definition 5.17. A random variable is *memoryless* when

$$\mathbf{P}[X-h \geq x | X > h] = \mathbf{P}[X > x]$$

That is, conditional on $X > h$, the $X - h$ has the same distribution as X does, unconditionally.

In more intuitive language, this means that if we observe a sequence of h Bernoulli trials and have observed no successes, the number of trials until the first success has the same distribution as when we started.

NEGATIVE BINOMIAL DISTRIBUTION

Definition 5.18. Consider a sequence of Bernoulli trials, let r be a positive integer, and let S_r be the number of trials required until the process achieves r successes. Then S_r follows the success-variant of the *negative binomial distribution*. Let F_r be the number of failures that occur before r successes occur. Then F_r follows the failure variant of the *negative binomial distribution*.

There are two variants of the negative binomial, and each one corresponds to one of the variants of the geometric distribution we discussed. In particular, the random variable S_r is the sum of r geometric random variables of the kind we have focused on.[1]

Theorem 5.19. *The random variable S_r has the probability mass function*

$$f_{S_r}(k) = \binom{k-1}{r-1} p^r (1-p)^{k-r}.$$

Proof. We use the standard technique for random variables for Bernoulli processes. For a Bernoulli process to be admissible, the rth success must occur on the kth trial. The probability that the kth trial is successful is p. Suppose the other $r-1$ successes occur in the first $r-1$ trials, and the remaining trials are all failures. The probability that this occurs is $p^{r-1}(1-p)^{k-r}$. Sequences that differ only in their order are equally probable, and there are $\binom{k-1}{r-1}$ permutations that keep the rth success fixed. This implies that

$$f_{S_r}(k) = \binom{k-1}{r-1} p^r (1-p)^{k-r}.$$ ■

The failure variant F_r is closely related. In particular, for any r, $F_r = S_r - r$, so that F_r is a translation of S_r. We leave the derivation of the probability mass function for F_r as an exercise.

Theorem 5.20. *The random variable S_r has expectation*

$$\mathbf{E}[S_r] = \frac{r}{p}.$$

Proof. We can write S_r as a sum of r independent, identically distributed geometric random variables, so that

$$\mathbf{E}[S_r] = \mathbf{E}[G_1] + \cdots + \mathbf{E}[G_r] = \frac{r}{p}.$$

■

1 We call a random variable geometric if it counts the number of trials until the first success in a sequence of Bernoulli trials. Other authors call a random variable geometric when it counts the number of failures before the first success in a sequence of Bernoulli trials.

Theorem 5.21. *The random variable S_r has variance*

$$\mathbf{V}[S_r] = \frac{r(1-p)}{p^2}.$$

Proof. We can write S_r as a sum of r independent, identically distributed geometric random variables, so that

$$\mathbf{V}[S_r] = \mathbf{V}[G_1] + \cdots + \mathbf{V}[G_r] = \frac{r(1-p)}{p^2}.$$

■

Theorem 5.22. *The random variable S_r has moment generating function*

$$M_{S_r}(t) = \left(\frac{p}{1-(1-p)e^t}\right)^n.$$

HYPERGEOMETRIC DISTRIBUTION

The hypergeometric distribution models an experiment where n balls are drawn from and urn containing r red balls and b black balls without replacement. A random variable that follows the hypergeometric distribution counts the number of red balls drawn.

Definition 5.23. A random variable X follows the hypergeometric distribution when it has the probability mass function

$$f_X(k) = \frac{\binom{r}{k}\binom{b}{n-k}}{\binom{r+b}{n}}.$$

Theorem 5.24. *The expected value of a hypergeometric random variable X is*

$$\mathbf{E}[X] = \frac{r}{r+b}.$$

Proof. Let X_k be an indicator variable for the event that the kth draw is a red ball. The probability that the kth ball drawn is red is

$$\frac{r}{r+b},$$

so that

$$\mathbf{E}[X_k] = \frac{r}{r+b}.$$

The linearity of expectation implies the result. ■

Theorem 5.25. *The variance of a hypergeometric random variable* X *is*

$$\mathbf{V}[X] = \frac{nrb}{(r+b)^2}\frac{r+b-n}{r+b-1}.$$

Proof. Let X_k be an indicator variable for the event that the kth draw is a red ball. The previous result implies that

$$\mathbf{V}[X_k] = \frac{rb}{(r+b)^2}.$$

If $j \neq k$, then $X_jX_k = 1$ only when both X_j and X_k are 1. The probability that X_jX_k is one is

$$\mathbf{E}[X_jX_k] = \frac{r(r-1)}{(r+b)(r+b-1)}.$$

This implies the covariance of X_j and X_k is

$$\mathbf{C}[X_j, X_k] = \frac{-rb}{(r+b)^2(r+b-1)}.$$

Finally, the variance of X is

$$\mathbf{V}[X] = \frac{nrb}{(r+b)^2}\left(1 - \frac{n-1}{r+b-1}\right).$$ ■

POISSON DISTRIBUTION

We saw that there are several probability distributions related to the Bernoulli process. The binomial distribution counts the number of successes in a fixed number of Bernoulli trials, and the geometric distribution counts the number of trials between each success. We now consider a continuous time analog of the Bernoulli process. Suppose we use a Bernoulli process to model the times in which customers arrive to a store between times 0 and t. We say that a time interval $[k, k+1)$, for $k \in \mathbf{N}^+$ is a success if a customer arrives in that interval. In order for this to be a realistic model, the probability that a customer arrives in the kth interval must be relatively small. Now, consider what happens as the number of trials n increases, while keeping $\lambda = np$ constant. In the limit as n increases, the Bernoulli process converges to the Poisson process. And just as the binomial distribution counts the number of successes in n trials, the Poisson distribution counts the number of arrivals between times 0 and t.

Definition 5.26. A random variable X follows the Poisson distribution with parameter λ if its probability mass function is

$$\mathbf{P}\left[X = k\right] = e^{-\lambda}\frac{\lambda^k}{k!} \text{ for } k \geq 0.$$

Theorem 5.27. *Let X follow the Poisson distribution with parameter λ. Then $\mathbf{E}\left[X\right] = \lambda$. Similarly, $\mathbf{V}\left[X\right] = \lambda$.*

Proof. We calculated the expectation in example 4.5 on page 89. We will calculate the variance in terms of $\mathbf{E}\left[X^2\right]$.

$$\begin{aligned}
\mathbf{E}\left[X^2\right] &= \sum_{k=0} k^2 e^{-\lambda}\frac{\lambda^k}{k!} = \sum_{k=1} k\frac{\lambda^k}{(k-1)!} \\
&= \lambda e^{-\lambda}\sum_{k=0}(k+1)\frac{\lambda^k}{k!} = \lambda e^{-\lambda}\left(\sum_{k=0} k\frac{\lambda^k}{k!} + \sum_{k=0}\frac{\lambda^k}{k!}\right) \\
&= \lambda\left(\mathbf{E}\left[X\right] + 1\right) = \lambda^2 + \lambda.
\end{aligned}$$

From this, we calculate

$$\mathbf{V}[X] = \mathbf{E}\left[X^2\right] - \mathbf{E}[X]^2 = \lambda^2 + \lambda - \lambda^2 = \lambda. \qquad \blacksquare$$

Theorem 5.28. *Let X and Y be independent Poisson random variables with parameters λ and μ, respectively. Then X + Y follows a Poisson distribution with parameter λ + μ.*

Proof. The proof is a straight-forward calculation.

$$\begin{aligned}
\mathbf{P}[X + Y = n] &= \sum_{k=0}^{n} \mathbf{P}[X = n-k]\,\mathbf{P}[Y = k] \\
&= \sum_{k=0}^{n} \frac{e^{-\lambda}\lambda^{n-k}}{(n-k)!} \cdot \frac{e^{-\mu}\mu^k}{k!} \\
&= \frac{e^{-(\lambda+\mu)}}{n!} \sum_{k=0}^{n} \binom{n}{k} \lambda^{n-k}\mu^k.
\end{aligned}$$

The binomial theorem implies that

$$= \frac{e^{-(\lambda+\mu)}(\lambda+\mu)^n}{n!}. \qquad \blacksquare$$

We can alternatively derive the moments for the Poisson distribution from its moment generating function, which we derive now.

Theorem 5.29. *Let X follow the Poisson distribution with parameter λ. Then the moment generating function for X is*

$$M_X(t) = e^{\lambda(e^t - 1)}.$$

Proof. This is a straight-forward calculation.

$$\begin{aligned}
M_X(t) = \mathbf{E}\left[e^{tX}\right] &= \sum_{k=0}^{\infty} e^{tk} e^{-\lambda} \frac{\lambda^k}{k!} \\
&= e^{-\lambda} \sum_{k=0}^{\infty} \frac{(\lambda e^t)^k}{k!} \\
&= e^{-\lambda} e^{\lambda e^t} = e^{\lambda(e^t - 1)}. \qquad \blacksquare
\end{aligned}$$

The moment generating function makes it easy to calculate moments and other interesting quantities for the Poisson distribution. As we saw before, the sum of independent Poisson random variables is a Poisson random variable. Proving this is very easy with moment generating functions.

Theorem 5.30. *Let X and Y be independent Poisson random variables with parameters λ and μ, respectively. Then $X+Y$ follows the Poisson distribution with parameter $\lambda+\mu$.*

Proof. The moment generating function for $X+Y$ is

$$\begin{aligned} M_{X+Y}(t) &= M_X(t)M_Y(t) \\ &= e^{\lambda(e^t-1)}e^{\mu(e^t-1)} \\ &= e^{(\lambda+\mu)(e^t-1)}. \end{aligned}$$ ■

EXPONENTIAL DISTRIBUTION

As we discussed in section 5.6, the exponential distribution models the time between arrivals in a Poisson process, but it is used to model a variety of phenomena.

Definition 5.31. A random variable X follows the exponential distribution with parameter λ if it has the probability density function

$$f_X(x) = \lambda e^{-\lambda x}, \text{ for } x > 0.$$

Theorem 5.32. *The probability distribution function for an exponentially distributed random variable X is*

$$F_X(x) = 1 - e^{-\lambda x}$$

Proof. The proof is a straight-forward calculation.

$$F_X(x) = \int_0^x \lambda e^{-\lambda x} = \left(-e^{-\lambda x}\Big|_0^x\right) = 1 - e^{-\lambda x}.$$ ■

Theorem 5.33. *The exponential distribution is memoryless. That is, an exponential random variable X satisfies*

$$\mathbf{P}[X - h \geq x | X > h] = \mathbf{P}[X > x]$$

Proof. This is a straight-forward calculation.

$$\mathbf{P}\big[X - h > x | X > h\big] = \frac{\mathbf{P}\big[\,[X > x + h] \wedge [X > h]\,\big]}{\mathbf{P}\big[X > h\big]} = \frac{\mathbf{P}\big[X > x + h\big]}{\mathbf{P}\big[X > h\big]}$$

$$= \frac{e^{-\lambda(x+h)}}{e^{-\lambda h}} = e^{-\lambda x} = \mathbf{P}\big[X > x\big]\,. \qquad \blacksquare$$

Theorem 5.34. *The moment generating function for an exponential random variable* X *is*

$$M_X(t) = \frac{\lambda}{\lambda - t}.$$

Proof. We proved this result in example 4.40 on page 111. ■

Theorem 5.35. *Let* X *be an exponential random variable with parameter* λ*. The* k^{th} *moment* $\mathbf{E}\big[X^k\big]$ *is*

$$\mathbf{E}\Big[X^k\Big] = \frac{k!}{\lambda^k}.$$

Proof. We will prove this with the method of generating functions. We begin by proving that the kth derivative of the moment generating function is

$$M_X^{(k)}(t) = \frac{k!\lambda}{(\lambda - t)^{k+1}}.$$

We will prove this by induction. For $k = 1$,

$$M_X^{(1)}(t) = \frac{d}{dt}\frac{\lambda}{\lambda - t} = \frac{(\lambda - t)0 - \lambda(-1)}{(\lambda - t)^2} = \frac{\lambda}{(\lambda - t)^2}.$$

Now, assume that

$$M_X^{(k)}(t) = \frac{k!\lambda}{(\lambda - t)^{k+1}}$$

and take the derivative

$$M_X^{(k+1)}(t) = \frac{d}{dt}M^{(k)}(t) = \frac{d}{dt}\frac{k!\lambda}{(\lambda - t)^{k+1}}$$

$$= \frac{(\lambda - t)^{k+1}0 - k!\lambda(k+1)(-1)(\lambda - t)^k}{(\lambda - t)^{2k+2}}$$

$$= \frac{(k+1)!\lambda}{(\lambda - t)^{k+2}}.$$

This argument by induction implies that

$$M_X^{(k)}(t) = \frac{k!\lambda}{(\lambda - t)^{k+1}},$$

so that

$$\mathbf{E}\left[X^k\right] = M_X^{(k)}(0) = \frac{k!}{\lambda^k}. \qquad \blacksquare$$

Using this formula, we see that

Theorem 5.36. *The expectation for an exponentially distributed random variable X is*

$$\mathbf{E}[X] = \frac{1}{\lambda},$$

and the second moment of X is

$$\mathbf{E}\left[X^2\right] = \frac{2}{\lambda^2},$$

so that

$$\mathbf{V}[X] = \mathbf{E}\left[X^2\right] - \mathbf{E}[X]^2 = \frac{1}{\lambda^2}.$$

CONTINUOUS UNIFORM DISTRIBUTION

Definition 5.37. A random variable follows the *continuous uniform distribution* on a set if the probability that X is an element of some event A is proportional to the area of A.

Because of the proportionality property for the continuous uniform distribution on a set Ω, calculating probabilities that an event A occurs is very straight-forward. We calculate the size of A, and divide by the size of Ω.

Example 5.38. A beginner dart player's throws are uniformly distributed on the dart board, which has a radius of 10 inches. If the bullseye has a radius of 0.75 inches, what is the probability that the beginner gets a bullseye?

Solution. The dart board has area $|\Omega| = \pi 10^2$. The bullseye has area $\pi 0.75^2$. The probability that the beginner gets a bullseye is approximately 0.0056. ∎

Definition 5.39. A random variable X is a standard uniform random variable if it is uniformly distributed on $[0, 1]$. In this case, the probability density function is

$$f_X(x) = 1, \text{ for } 0 \leq x \leq 1.$$

We are often interested in random variables that are uniformly distributed on an interval $[a, b]$ of real numbers. We can transform a standard uniform random variable X into a random variable Y that is distributed on $[a, b]$ by defining

$$Y = a + (b - a)X$$

Theorem 5.40. *Let X be a standard uniform random variable, and let Y be uniformly distributed on $[a, b]$. Then*

$$\mathbf{E}[X] = \frac{1}{2}$$

and

$$\mathbf{E}[Y] = \frac{a+b}{2}.$$

Proof. We calculate $\mathbf{E}[X]$ directly.

$$\mathbf{E}[X] = \int_0^1 x\,dx = \left(\frac{x^2}{2}\bigg|_0^1\right) = \frac{1}{2}.$$

Given that we have calculated $\mathbf{E}[X]$, we calculate

$$\mathbf{E}[Y] = \mathbf{E}[a + (b-a)X] = a + (b-a)\mathbf{E}[X] = a + \frac{b-a}{2} = \frac{a+b}{2}.$$

∎

We can calculate the variance for Y using a similar construction.

Theorem 5.41. *Let X be a standard uniform random variable, and let Y be uniformly distributed on* (a, b)*. Then*

$$\mathbf{V}[X] = \frac{1}{12}$$

and

$$\mathbf{V}[Y] = \frac{(b-a)^2}{12}.$$

Proof. We calculate $\mathbf{E}[X^2]$.

$$\mathbf{E}\left[X^2\right] = \int_0^1 x^2\,dx = \left(\frac{x^3}{3}\bigg|_0^1\right) = \frac{1}{3}.$$

With this, we can calculate the variance

$$\mathbf{V}[X] = \mathbf{E}\left[X^2\right] - \mathbf{E}[X]^2 = \frac{1}{3} - \frac{1}{4} = \frac{1}{12}.$$

Since $Y = a + (b-a)X$, we find

$$\mathbf{V}[Y] = \mathbf{V}[a + (b-a)X] = \mathbf{V}[(b-a)X] = (b-a)^2\mathbf{V}[X] = \frac{(b-a)^2}{12}.$$

■

PARETO DISTRIBUTION

The Pareto distribution is not on the Exam P syllabus, but it is worth learning about, since it is frequently used for exam problems and in the insurance industry. It is commonly used as a model of the distribution of income, especially when modeling the incomes of high net worth individuals.

Definition 5.42. A random variable X follows the *Pareto distribution* if it has the probability density function

$$f_X(x) = \frac{\alpha x_0^\alpha}{x^{\alpha+1}} \text{ for } x_0 < x.$$

Theorem 5.43. *The probability distribution function for a Pareto random variable X is*

$$F_X(x) = 1 - \left(\frac{x_0}{x}\right)^\alpha.$$

Proof. We integrate

$$\begin{aligned}
F_X(x) &= \int_{x_0}^{x} \frac{\alpha x_0^\alpha}{x^{\alpha+1}}\,dx \\
&= \alpha x_0 \int_{x_0}^{x} \frac{1}{x^{\alpha+1}}\,dx \\
&= \alpha x_0 \left(-\frac{1}{\alpha x^\alpha}\bigg|_{x_0}^{x} \right) \\
&= 1 - \left(\frac{x_0}{x}\right)^\alpha.
\end{aligned}$$

■

Theorem 5.44. *The expectation for a Pareto random variable X is*

$$\mathbf{E}[X] = \frac{\alpha x_0}{\alpha - 1}.$$

Proof. We integrate

$$\begin{aligned}
\mathbf{E}[X] &= \int_{x_0}^{\infty} x \frac{\alpha x_0^\alpha}{x^{\alpha+1}}\,dx \\
&= \int_{x_0}^{\infty} \frac{\alpha x_0^\alpha}{x^{\alpha}}\,dx \\
&= \left(-\frac{\alpha x_0^\alpha}{(\alpha - 1) x_0^{\alpha-1}}\bigg|_{x_0}^{\infty} \right) \\
&= \frac{\alpha x_0}{\alpha - 1}.
\end{aligned}$$

■

Theorem 5.45. *The variance for a Pareto random variable X is*

$$\mathbf{V}[X] = \frac{\alpha x_0}{(\alpha - 1)^2(\alpha - 2)}.$$

Proof. We calculate that

$$\begin{aligned}\mathbf{E}\left[X^2\right] &= \int_{x_0}^{\infty} x^2 \frac{\alpha x_0^{\alpha}}{x^{\alpha+1}}\,dx \\ &= \alpha x_0^{\alpha} \int_{x_0}^{\infty} \frac{1}{x^{\alpha-1}}\,dx \\ &= \alpha x_0^{\alpha} \left(\frac{1}{(\alpha-2)x^{\alpha-2}} \Big|_{x_0}^{\infty} \right) \\ &= \frac{\alpha x_0^2}{\alpha - 2}.\end{aligned}$$

We have shown that

$$\mathbf{E}[X] = \frac{\alpha x_0}{\alpha - 1},$$

so we calculate

$$\begin{aligned}\mathbf{V}[X] &= \frac{\alpha x_0^2}{\alpha - 2} - \frac{\alpha^2 x_0^2}{(\alpha-1)^2} \\ &= \frac{x_0^2 \alpha(\alpha^2 - 2\alpha + 1) - x_0^2(\alpha^3 - 2\alpha)}{(\alpha-1)^2(\alpha-2)} \\ &= \frac{\alpha x_0}{(\alpha-1)^2(\alpha-2)}.\end{aligned}$$

■

NORMAL DISTRIBUTION

Definition 5.46. A normal random variable with mean μ and standard deviation σ has the probability density function

$$f_X(x) = \frac{1}{\sigma\sqrt{2\pi}} e^{-\frac{(x-\mu)^2}{2\sigma^2}}.$$

As we might know from previous courses in mathematics, the cumulative distribution function for the normal distribution cannot be expressed in closed-form. In other words, there is no formula for the integral

$$F_X(x) = \int_{-\infty}^{x} \frac{1}{\sigma\sqrt{2\pi}} e^{-\frac{(x-\mu)^2}{2\sigma^2}}.$$

Instead, we must use tables or electronic devices to calculate F. To aid in this process, we define the

Definition 5.47. The *standard normal distribution* is the normal distribution with mean 0 and standard deviation 1. We use Z to denote a standard normal random variable.

Definition 5.48. Given random variable X, we can define the standardized variable X^* by

$$X^* = \frac{X - \mu}{\sigma}.$$

Without the ability to standardize normal random variables, we would need a table of probabilities for each value of μ and σ. Instead, we can standardize the data we are given and use the standard normal distribution table. This table is also known as a Z-table.

Example 5.49. Male body weight is approximately normally distributed, with mean 175 and standard deviation 20. What proportion of the male population has a body weight below 190?

Solution. Let X be a male's body weight. We seek

$$\mathbf{P}[X < 190] = \mathbf{P}[X^* < 190^*] = \mathbf{P}\left[Z < \frac{190 - 175}{20}\right] = 0.77. \quad \blacksquare$$

Theorem 5.50 (Central Limit Theorem). *Given a sequence $\{X_n\}$ of independent, identically distributed random variables with means μ and finite standard deviations σ, the sum*

$$S = \sum_{i=1}^{n} X_i$$

is approximately normal with mean $n\mu$ and standard deviation $\sigma\sqrt{n}$.

The central limit theorem explains the common occurrence of the normal distribution. Many physical and social phenomena are caused by large numbers of random factors with additive effects. The central limit theorem implies that the random aggregate is approximately normally distributed.

Example 5.51. An experiment will be run 1000 times. Each experiment will be successful with probability $p = 0.65$. What is the probability that the experiment will be successful at least 625 times and at most 675 times?

Solution. In principle, we can solve this using the binomial distribution, but using that technique requires us to evaluate a very large sum. Instead, we will appeal to the central limit theorem. Since the number of successes is a binomial random variable, it is the sum of 1000 Bernoulli variables. The sum S is approximately normal, with mean $1000p = 650$ and standard deviation $\sigma = 15.08$. We calculate

$$\begin{aligned}\mathbf{P}\big[625 \leq S \leq 675\big] &= \mathbf{P}\left[\frac{625-650}{15.08} \leq Z \leq \frac{675-650}{15.08}\right] \\ &= \mathbf{P}\big[-1.66 \leq Z \leq 1.66\big] \\ &= \mathbf{P}\big[Z \leq 1.66\big] - \mathbf{P}\big[Z < -1.66\big] \\ &= 0.903\end{aligned}$$

■

As we have seen, the normal distribution is specified in terms of is expectation μ and standard deviation σ. Deriving the moment generating function for the normal distribution is beyond the scope of this volume, but it is still worth knowing. We state the following theorem without proof:

Theorem 5.52. *Let X be a normal random variable. Then*

$$M_X(t) = \exp\left\{\mu t + \frac{1}{2}\sigma^2 t^2\right\}.$$

We use moment generating functions to deduce an important result about the normal distribution.

Theorem 5.53. *Let X and Y be independent normally distributed random variables with means and standard deviations μ_X and σ_X, and μ_Y and σ_Y, respectively. Then $X + Y$ is normally distributed with mean $\mu_X + \mu_Y$ and standard deviation $\sqrt{\sigma_X^2 + \sigma_Y^2}$.*

Proof. We calculate the moment generating function of $X+Y$ as

$$\begin{aligned} M_{X+Y}(t) = M_X(t)M_Y(t) &= \exp\left\{\mu_X t + \sigma_X^2 t^2\right\}\exp\left\{\mu_Y t + \sigma_Y^2 t^2\right\} \\ &= \exp\left\{(\mu_X + \mu_Y)t + (\sigma_X^2 + \sigma_Y^2)t^2\right\}, \end{aligned}$$

which we recognize is the moment generating function for a normal random variable with mean $\mu_X + \mu_Y$ and standard deviation $\sqrt{\sigma_X^2 + \sigma_Y^2}$. ■

LOG-NORMAL DISTRIBUTION

The log-normal distribution is closely related to the normal distribution.

Definition 5.54. Let X be a normally distributed random variable with parameters μ and σ. Then $Y = e^X$ follows a log-normal distribution with parameters μ and σ.

We can remember this definition by noting that if Y is lognormal, then $\log Y$ is normally distributed. We remind you that we are using 'traditional' mathematics notation here, so that log is the *natural logarithm*.

Example 5.55. Annual savings account returns follow a log-normal with parameters $\mu = 0.1$ and $\sigma = 0.5$. If you deposit 100 today, what is the probability that the account will have at least 110 at the end of the year?

Solution. Notice that this example is asking us to assume that the interest rate the account earns is normally distributed. The problem asks us to calculate

$$\begin{aligned} \mathbf{P}[100R \geq 110] = \mathbf{P}\left[100e^X \geq 110\right] &= \mathbf{P}\left[X \geq \log\frac{110}{100}\right] \\ &= \mathbf{P}\left[Z \geq \frac{\log\left(\frac{110}{100}\right) - \mu}{\sigma}\right] = 1 - \mathbf{P}[Z < 0.391] \\ &\approx 0.35. \end{aligned}$$

■

The log-normal distribution plays a similar role for multiplicative effects as the normal distribution plays for additive effects. We can see that the exponential e in $Y = e^X$ 'translates' the additive effects that lead to the outcome X into a multiplicative effects that lead to the outcome Y. We will see the lognormal distribution in detail when we prepare for Exam MFE. It is especially useful for modeling the behavior of stock prices, since we calculate stock prices in terms of returns by multiplying the original stock price by the return's accumulation factor, just as we do for interest earned.

EXERCISES

1° An aeronautics company tests each component it makes 3 times. If a component is destroyed if it fails a test. The probability that a component passes the first test is 90%. If a component passes the first test, the probability that it passes the second test is 95%. The probability that it passes the third test, given that it passed the first two, is 98%.

Four components are tested. What is the probability that at least two pass the test?

2° A company runs three simultaneous training courses. Each course has 15 students. The company has a policy that a student fails if he or she misses 2 or more days. Each student has a 1.5% probability of missing a day, independently of the others. The class is 60 days long. Let K be the number of classes that pass at least 12 students. What is the variance of K?

3° Suppose a fair coin is tossed an even number of times. How many tosses are required so that the probability of tossing an equal number of heads and tails is less than 1%?

4° In each minute of a basketball game, the probability that a team scores a basket is 0.6. What is the expected time until the team scores its 12th basket?

5° A game consists of rolling a single die. If a 1 is rolled, the player wins. If a 3 or 5 are rolled, the player loses. If an even number is rolled, the player rolls again, until he either wins or loses. If the player wins, he gains a dollar for each roll made. What is the expected payoff for the game?

6° Let X be a random variable with probability mass function

$$f_X(k) = \frac{4}{5^k}.$$

What is the conditional expectation of X, given that X is even?

7° 10 red balls and 12 black balls are placed in an urn. An experiment consists of rolling a fair four sided die with labels 1, 2, 3 and n. If the result of the throw is X, X balls are drawn from the urn without replacement. After many repetitions of the experiment, it is found that the average number of red balls drawn is approximately 1.3636. What is n?

8° Let X and Y be independent Poisson random variables with means $\lambda_X = 8$ and $\lambda_Y = 12$, respectively. Find the mean of X, given that $X + Y = 10$.

9° Let X be a Poisson random variable with parameter $\lambda = 0.25$. Find the expectation of $\frac{1}{1+X}$.

10° In a certain game, the player can take any one of three actions in a turn. Once the player takes an action, he sees the consequences of his choice and begins a new turn. The number of turns in a game is a Poisson random variable with mean 8. What is the expected number of sequences of choices a player can make?

11° Let X be an exponential random variable with $\lambda = 3$ and let $Y = X^2$. Find $\mathbf{E}\left[Y^2\right]$.

12° A business insures 5 laptop computers. The lifetime of a laptop computer is an exponential random variable with a mean of 2 years. What is the expected value of the time until the last laptop fails?

13° A life insurance company classifies people as either non-smokers, light smokers, or heavy smokers. The survival functions for non-smokers, light smokers, and heavy smokers are

$$S_N(x) = e^{-\frac{1}{75}x} \qquad S_L(x) = e^{-\frac{1}{65}x} \qquad S_H(x) = e^{-\frac{1}{55}x}.$$

respectively. The probability that a customer is a non-smoker is 0.6. The probability that a customer is a light smoker is 0.25. The probability that a customer is a heavy smoker is 0.15. Given that a customer has lived to 55, what is the probability that he lives to 65?

14° Let (X, Y) be uniformly distributed on the region $\frac{1}{2}x < y < 2x$, $0 < x < 1$. Find $\mathbf{P}\left[X + Y > \frac{3}{2}\right]$.

15° A random variable X has the probability density function

$$f_X(x) = \frac{c}{\sqrt{2\pi}} e^{-\frac{x^2}{2}} \text{ for } x > 0.$$

Calculate $\mathbf{E}\left[X\right]$.

16° A random variable X is normally distributed with mean $\mu = 100$ and standard deviation σ. It is known that $\mathbf{E}\left[X^3\right] = 1067500$. Find σ.

17° The Phoebus Group takes 100 random samples from Generic Electronics' light bulb factory and fines Generic Electronics 100000 for each light bulb it finds with a lifetime of more than 1000 hours. The lifetimes for Generic Electronics' bulbs are normally distributed with a mean of 940 and a standard deviation of 35. How much can Generic Electronics expect to pay in fines?

18° A lognormal random variable X has parameters $\mu = 0.1$ and $\sigma = 0.2$. What is the probability that X is greater than 1.4?

19° A random variable X is lognormally distributed, and

$$\mathbf{P}\left[83.4 < 100X < 133.5\right] = 0.95.$$

What is the expected value of 100X?

SOLUTIONS

1° Let S be the event that a component passes all the tests successfully. Let A be the event that a component passes the first test. Let B be the event that a component passes the second test. Let C be the event that a component passes the third test. We can use the chain rule for conditional probabilities to compute

$$\mathbf{P}[S] = \mathbf{P}[ABC] = \mathbf{P}[C|AB]\,\mathbf{P}[B|A]\,\mathbf{P}[A] \approx 0.8379.$$

Let N be the number of components that pass. We see that N is a binomial random variable with parameters $p = 0.8379$ and $n = 4$. We calculate

$$\begin{aligned}\mathbf{P}[N \geq 2] &= \binom{4}{2}\mathbf{P}[S]^2\,\mathbf{P}[S']^2 + \binom{4}{3}\mathbf{P}[S]^4\,\mathbf{P}[S'] + \binom{4}{4}\mathbf{P}[S]^4 \\ &\approx 0.985.\end{aligned}$$

2° The number of days that a student misses is a binomial random variable with parameters $n = 60$ and $p = 0.015$. The probability that a student passes is q in

$$q = \binom{60}{0}(1-p)^{60} + \binom{60}{1}p(1-p)^{59} \approx 0.773.$$

The number of passing students in a class that pass the course is a binomial random variable with parameters $p = q$ and $n = 15$. This means the probability that at least 12 students will pass the course is r in

$$\begin{aligned}r &= \binom{15}{12}q^{12}(1-q)^3 + \binom{15}{13}q^{13}(1-q)^2 \\ &\quad + \binom{15}{14}q^{14}(1-q)^1 + \binom{15}{13}q^{15}(1-q)^0 \\ &\approx 0.545.\end{aligned}$$

Finally, the number of classes that passes with at least 12 students is a binomial random variable with parameters $n = 3$ and $p = r$, so that the variance is $nr(1-r) = 0.744$.

3° We seek the smallest integer n that satisfies

$$0.01 > \binom{n}{\frac{n}{2}} \left(\frac{1}{2}\right)^{\frac{n}{2}} \left(\frac{1}{2}\right)^{\frac{n}{2}}.$$

Intuition suggests that n will be 'large', so we use approximate methods to estimate $n!$. We use Stirling's approximation:

$$\begin{aligned}
&\approx \frac{\sqrt{2\pi n}}{\pi n} \frac{\left(\frac{n}{e}\right)^n}{\left(\frac{n}{2e}\right)^n} \left(\frac{1}{2}\right)^n \\
&= \frac{\sqrt{2}}{\sqrt{\pi n}} (2^n) \left(\frac{1}{2}\right)^n \\
&= \frac{\sqrt{2}}{\sqrt{\pi n}}.
\end{aligned}$$

This implies that

$$\begin{aligned}
\frac{\sqrt{\pi n}}{\sqrt{2}} &\geq 100 \\
\sqrt{\pi n} &> 100\sqrt{2} \\
\sqrt{n} &> \frac{100\sqrt{2}}{\sqrt{\pi}} \\
n &> \left(\frac{100\sqrt{2}}{\sqrt{\pi}}\right)^2 \\
&> 6366.19.
\end{aligned}$$

This implies that $n \approx 6367$.

4° We treat each minute as a Bernoulli trial, so that the game is a sequence of Bernoulli trials. We see that the time T_1 until the first basket is a geometric random variable. Because of the memorylessness property, the time T_2 until the next basket is a geometric random variable with the same distribution. In general, the time T_{k+1} between the kth basket and the $(k+1)^{st}$ basket is a geometric random variable with the same distribution. The total time until the 12th basket is

$$T = T_1 + T_2 + \cdots + T_{12},$$

so that

$$\mathbf{E}[T] = \mathbf{E}[T_1] + \mathbf{E}[T_2] + \cdots + \mathbf{E}[T_{12}] = 12\mathbf{E}[T_i] = 20.$$

5° To win in the first roll, the player must roll a 1. We see that the probability of winning in the first turn is $\frac{1}{6}$. To win in the second turn, the player must roll and even number and then a 1. The probability is $\frac{1}{2}\frac{1}{6}$. In general, to win in the k-th turn, the player must roll an even number $k-1$ times and then roll a 1. The probability of winning in the k-th turn is $\left(\frac{1}{2}\right)^{k-1}\left(\frac{1}{6}\right)$. We see that the expected payoff is

$$\begin{aligned}
\mathbf{E}[X] &= 1 \cdot \frac{1}{6} + 2\frac{1}{2}\frac{1}{6} + 3\left(\frac{1}{2}\right)^2 \frac{1}{6} + \cdots \\
&= \frac{1}{6}\left(1 + 2 \cdot \frac{1}{2} + 3 \cdot \left(\frac{1}{2}\right)^2 + \cdots\right) \\
&= \frac{1}{3}\left(\frac{1}{2} + 2 \cdot \left(\frac{1}{2}\right)^2 + 3 \cdot \left(\frac{1}{2}\right)^3 + \cdots\right)
\end{aligned}$$

We see that the sum is the expected value of a geometric random variable with parameter $p = \frac{1}{2}$, so that $\mathbf{E}[X] = 2/3$.

6° Let E denote the event that X is even. We must calculate

$$\mathbf{E}[X|E] = \sum_{k=0}^{\infty} k\mathbf{P}[X = k|E]\,\mathbf{P}[E] = \sum_{k=0}^{\infty} k\frac{\mathbf{P}[(X = k)E]}{\mathbf{P}[E]}.$$

To that end, we begin by calculating

$$\begin{aligned}\mathbf{P}[E] &= \frac{4}{5^2} + \frac{4}{5^4} + \frac{4}{5^6} + \cdots \\ &= 4\left(\left(\frac{1}{25}\right) + \left(\frac{1}{25}\right)^2 + \left(\frac{1}{25}\right)^3 + \cdots\right.\end{aligned}$$

Since the geometric series is

$$\sum_{k=0}^{\infty} r^k = \frac{1}{1-r},$$

we find that $\mathbf{P}[E] = 1/6$. We now calculate

$$\begin{aligned}\mathbf{E}[X|E] &= \frac{1}{\mathbf{P}[E]}\sum_{k=1}^{\infty} k\mathbf{P}[[X = k]E] \\ &= 6 \times \left(2\frac{4}{5^2} + 4\frac{4}{5^4} + 6\frac{4}{5^6}\cdots\right. \\ &= 6 \times 2 \times 4\left(1\frac{1}{25} + 2\frac{1}{25^2} + 3\frac{1}{25^3}\cdots\right.\end{aligned}$$

We recognize that the series in parentheses is the expectation of a geometric random variable with parameter $p = 1/25$. This implies that the series converges to 25, and $\mathbf{E}[X|E] = 1200$.

7° Let R be the number of red balls drawn. We see that for a fixed X, (R|X) is hypergeometric, so that $\mathbf{E}\left[R|X\right] = \frac{Xr}{r+b} = \frac{10X}{22}$. We use the law of total probability to write

$$\begin{aligned}
1.3636 &= \mathbf{E}\left[R\right] \\
&= \mathbf{E}\left[R|X=1\right]\mathbf{P}\left[X=1\right] + \mathbf{E}\left[R|X=2\right]\mathbf{P}\left[X=2\right] \\
&\quad + \mathbf{E}\left[R|X=3\right]\mathbf{P}\left[X=3\right] + \mathbf{E}\left[R|X=n\right]\mathbf{P}\left[X=n\right] \\
&= \frac{1}{4}\frac{10}{22}(1+2+3+n) \\
&= \frac{10}{88}(6+n),
\end{aligned}$$

so that $6+n \approx 11.99$ and $n \approx 6$.

8° As we saw in theorem 5.28 on page 145, $X+Y$ is a Poisson random variable with parameter $\lambda_X + \lambda_Y$. We calculate

$$\begin{aligned}
\mathbf{P}\left[X=k|X+Y=n\right] &= \frac{\mathbf{P}\left[(X=k)(X+Y=n)\right]}{\mathbf{P}\left[X+Y=n\right]} \\
&= \frac{\mathbf{P}\left[(X=k)(Y=n-k)\right]}{\mathbf{P}\left[X+Y=n\right]} \\
&= \frac{\mathbf{P}\left[(X=k)\right]\mathbf{P}\left[(Y=n-k)\right]}{\mathbf{P}\left[X+Y=n\right]} \\
&= \frac{e^{-\lambda_X}\frac{\lambda_X^k}{k!}e^{-\lambda_Y}\frac{\lambda_Y^{n-k}}{(n-k)!}}{\frac{e^{-(\lambda_X+\lambda_Y)}(\lambda_X+\lambda_Y)^n}{n!}} \\
&= \binom{n}{k}\frac{\lambda_X^k\lambda_Y^{n-k}}{(\lambda_X+\lambda_Y)^n}.
\end{aligned}$$

This implies that the conditional distribution $(X|X+Y=n)$ is the binomial distribution, with parameters n and $p = \frac{\lambda_X}{\lambda_X+\lambda_Y}$. Since $(X|X+Y=n)$ is binomial, the expected value is $\mathbf{E}\left[X|X+Y=n\right] = np = 4$.

9° By definition,

$$\mathbf{E}\left[\frac{1}{1+X}\right] = \sum_{n=0}^{\infty} \frac{1}{1+n} e^{-\lambda} \frac{\lambda^n}{n!},$$

which we simplify as

$$\begin{aligned} e^{-\lambda} \sum_{n=0}^{\infty} \frac{\lambda^n}{(n+1)!} &= \frac{e^{-\lambda}}{\lambda} \sum_{n=0}^{\infty} \frac{\lambda^{n+1}}{(n+1)!} \\ &= \frac{e^{-\lambda}}{\lambda} \sum_{n=1}^{\infty} \frac{\lambda^n}{n!} \\ &= \frac{e^{-\lambda}}{\lambda} \left(e^{\lambda} - 1\right) \\ &= \frac{1}{\lambda} \left(1 - e^{-\lambda}\right) \\ &\approx 0.88 \end{aligned}$$

10° Let N be the number of turns in a game. For a game with N turns, there are 3^N possible sequences of choices the player can make. We must calculate $\mathbf{E}\left[3^N\right]$. This is done easily with moment generating functions, since

$$\mathbf{E}\left[3^N\right] = \mathbf{E}\left[e^{N \log 3}\right] = M_N(\log 3) = \exp\left[8(e^{\log 3} - 1)\right] \approx 8886110.$$

11° We see that $Y^2 = X^4$, so that we seek the fourth moment of X. Since X is an exponential random variable, we can use the formula

$$\mathbf{E}[X^n] = \frac{n!}{\lambda^n},$$

so that $\mathbf{E}[Y^2] = \mathbf{E}[X^4] = \frac{4!}{3^4} = \frac{8}{27}$.

Alternatively, you could use the method of moment generating functions. Recall that

$$M_X(t) = \frac{\lambda}{\lambda - t}.$$

We can calculate $\mathbf{E}[X^4]$ using the formula

$$\mathbf{E}\left[X^4\right] = M_X^{(4)}(0).$$

In particular, we take derivatives:

$$\begin{aligned}
M_X'(t) &= \frac{1\lambda}{(\lambda - t)^2} \\
M_X''(t) &= \frac{2\lambda}{(\lambda - t)^3} \\
M_X^{(3)}(t) &= \frac{6\lambda}{(\lambda - t)^4} \\
M_X^{(4)}(t) &= \frac{24\lambda}{(\lambda - t)^5}
\end{aligned}$$

so that $\mathbf{E}[X^4] = M_X^{(4)}(0) = \frac{24}{\lambda^4} = \frac{8}{27}$.

12° We begin by calculating the probability distribution function of the minimum of n exponential random variables. This is a useful formula to know. Let $X_1, X_2, \ldots, X_n$ be independent exponential random variables with parameter λ.

$$\begin{aligned}
\mathbf{P}[\min\{X_1, \ldots, X_n\} < t] &= 1 - \mathbf{P}[\min\{X_1, \ldots, X_n\} > t] \\
&= 1 - \mathbf{P}[X_1 > t]\,\mathbf{P}[X_2 > t] \cdots \mathbf{P}[X_n > t] \\
&= 1 - \left(e^{-\lambda t}\right)^n \\
&= 1 - e^{-n\lambda t}.
\end{aligned}$$

We see that the minimum is an exponential random variable with parameter $n\lambda$, so that

$$\mathbf{E}\big[\min\{X_1, \ldots, X_n\}\big] = \frac{1}{n\lambda}.$$

Now, the times at which the 5 computers break down are random variables. Define $X_{(i)}$ as the ith smallest of these. Since X_1 is the smallest time, we see that $\mathbf{E}\big[X_1\big] = 1/5\lambda$. The memoryless property of X_2 implies that $X_2 - X_1$ is distributed as the minimum of 4 independent exponentially distributed random variables with common parameter λ. Proceeding in this way, we write

$$\begin{aligned}
\mathbf{E}\big[X_5\big] &= \mathbf{E}\big[X_{(1)} + (X_{(2)} - X_{(1)}) + \cdots + (X_{(5)} - X_{(4)})\big] \\
&= \mathbf{E}\big[X_{(1)}\big] + \mathbf{E}\big[X_{(2)} - X_{(1)}\big] + \cdots + \mathbf{E}\big[X_{(5)} - X_{(4)})\big] \\
&= \frac{1}{5\lambda} + \frac{1}{4\lambda} + \frac{1}{3\lambda} + \frac{1}{2\lambda} + \frac{1}{1\lambda} \\
&= \frac{2}{5} + \frac{2}{4} + \frac{2}{3} + \frac{2}{2} + \frac{2}{1} \\
&= 4.57.
\end{aligned}$$

13° Let X be the customer's lifespan. We must calculate

$$\begin{aligned}
\mathbf{P}\big[X > 65|X > 55\big] &= \mathbf{P}\big[X > 65|X > 55, N\big]\,\mathbf{P}\big[N\big] \\
&\quad + \mathbf{P}\big[X > 65|X > 55, L\big]\,\mathbf{P}\big[L\big] \\
&\quad + \mathbf{P}\big[X > 65|X > 55, H\big]\,\mathbf{P}\big[H\big] \\
&= \frac{\mathbf{P}\big[X > 65|N\big]}{\mathbf{P}\big[X > 55|N\big]}\mathbf{P}\big[N\big] + \frac{\mathbf{P}\big[X > 65|L\big]}{\mathbf{P}\big[X > 55|L\big]}\mathbf{P}\big[L\big] \\
&\quad + \frac{\mathbf{P}\big[X > 65|H\big]}{\mathbf{P}\big[X > 55|H\big]}\mathbf{P}\big[H\big] \\
&= 0.6\frac{e^{-\frac{65}{75}}}{e^{-\frac{55}{75}}} + 0.25\frac{e^{-\frac{65}{65}}}{e^{-\frac{55}{65}}} + 0.15\frac{e^{-\frac{65}{55}}}{e^{-\frac{55}{55}}} \\
&\approx 0.865
\end{aligned}$$

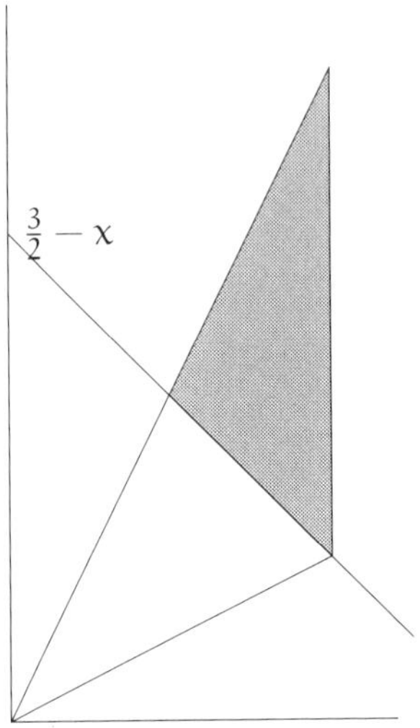

Figure 11: We must integrate over the region in gray.

14° We determine the limits of integration by drawing figure 11. Since the pair (X, Y) is uniformly distributed in the region, we can calculate that

$$1 = c \int_0^1 \int_{\frac{x}{2}}^{2x} dy dx = c \int_0^1 2x - \frac{x}{2} dx = c \int_0^1 \frac{3}{2} x \, dx$$

$$= c \left(\frac{3}{4} x^2 \Big|_0^1 \right) = \frac{3}{4} c,$$

so that $c = 4/3$. This implies that the probability we seek is

$$\begin{aligned}
\mathbf{P}\left[X+Y>\frac{3}{2}\right] &= c\int_{\frac{1}{2}}^{1}\int_{\frac{3}{2}-x}^{2x} 1\,dy\,dx \\
&= c\int_{\frac{1}{2}}\left(y\Big|_{\frac{3}{2}-x}^{2x} y\right) dx \\
&= c\int_{\frac{1}{2}}^{1} 3x-\frac{3}{2}\,dx \\
&= c\left(\frac{3}{2}x^2-\frac{3}{2}x\Big|_{\frac{1}{2}}^{1}\right) \\
&= \frac{9}{32}.
\end{aligned}$$

15° We find c, by solving for it in

$$1 = c\int_0^{\infty}\frac{1}{\sqrt{2\pi}}e^{-\frac{x^2}{2}}\,dx.$$

We see that the integral, excluding the c term, represents the probability that a standard normal random variable is greater than 0. This implies that $c = 2$. Now, we calculate the expectation

$$\mathbf{E}[X] = \frac{2}{\sqrt{2\pi}}\int_0^{\infty} xe^{-\frac{x^2}{2}}\,dx$$

so that, by u-substitution,

$$\begin{aligned}
&= -\frac{2}{\sqrt{2\pi}}\int_0^{\infty} d\left(e^{-\frac{x^2}{2}}\right) \\
&= -\frac{2}{\sqrt{2\pi}}e^{-\frac{x^2}{2}}\Big|_0^{\infty} \\
&= \sqrt{\frac{2}{\pi}}.
\end{aligned}$$

16° Recall that the moment generating function for X is given by

$$M_X(t) = \exp\left\{\mu t + \frac{1}{2}\sigma^2 t^2\right\}.$$

We calculate $\mathbf{E}\left[X^3\right]$ by calculating the third derivative of $M_X(t)$ and evaluating at 0.

$$\begin{aligned}
M_X'(t) &= (\mu + \sigma^2 t) M_X(t) \\
M_X''(t) &= (\mu + \sigma^2 t)^2 M_X(t) + \sigma^2 M_X(t) \\
M_X'''(t) &= (\mu + \sigma^2 t)^3 M_X(t) + 2\sigma^2(\mu + \sigma^2 t) M_X(t) + \sigma^2(\mu + \sigma^2 t) M_X(t)
\end{aligned}$$

so that

$$\mathbf{E}\left[X^3\right] = \mu^3 + 3\sigma^2\mu = 1067500.$$

This implies that $\sigma = 15$.

17° Let T be the lifetime of a randomly chosen bulb. We standardize the variable to find

$$\mathbf{P}\left[T < 1000\right] = \mathbf{P}\left[Z < \frac{1000 - \mu}{\sigma}\right] = \mathbf{P}\left[Z < 1.7143\right] \approx 0.9564,$$

so that $\mathbf{P}\left[Z > 1000\right] \approx 0.0436$.

The number of defective bulbs the Phoebus group finds is a binomial random variable with parameters $n = 100$ and $p = 0.0436$, so that the expected fine is approximately $436,000$.

18° We seek the probability $\mathbf{P}\left[X > 1.4\right]$, which we calculate as

$$\begin{aligned}
\mathbf{P}\left[X > 1.4\right] = \mathbf{P}\left[e^{\mu + \sigma Z} > 1.4\right] &= \mathbf{P}\left[Z > \frac{\log(1.4) - \mu}{\sigma}\right] \\
&= \mathbf{P}\left[Z > 1.18\right] = 1 - \mathbf{P}\left[Z < 1.18\right] \approx 0.12.
\end{aligned}$$

19° Since X is lognormally distributed, we calculate

$$\mathbf{P}\left[83.4 < 100X < 133.5\right] = \mathbf{P}\left[\frac{\log\left(\frac{83.4}{100}\right) - \mu}{\sigma} < Z < \frac{\log\left(\frac{133.5}{100}\right) - \mu}{\sigma}\right],$$

where Z is a standard normal random variable. We use a standard normal table to find that

$$\frac{\log\left(\frac{83.4}{100}\right) - \mu}{\sigma} = -1.96$$

$$\frac{\log\left(\frac{133.5}{100}\right) - \mu}{\sigma} = 1.96$$

so that

$$\log\left(\frac{133.5}{100}\right) + \log\left(\frac{83.4}{100}\right) = 2\mu,$$

and $\mu = 0.0537$. This implies that

$$\sigma = \frac{\log\left(\frac{133.5}{100}\right) - \mu}{1.96} = 0.12.$$

With this data, we calculate

$$\mathbf{E}\left[100X\right] = 100\mathbf{E}\left[X\right] = 100e^{\mu + \frac{\sigma^2}{2}} = 106.28.$$

6

INSURANCE

Insurance companies *write*, or sell, insurance policies. The customer is known as a policy holder, and the policy gives the policy holder the right, but not the obligation, to file *claims* for *benefits* under specific conditions. These claims are meant to pay the policy holder when, for example, accidental damage occurs to the policy holder's property, or when the policy holder requires emergency medical treatment. Of course, the policy defines which events are covered by the policy—a healthy insurance policy typically does not pay to repair damage to one's home. In other words, an insurance policy provides protection against specific *perils*, which we can think of as sources of risk. Summing up, we have

Definition 6.1. An *insurance policy* is a contract between an insurance company and the *policy holder* that gives the policy holder the right, but not the obligation, to file claims when specific perils cause the policy holder financial damage.

MODELING POLICIES

Definition 6.2. An insurance policy's *net premium* or *pure premium* is the expected value of the benefits paid by the insurance company.

Example 6.3. In a certain city, the probability that a major earthquake occurs in the next year is 10%. If an earthquake occurs, the damage to a home due to the earthquake is exponentially distributed with mean $25,000$. Calculate the net premium for an earthquake insurance policy for this home. Assume that at most one major earthquake occurs in a single year.

Solution. Let X be the total damage due to earthquakes and E be the event that a major earthquake occurs. We have two cases consider. We see that $(X|E')$, the damage due to earthquakes given that no earthquakes occur, is 0. Similarly, we see that $(X|E)$ is exponentially distributed with mean 25000. We use the law of total probability to calculate

$$\mathbf{E}[X] = \mathbf{E}[X|E']\,\mathbf{P}[E'] + \mathbf{E}[X|E]\,\mathbf{P}[E] = (0.1 \times 25000) = 2500. \quad \blacksquare$$

Many kinds of perils can occur more than once over the term of the insurance policy. For example, it is possible that a driver has more than one accident in a single year. In this case, we have two probability distributions to consider. The random variable N, which tells us how many accidents occur, follows the *frequency distribution*, while the random variable D, which tells us how much damage occurs in a single accident, follows the *severity distribution*.

Example 6.4. If a hurricane hit a certain city, the damage to a home is exponentially distributed with mean $50,000$. The number of hurricanes that hit this city is a Poisson random variable with mean $\frac{1}{15}$. What is the net premium for a home in this city?

Solution. Let X be the damage due to hurricanes. The net premium is

$$\begin{aligned}
\mathbf{E}[X] &= \mathbf{E}[\mathbf{E}[D_1 + D_2 + \cdots + D_N | N]] \\
&= \mathbf{E}[\mathbf{E}[ND|N]] \\
&= \mathbf{E}[N\mathbf{E}[D]] \\
&= \mathbf{E}[D]\,\mathbf{E}[N] \\
&= 3333.
\end{aligned}$$

$\blacksquare$

So far, we have considered insurance policies where the insurance company pays for the complete cost of the damage due to the covered peril. In general, both insurance companies and customers prefer to limit the amount that the insurance company pays. Insurance companies prefer these limits because they ensure that the customer faces some risk. Since the customer must pay for some of the damage, they are more likely to take actions to avoid losses due to covered perils, which has the effect of lowering the number of accidents that occur. Customers prefer these limits because they lower the premiums that must be paid. These policy limits can be implemented in two main ways.

Definition 6.5. For a policy with a *deductible* d, the customer must pay at most a quantity d for damages due to covered perils. Symbolically, if X is the damage due to a peril, the benefit B paid by a policy with a deductible d is given by

$$B = \begin{cases} 0, & \text{if } X \leq d, \\ X - d, & \text{if } X > d. \end{cases}$$

Definition 6.6. For a policy with a *policy limit* u, the insurance policy will pay a benefit B given by

$$B = \begin{cases} X, & \text{if } 0 < X \leq u, \\ u, & \text{if } X > u. \end{cases}$$

We can also create policies with a deductible and a policy limit. In this case, the benefit B is given by

$$B = \begin{cases} 0, & \text{if } X \leq d, \\ X - d, & \text{if } d < X < u, \\ u - d, & \text{if } X > u. \end{cases}$$

MANAGING RESERVES

An insurance company operates by collecting premiums, and then using these premiums to pay for insured losses. The possibility of doing this depends essentially on the central limit theorem, and we can use the central limit theorem to calculate various useful and important quantities.

Example 6.7. An insurance company has a portfolio of 50 identical policies. The benefit for a policy has expected value $\mathbf{E}[B] = 300$ and variance $\mathbf{V}[B] = 900$. If the company charges a premium of 307 for each policy, what is the probability that the company will be able to pay all its claims?

Solution. Let S be the total benefit paid for all policies. Since the company charges 307 for each policy, the company collects 15350 in total. We seek the probability that $S < 15350$. We use a normal approximation for S, as justified by the central limit theorem, so that S is approximately normally distributed with mean 15000 and standard deviation $\sqrt{50}\sqrt{900} = 212.13$. We calculate

$$\begin{aligned} \mathbf{P}[S < 15350] &= \mathbf{P}\left[Z < \frac{15350 - 15000}{212.13}\right] \\ &= \mathbf{P}[Z < 1.649] \\ &= 0.95 \end{aligned}$$ ■

Another important variation on this problem is finding how much the insurance company should charge to ensure that it can pay all its claims with some specified probability.

Example 6.8. An insurance company has a portfolio of 50 identical policies. The benefit for each policy has an expected value $\mathbf{E}[B] = 300$ and variance $\mathbf{V}[B] = 400$. What should the company charge for a policy to ensure that there is a 99% probability that it can pay all its claims?

Solution. Let k be the premium charged, and let S be the total benefit paid for all policies. By the central limit theorem, S is approximately normal, with mean $\mathbf{E}[S] = n\mathbf{E}[B] = 15000$ and variance $\mathbf{V}[S] = \sqrt{n}\mathbf{V}[B] = 1000000$. Since the company charges k, the company will collect a total of 50k. We seek k such that

$$\mathbf{P}[S < 50k] = \mathbf{P}\left[Z < \frac{50k - \mathbf{E}[S]}{\sigma_S}\right] = 0.99.$$

With the aid of a table of normal values, we find that

$$\frac{50k - \mathbf{E}[S]}{\sigma_S} = 2.33,$$

so that $k = 346.6$. ■

In these examples, we have been given the mean and variance for each policy. One common variation of these problems is to describe a policy in terms of its loss or benefit distribution, so that we must calculate the mean and variance of the benefit ourselves.

Example 6.9. An insurance company has a portfolio of 100 home insurance policies, each with policy limit of $75,000. The probability that a homeowner will file a policy is 5%, and the loss distribution is exponentially distributed with mean 65,000. How much should the company charge for a policy so that there is a 95% probability that the company can pay all its claims?

Solution. Let C be the event that the policyholder files a claim. We see that $\mathbf{P}[C] = 5\%$. The benefit paid, given that there is a claim, is

$$(B|C) = \begin{cases} X, & \text{if } X \leq 75,000 \\ 75,000 & \text{if } X > 75,000 \end{cases}$$

We will begin by calculating $\mathbf{P}[X \leq 75,000]$ and $\mathbf{P}[X > 75,000]$, using

$$F_X(x) = 1 - e^{-\lambda x},$$

so that $\mathbf{P}[X \leq 75000] = 0.6846$ and $\mathbf{P}[X > 75,000] = 0.3154$. Now we must calculate

$$\begin{aligned} \mathbf{E}[B|C] = \mathbf{E}[B|X \leq 75,000]\, \mathbf{P}[X \leq 75,000] \\ +\mathbf{E}[B|X > 75,000]\, \mathbf{P}[X > 75,000] \end{aligned}$$

We see that the latter term is

$$\mathbf{E}[75000|X > 75,000]\, \mathbf{P}[X > 75000] = 23655,$$

so we focus on calculating $\mathbf{E}[B|X \leq 75000]\,\mathbf{P}[X \leq 75000]$

$$
\begin{aligned}
&= \left(\int_0^{75000} x f_{(X|X \leq 75,000)}(x)\, dx \right) \mathbf{P}[X \leq 75000] \\
&= \left(\int_0^{75000} x f_X(x)\, dx \right) \\
&= \left(\int_0^{75000} x (\lambda e^{-\frac{x}{75000}})\, dx \right) \\
&= 20841.02
\end{aligned}
$$

We used integration by parts to calculate the last integral. We can now calculate $\mathbf{E}[B|C] = 44496$. We use a similar technique to calculate $\mathbf{E}[B^2|C]$. Clearly, $\mathbf{E}[B^2|X > 75000]\,\mathbf{P}[X > 75000] = 75000^2\mathbf{P}[X > 75000] = 1774125000$. We use repeated integration by parts to calculate

$$
\mathbf{E}\left[B^2|X \leq 75000\right] = \int_0^{75000} x^2 \left(\lambda e^{-\lambda x}\, dx\right) = 935088132,
$$

so that $\mathbf{E}[B^2|X \leq 75000]\,\mathbf{P}[X \leq 75000] = 640161335$. From this, we can conclude that $\mathbf{E}[B^2|C] = 2414286335$. From here, we can calculate $\mathbf{E}[B]$ as

$$
\mathbf{E}[B] = \mathbf{E}[B|C]\,\mathbf{P}[C] + \mathbf{E}[B|C']\,\mathbf{P}[C'] = 2224.8
$$

and

$$
\mathbf{E}\left[B^2\right] = \mathbf{E}\left[B^2|C\right]\mathbf{P}[C] + \mathbf{E}\left[B^2|C'\right]\mathbf{P}[C'] = 120714317,
$$

so that

$$
\mathbf{V}[B] = \mathbf{E}\left[B^2\right] - \mathbf{E}[B]^2 = 115764582
$$

and $\sigma_B = 10759$. At this stage, we have enough information to estimate the distribution of total benefits paid by the insurance company. Let P be the premium the insurance company charges and let S be the total benefit paid to customers. By the central limit theorem, S is approximately normal with mean $\mu_S = 222480$ and standard deviation $\sigma_S = 107590$. Since the company has 100 policies, the company collects $100P$. We require that P satisfies

$$\mathbf{P}\left[S < 100P\right] = \mathbf{P}\left[Z \leq \frac{100P - \mu_S}{\sigma_S}\right] = 0.95.$$

We use a standard normal table to estimate that

$$\frac{100P - \mu_S}{\sigma_S} \approx 1.645.$$

We solve this equation so that the minimum premium is $P = 3995$. ■

In this example, the premium is significantly higher than the expected loss per policy. This is because the benefit paid per policy has a relatively high variance. The amount that the company will pay to each policy holder is very uncertain. This translates into wide variations in the total amount paid by the company. In general, the higher the variance of the total benefits paid, the higher the minimum premium required.

This example highlights the major purpose of insurance. Without insurance, the homeowner faces the risk of losing the entire value of her home. In order to replace her home in the event of a loss, she would need to keep the entire value of her home in a savings account or similar financial instrument. This may or may not be feasible. Even if keeping that much money in an account is feasible, it means that her money is 'spent' on self-insurance—it sits idle, unable to be spent for other purposes while still providing protection against a loss. Instead, the homeowner has the option of purchasing insurance, which allows her to transfer much of her risk onto the insurance company for a much smaller fee than the total risk she faces. Both the home owner and insurance company are better off.

If we assume that the insurance company's portfolio contains 1000 of these policies, we calculate that the the minimum premium is $P = 2784$. In general, the more policies a portfolio contains, the lower the minimum premium required, up to a lower limit of $\mathbf{E}[B]$. This highlights the importance of sales to an insurance company. A sale not only increases the company's income, but lowers the average per policy operating cost.

This example has put together many of the techniques we have learned in order to calculate reserves. We see that the process is, in general, quite involved. We must calculate the expectation and standard deviation of the total benefit paid, which can require multiple calculations of conditional expectations and variances which we consolidate with the laws of total expectations and variance. And finally, we use these statistics, together with the central limit theorem, to estimate the distribution of the total benefit paid. For the purposes of the exam, it is essential that we understand this general process. Exam problems on this topic will typically not be as involved as our example, but they will certainly exercise your ability to apply each of these steps, or even the entire process.

EXERCISES

1° A laptop computer costs 900, and will fail in the kth year with probabilities

k	p_k
1	0.1
2	0.25
3	0.35
4	0.3

A 3 year insurance policy has a deductible of 300, and will replace the laptop computer once. What is the net premium for the policy?

2° A laptop computer costs X, and will fail in the kth year with probabilities

k	p_k
1	0.2
2	0.25
3	0.35
4	0.1

A 3 year insurance policy has a deductible of 200, and will replace the laptop computer once. How much does the laptop cost if the net premium for the policy is 300?

3° A smart phone costs X. A 1 year insurance policy for a smart phone has a deductible of 250, and the standard deviation of the benefit paid is 119.87. The probability that the smart phone fails in the kth year is given by

k	p_k
1	0.05
2	0.25
3	0.35
4	0.35

What is X?

4° A factory relies on a machine worth 100,000 for its operations. The probability that the machine will break down irreparably this year is 20%. If the machine breaks down, the factory will have to close. To protect itself, the factory joins a group of 29 other factories with identical machines and risks, each of which pays 20,000 into a fund devoted to paying for replacement machines. What is the probability that the fund will pay for all of the required replacements this year?

5° A factory relies on a machine worth 100,000 for its operations. The probability that the machine will break down irreparably this year is 20%. If the machine breaks down, the factory will have to close. To protect itself, the factory joins a group of 29 other factories with identical machines and risks, each of which pays 20,000 into a fund devoted to paying for replacement machines.

What is the expected fund balance at the end of the year?

6° A recent study has shown that each household spent an average of 8910 on health care last year, with a variance of 12257000. Projections estimate that health care costs will increase by 7% this year. A small insurance company has 500 policies and pays 85% of the policy holder's health care costs. What is the standard deviation of the total benefit it will pay?

7° An automobile insurance company classifies accidents as low severity, moderate severity, and high severity. The probability that an accident is low severity is 20%, and the damage due to a low severity accident is normally distributed with mean 300. The probability that an accident is moderate severity is 0.75, and the damage due to a moderate severity accident is exponentially distributed with mean 5000. The probability that an accident is severe is 0.05, and the damage due to a severe accident is exponentially distributed with mean 50000. The number of accidents a good driver has in a year follows a Poisson distribution with $\lambda = 1/7$. What is a good driver's net premium?

8° An insurance policy pays $\max\{0, 10,000 - 2500(K-1)\}$ if a machine fails before the end of the Kth year. The random variable K is distributed with the probability mass function

$$f_K(k) = (1-p)^{k-1}p,$$

where p = 0.15. How many policies must be sold for 4000, so that the probability that the insurer can pay for all claims is greater than 0.975?

SOLUTIONS

1° Let K be the year in which the laptop fails. The policy will pay a benefit B of 600 in the event of a loss in the first three years, and 0 if the loss occurs in the 4th year. The expected benefit is

$$\mathbf{E}[B] = 600\left(\mathbf{P}[K=1] + \mathbf{P}[K=2] + \mathbf{P}[K=3]\right) = 420.$$

2° Let K be the year in which the laptop fails. The policy will pay a benefit $B = X - 200$ if the laptop fails in the first three years, and 0 if it fails in the 4th year. The net premium is

$$300 = (X - 200)\left(\mathbf{P}[K=1] + \mathbf{P}[K=2] + \mathbf{P}[K=3]\right),$$

so that

$$X = \frac{300}{\mathbf{P}[K=1] + \mathbf{P}[K=2] + \mathbf{P}[K=3]} + 200 = \xcancel{533.33}\ 575.$$

3° We see that the benefit paid is $B = X - d$, where the deductible $d = 250$. The standard deviation of B is 119.87, so that

$$\begin{aligned}
\mathbf{V}[B] &= 14368.81 \\
&= \mathbf{E}\left[B^2\right] - \mathbf{E}[B]^2 \\
&= (X-d)^2\mathbf{P}[K=1] + \left((X-d)\mathbf{P}[K=1]\right)^2 \\
&= (X-d)^2\left(\mathbf{P}[K=1] - \mathbf{P}[K=1]^2\right)
\end{aligned}$$

so that $(X-d)^2 = 302501.408$, and $X - d = 550$. From this it follows that $X = 800$.

4° Let N be the number of machines that must be replaced. N is a binomial random variable with parameters $p = 0.2$ and $n = 30$. Before any breakdowns, the fund contains $30 \times 20,000 = 600,000$, which is enough to pay for 6 replacements. We calculate

$$\begin{aligned}\mathbf{P}[N \leq 6] = &\binom{30}{0}(1-p)^{30} + \binom{30}{1}(1-p)^{29}p + \binom{30}{2}(1-p)^{28}p^2 \\ &+\binom{30}{3}(1-p)^{27}p^3 + \binom{30}{4}(1-p)^{26}p^4 \\ &+\binom{30}{5}(1-p)^{25}p^5 + \binom{30}{6}(1-p)^{24}p^6\end{aligned}$$

so that $\mathbf{P}[N \leq 6] \approx 0.61$.

5° Let N be the number of machines that must be replaced. N is a binomial random variable with parameters $p = 0.2$ and $n = 30$. Before any breakdowns, the fund contains $30 \times 20,000 = 600,000$, which is enough to pay for 6 replacements. The fund balance at the end of the year is $B = 100,000 \cdot \max\{0, 6 - N\}$. We calculate

$$\begin{aligned}\mathbf{E}[B] = 100,000\Bigg(&6(1-p)^{30} + 5\binom{30}{1}p(1-p)^{29} + 4\binom{30}{2}p^2(1-p)^{28} \\ &+3\binom{30}{3}p^3(1-p)^{27} + 2\binom{30}{4}p^4(1-p)^{26} + 1\binom{30}{5}p^5(1-p)^{25}\Bigg)\end{aligned}$$

so that $\mathbf{E}[B] \approx 18855$.

6° Let X be the health care cost for a policy. We are given that $\mathbf{V}[X] = 12557000$, and we must find

$$\begin{aligned}\sqrt{\mathbf{V}[500 \cdot 0.85 \cdot 1.07 \cdot X]} &= \sqrt{500^2 \cdot 0.85^2 \cdot 1.07^2 \cdot \mathbf{V}[X]} \\ &= 500 \cdot 0.85 \cdot 1.07\sqrt{\mathbf{V}[X]} \approx 1592080.\end{aligned}$$

7° We begin by calculating $\mathbf{E}[D]$. Let L represent the event that an accident is of low severity, M represent moderate severity, and S represent high severity. We use the law of total expectation:

$$\mathbf{E}[D] = \mathbf{E}[D|L]\,\mathbf{P}[L] + \mathbf{E}[D|M]\,\mathbf{P}[M] + \mathbf{E}[D|H]\,\mathbf{P}[H] =$$ ~~6130.~~ 6310

Now we use the tower rule to calculate

$$\begin{aligned}
\mathbf{E}[X] &= \mathbf{E}[\mathbf{E}[D_1 + D_2 + \cdots + D_N | N]] \\
&= \mathbf{E}[\mathbf{E}[ND|N]] \\
&= \mathbf{E}[N\mathbf{E}[D]] \\
&= \mathbf{E}[D]\,\mathbf{E}[N]
\end{aligned}$$

Since N follows a Poisson distribution with $\lambda = 1/7$, the mean number of accidents a good driver has in a year is $\mathbf{E}[N] = 1/7$. From this it follows that $\mathbf{E}[X] = 901.43$.

8° We see the policy pays

k	B	p_k
1	10000	0.15
2	7500	0.1275
3	5000	0.10838
4	2500	0.09212

With this data, we calculate that $\mathbf{E}[B] = 3228.45$ and $\mathbf{E}[B^2] = 25457125$, so that $\mathbf{V}[B] = 15034235.6$ and $\sigma_B = 3877.4$. With this data, we can use the central limit theorem to estimate the total benefit paid. In particular, if n policies are sold, the total benefit paid is approximately normally distributed random variable with mean $3228.45n$ and standard deviation $3877.4\sqrt{n}$. We seek n such that

$$\mathbf{P}[S < 4000n] = \mathbf{P}\left[Z < \frac{4000n - 3228.45n}{3877.4\sqrt{n}}\right] = 0.975.$$

We use a normal distribution table to find that

$$\frac{4000n - 3228.45n}{3877.4\sqrt{n}} \approx 1.96,$$

so that

$$771.55n - 7599.55\sqrt{n} = 0.$$

we solve for $\sqrt{n}$ using the quadratic formula, and find that $\sqrt{n} \approx 9.85$ and $n = 97$.

PRACTICE EXAM

1° A game consists of rolling a die until a 1 is rolled. In each roll, including the last, the player wins a dollar for each point rolled. What are the expected winnings?

A. 21 B. 22 C. 23 D. 24 E. 25

2° An actuary is interested in the minimum premium required so that the company can pay all its claims with a 99% probability. Which of the following are true?

i. The minimum premium required is greater than the expected benefit per policy.

ii. The minimum premium required increases as the number of policies increases.

iii. The minimum premium required increases as the standard deviation of the total benefit paid increases.

A. i. only B. ii. only C. i. and ii. D. i. and iii. E. i., ii. and iii.

3° Ellie has forgotten the combination for her locker. She remembers that two of the numbers are 17 and 24, but has forgotten the third number, and does not know the order of the numbers. There are 40 possibilities for the third number. At 10 seconds per try, at most how long will it take her to find the combination?

A. 36 B. 37 C. 38 D. 39 E. 40

4° A probability mass for a random variable K is defined by the probabilities p_k, for $k \geq 0$, which satisfy

$$p_{k+1} = \frac{e}{k+1} p_k.$$

Calculate $\mathbf{E}\left[K | K > 0\right]$.

A. 2.3 B. 2.5 C. 2.7 D. 2.9 E. 3.1

5° A number is admissible if it is composed of the digits 1, 2, and 3, in such a way that 1 is never immediately followed by 2, 2 is never immediately followed by 3, and 3 is never immediately followed by 1. Let X be a randomly chosen admissible number. Calculate $\mathbf{P}\left[X < \mathbf{E}\left[X\right]\right]$.

A. $\frac{5}{21}$ B. $\frac{7}{18}$ C. $\frac{5}{9}$ D. $\frac{49}{81}$ E. $\frac{15}{24}$

6° An insurance company estimates that if every policy has deductible $d < 1500$, the number of claims filed is a Poisson random variable N_d with mean $1500 - d$. The expected loss is $10,000$ and the standard distribution of the loss is 1000. It is found that the expected total benefit paid is $5,000,000$. What is the deductible d?

A. 950 B. 1000 C. 1050 D. 1100 E. 1150

7° We are given the following information about the events A and B:

i. $\mathbf{P}\left[A\right] = 0.25$

ii. $\mathbf{P}\left[A'B\right] = 0.25$

iii. $\mathbf{P}\left[AB\right] - \mathbf{P}\left[A\right]\mathbf{P}\left[B\right] = 0.05$

Calculate $\mathbf{P}\left[A | B'\right]$.

A. 0.1 B. 0.167 C. 0.2 D. 0.25 E. 0.333

8° Five fair dice are thrown. Let X be the probability of throwing 3 of the same value and 2 with some other value. Five cards are drawn from a deck of 52 cards. Let Y be the probability of drawing 3 cards with the same rank and 2 of another rank. Calculate X − Y.

A. 1.1% B. 1.6% C. 3.7% D. 5.1% E. 8.4%

9° A random variable X has the probability density function

$$f_X(x) = \frac{3x^2}{1000}, \text{ for } 0 \leq x \leq 10.$$

Jacob plays a game where he chooses a real number c. If the random variable X is at least c, Jacob wins c. Otherwise, Jacob wins nothing. What is the maximum expected value of Jacob's winnings?

A. 3.8 B. 4.7 C. 5.3 D. 6.3 E. 8.1

10° An analyst is studying the distribution of damage due to earthquakes and finds that if the last major earthquake occurred Y years ago, then the damage is normally distributed with mean Y^2 and standard deviation Y. Moreover, she finds that the time between major earthquakes is exponentially distributed with an average of 15.

Calculate the coefficient of variation for damage due to major earthquakes.

A. 2.2 B. 2.4 C. 2.6 D. 2.8 E. 3.0

11° An analyst estimates that if the risk free interest rate R is 0.035 this year, there is a 45% chance of an increase in aggregate production. If the risk free interest rate is 0.065, there is a 25% chance of an increase in aggregate production. If the risk free interest rate is 0.085, there is a a 10% chance of an increase in aggregate production. The probability that the risk free rate will be 0.035 is 20%. The probability that it will be 0.065 is 70%. The probability that it will be 0.085 is 10%.

Given that there is an observed increase, what is the expected value of $100e^R$?

A. 102.3 B. 103.7 C. 105.8 D. 108.4 E. 113.0

12° Let X be a normal random variable with mean μ and standard deviation $\sigma = 0.4$. Let $Y = e^X$. The integral

$$\int_0^\infty |y - m| f_Y(y)\, dy$$

is minimal for the value $m = 1.1052$. Calculate the probability that $Y < 1$.

A. 0.25 B. 0.30 C. 0.35 D. 0.40 E. 0.45

13° A random variable X has the probability distribution function

$$F(x) = 1 - e^{-\left(\frac{x}{2}\right)^3},$$

for $x > 0$. Find the mode of X.

A. 1.0 B. 1.25 C. 1.5 D. 1.75 E. 2.0

14° Which of the following are true?

i. Suppose that $\mathbf{E}[X|Y] = 0$ and $\mathbf{E}[X|Z] = 0$. Then $\mathbf{E}[X|Y, Z] = 0$.

ii. Suppose that $\mathbf{E}[X] = \mathbf{E}[1 - X]$. Then $\mathbf{E}[X] = \frac{1}{2}$.

iii. Suppose that $\mathbf{E}[X|Y] = \mathbf{E}[Y|X]$. Then $\mathbf{E}[X] = \mathbf{E}[Y]$.

A. ii. only B. i. and ii. C. i. and iii. D. ii. and iii. E. i., ii., and iii.

15° Four nickles, five dimes, and two quarters are randomly tossed into two urns. If the two urns contain the same amount of money, the player wins a dollar. What is the probability the player wins?

A. 0.10 B. 0.11 C. 0.12 D. 0.13 E. 0.14

16° Let X be a random variable with the moment generating function

$$M_X(t) = \frac{1}{1-\frac{t}{2}} \cdot \left(\frac{1}{3} + \frac{2}{3}e^t\right)^4.$$

Calculate the probability that X is greater than 1.5.

A. 0.91 B. 0.93 C. 0.95 D. 0.97 E. 0.99

17° 36 bar magnets are placed in a line, end to end, with randomly chosen orientations. Opposite poles attract, and ends with opposite poles join to form contiguous blocks. Of course, similar poles repel. Let N be the number of contiguous blocks. Calculate the expected number for N.

A. 17.5 B. 18 C. 18.5 D. 19 E. 19.5

18° A beach-side lemonade stand is concerned about rain, and asks its insurance company about rain insurance for the upcoming summer. The insurance company has historically found that, for the 90 days of summer, the probability that it does not rain for n days is $\frac{12}{11}$ times the probability that it does not rain for $n+1$ days. The insurance company offers the lemonade stand a policy with a 250 benefit for each day of rain in the 90 days of summer, for up to 5 days. What is the net premium for the policy?

A. 1000 B. 1100 C. 1200 D. 1300 E. 1400

19° Let A and B be independent events such that $\mathbf{P}[AB] = \frac{1}{7}$, $\mathbf{P}[A|B] + \mathbf{P}[B|A] = 1$, and $\mathbf{P}[A] < \mathbf{P}[B]$. What is $\mathbf{P}[A]$?

A. 0.173 B. 0.205 C. 0.434 D. 0.759 E. 0.827

20° The random variable X has density

$$f(x) = c(x^3 + x^2) \text{ on } 0 < x < 10.$$

Find $\mathbf{V}[X|5 < X < 7]$.

A. 0.1 B. 0.3 C. 0.5 D. 0.7 E. 0.9

21° Lightbulbs manufactured at Generic Electronics' factory have lifespans that are normally distributed with mean 940 and standard deviation 35. The Phoebus Group takes 100 random samples from Generic Electronics' lightbulb factory. If the Phoebus Group finds more than 3 bulbs that last more than 1000 hours, it fines Generic Electronics 100,000 for each light bulb it finds. How much can Generic Electronics expect to pay in fines?

A. 150000 B. 200000 C. 250000 D. 300000 E. 350000

22° The random variables X and Y have the joint moment generating function

$$M_{X,Y}(s,t) = 0.3e^{s+t} + 0.2e^{2s+t} + 0.17e^{s+2t} + 0.08e^{s+3t} + 0.1e^{2s+3t}.$$

Calculate $\mathbf{V}\left[Y^2|X+Y>3\right]$.

A. 0.09 B. 0.25 C. 0.49 D. 0.81 E. 1.21

23° Each day, a stock price will either increase by 8 cents or decrease by 5 cents, with probabilities 0.55 and 0.45 respectively. What is the expected gain (or loss) over 5 days?

A. 0.10 B. 0.11 C. 0.12 D. 0.13 E. 0.14

24° Let X_k be identically distributed, independent random variables with probability density function $f(x) = 1$ for each $0 < k < 9$, and let $Y_k = -k \log X_k$ be independent random variables. What is the probability that $\min\{Y_1, Y_2, \ldots Y_8\}$ is greater than $\frac{1}{2}$?

A. 0.25 B. 0.30 C. 0.35 D. 0.40 E. 0.45

25° Let N be a Poisson random variable and let $(M|N)$ be a binomial random variable with parameters $n = N$ and $p = 0.35$. Find the correlation between M and N.

A. 0.5 B. 0.6 C. 0.7 D. 0.8 E. 0.9

26° Player A, B, and C take turns rolling a pair of dice until one of them rolls a 5. Player A always rolls first. Player A insists on playing until he has won twice. What is the variance in the number of games they play?

A. 3.5 B. 4.0 C. 4.5 D. 5.0 E. 5.5

27° A lognormal random variable X satisfies

$$\mathbf{E}[X] = 1.5 \quad \text{and} \quad \mathbf{V}[X] = 0.3.$$

What is the median of X?

A. 1.30 B. 1.35 C. 1.40 D. 1.45 E. 1.50

28° Let T_1 and T_2 have joint density

$$f_{T_1,T_2}(t_1, t_2) = 200e^{-20t_1}e^{-10t_2}, \text{ for } t_1 > 0, t_2 > 0.$$

It is found that $\mathbf{P}[T_1 > kT_2] = 1/7$. Find k.

A. 1 B. 2 C. 3 D. 4 E. 5

29° A recent study has shown that each household spent an average of 8910 on health care last year, with a variance of 12257000. Projections estimate that health care costs will increase by 7% in the next year. A small insurance company has 500 policies and pays 85% of the policy holder's healthcare costs. What is the probability that it will spend more than 7,000,000 on benefits?

A. 0.005 B. 0.010 C. 0.015 D. 0.020 E. 0.025

30° Analyst Samantha examines batches of 10 claims for fraud. If she finds signs of fraud, she examines each claim until she finds a fraudulent claim, and then moves on to the next batch. A claim is fraudulent with probability $p = 0.04$, independent of the other claims. If Samantha examines 20 batches per day, what is the expected number of claims Samantha misses?

A. 1.0 B. 1.1 C. 1.2 D. 1.3 E. 1.4

SOLUTIONS

1° Let N be the number of rolls thrown, and let W be the amount won. Finally, let W_i be the number rolled in the ith roll. By construction, $W_N = 1$, and it is the first time a 1 is thrown. In particular, this means that if $i < N$, $W_i \neq 1$. We calculate the probability mass function for W_i by conditioning on the event that $W_i \neq 1$ as follows. For $k \in \{2, 3, 4, 5, 6\}$,

$$\mathbf{P}\left[W_i = k | W_i \neq 1\right] = \frac{\mathbf{P}\left[[W_i = k] \wedge [W_i \neq 1]\right]}{\mathbf{P}\left[W_i \neq 1\right]} = \frac{\mathbf{P}\left[W_i = k\right]}{\mathbf{P}\left[W_i \neq 1\right]},$$

which we calculate is $1/5$. We now calculate $\mathbf{E}\left[W_i\right]$ for $i < N$ as

$$\frac{1}{5}(2+3+4+5+6) = 4.$$

Now, we calculate that

$$\begin{aligned}
\mathbf{E}\left[W|N\right] &= \mathbf{E}\left[W_1 + W_2 + \cdots + W_N | N\right] \\
&= \mathbf{E}\left[W_1 + W_2 + \cdots + W_{N-1} + 1 | N\right] \\
&= \mathbf{E}\left[W_1 + W_2 + \cdots + W_{N-1} | N\right] + 1 \\
&= \mathbf{E}\left[(N-1)W_1 | N\right] + 1.
\end{aligned}$$

Finally, we use the tower property to calculate

$$\begin{aligned}
\mathbf{E}\left[W\right] &= \mathbf{E}\left[\mathbf{E}\left[W|N\right]\right] \\
&= \mathbf{E}\left[\mathbf{E}\left[(N-1)W_1|N\right] + 1\right] \\
&= \mathbf{E}\left[\mathbf{E}\left[(N-1)W_1|N\right]\right] + 1
\end{aligned}$$

In the next step, we pull out the known quantity.

$$= \mathbf{E}\left[(N-1)\mathbf{E}\left[W_i\right]\right] + 1$$

Since W_i does not depend on N, we can factor it out of the expectation

$$= \mathbf{E}\left[W_i\right] \mathbf{E}\left[(N-1)\right] + 1$$

We recognize that N is a geometric random variable, so that $\mathbf{E}[N] = 6$. This implies that

$$\mathbf{E}[W] = 21.$$

<u>A. 21</u> B. 22 C. 23 D. 24 E. 25

2° We see that

i. is true. The total benefit paid is approximately normally distributed. If the company collected the expected benefit, the probability of paying all its claims would be 0.5.

ii. is false. The minimum premium required decreases as the number of policies increases.

iii. is true, since a higher standard deviation makes larger total payments more likely.

A. i. only B. ii. only C. i. and ii. <u>D. i. and iii.</u> E. i., ii. and iii.

3° Consider the six sets of possible locker combinations

$$C_1 = \{(x, 17, 24) : 1 \leq x \leq 40\}$$
$$C_2 = \{(17, x, 24) : 1 \leq x \leq 40\}$$
$$C_3 = \{(17, 24, x) : 1 \leq x \leq 40\}$$
$$C_4 = \{(x, 24, 17) : 1 \leq x \leq 40\}$$
$$C_5 = \{(24, x, 17) : 1 \leq x \leq 40\}$$
$$C_6 = \{(24, 17, x) : 1 \leq x \leq 40\}$$

Each set has 40 elements. But the element $(17, 17, 24)$ belongs to both C_1 and C_2. The element $(17, 24, 24)$ belongs to both C_2 and C_3. Similarly, each of the combinations $(17, 24, 17)$, $(24, 17, 17)$, $(24, 24, 17)$ and $(24, 17, 17)$ belong to two sets. In total, six combinations belong to two sets. By the inclusion-exclusion principle,

$$|C_1 \cup C_2 \cup C_3 \cup C_4 \cup C_5 \cup C_6| = (40 \times 6) - 6 = 39 \times 6.$$

Since Ellie can check 6 combinations per minute, it will take her at most 39 minutes to find the correct combination.

A. 36 B. 37 C. 38 <u>D. 39</u> E. 40

4° We see that we calculate p_k from p_{k-1} by multiplying by $\frac{e}{k}$. In particular, this means we can calculate p_k from p_0 as

$$p_k = \frac{e^k}{k!} p_0.$$

Since p_k is a probability, we can write

$$\begin{aligned} 1 &= \sum_{k=0} \frac{e^k}{k!} p_0 \\ &= p_0 \sum_{k=0} \frac{e^k}{k!} \\ &= p_0 e^e, \end{aligned}$$

so that $p_0 = e^{-e} = 0.06599$. At this point, we recognize that K follows a Poisson distribution with parameter $\lambda = e$. This implies that $\mathbf{E}[K] = e$. We use the law of total expectation

$$\begin{aligned} \mathbf{E}[K] &= \mathbf{E}[K|K > 0]\, \mathbf{P}[K > 0] + \mathbf{E}[K|K = 0]\, \mathbf{P}[K = 0] \\ &= \mathbf{E}[K|K > 0]\, \mathbf{P}[K > 0], \end{aligned}$$

so that

$$\mathbf{E}[K|K > 0] = \frac{\mathbf{E}[K]}{\mathbf{P}[K > 0]} = \frac{e}{1 - p_0} = 2.91.$$

A. 2.3 B. 2.5 C. 2.7 <u>D. 2.9</u> E. 3.1

5° There are at least two ways to solve this problem. The first, straight-forward way, is time consuming. We begin by calculating the number of admissible numbers. We have 3 choices for the first number, and given a that we have chosen a digit, we can choose the same digit again or switch to another digit, three times. This means there are $3 \times 2 \times 2 \times 2$ admissible numbers. We now enumerate them:

1111	1113	1132	1133	1321	1322	1332	1333
2222	2221	2213	2211	2132	2133	2113	2111
3333	3332	3321	3322	3313	3211	3221	3222

Each of these numbers is equally likely. We add the numbers carefully and divide by 24, to find that $\mathbf{E}[X] = 2222$. We see that 2222 is the largest of the numbers starting with 2. There are 15 good numbers smaller than 2222. The probability $\mathbf{P}[X < \mathbf{E}[X]] = 15/24$.

The other solution is tricky to find, but can be much faster. Each number a embodies series of decisions. Given that we have chosen the first digit, each subsequent digit represents a choice to use the *same* digit, which we denote by S or to *change*, which we denote by C. The numbers in the first column all embody the choices SSS. Similarly, the numbers in the second column all embody the choices SSC, and so on. The we recognize that the choice C is the permutation $(1, 2, 3)$, and that S is the identity permutation, which changes nothing. Notice that if C is applied to different numbers, different numbers result. This implies that 1, 2, and 3 will appear as the second digit for only one good number in the column. Similarly for the third and fourth digits. As a consequence of this observation, we see that each column of numbers will add up to 6666. We know there must be 8 columns, since there are 2^3 sequences of choices. This implies that the sum of all the numbers is 53328, and that $\mathbf{E}[X] = 2222$, as before.

A. $\frac{5}{21}$ B. $\frac{7}{18}$ C. $\frac{5}{9}$ D. $\frac{49}{81}$ E. $\underline{\frac{15}{24}}$

6° Let B be the total benefit paid, X_i be the loss reported in the ith claim, and B_i be the benefit paid for the ith claim. Then

$$\begin{aligned}
\mathbf{E}[B] &= \mathbf{E}[\mathbf{E}[B_1 + \cdots + B_{N_d} | N_d]] \\
&= \mathbf{E}[N_d \mathbf{E}[B_i]] \\
&= \mathbf{E}[B_i]\,\mathbf{E}[N_d] \\
&= \mathbf{E}[X_i - d]\,\mathbf{E}[N_d] \\
&= (10000 - d)(1500 - d).
\end{aligned}$$

By hypothesis, $\mathbf{E}[B] = 5{,}000{,}000$, so we must solve for d in

$$d^2 - 11500d + 10000000 = 0.$$

We find that $d \in \{947.65, 10552.34\}$. We reject $d = 10552.34$, since $d < 1500$.

<u>A. 950</u> B. 1000 C. 1050 D. 1100 E. 1150

7° We calculate

$$\begin{aligned}
\mathbf{P}[AB] - \mathbf{P}[A]\,\mathbf{P}[B] &= \mathbf{P}[AB] - (1 - \mathbf{P}[A'])\,\mathbf{P}[B] \\
&= \mathbf{P}[AB] + \mathbf{P}[A']\,\mathbf{P}[B] - \mathbf{P}[B] \\
&= \mathbf{P}[A']\,\mathbf{P}[B] - (\mathbf{P}[B] - \mathbf{P}[AB]) \\
&= \mathbf{P}[A']\,\mathbf{P}[B] - \mathbf{P}[A'B] \\
&= 0.05.
\end{aligned}$$

We use the data we are given to solve for $\mathbf{P}[B] = 0.4$. Since we have $\mathbf{P}[B]$, we can solve for $\mathbf{P}[AB] = 0.05 + \mathbf{P}[A] + \mathbf{P}[B] = 0.15$. This implies that $\mathbf{P}[AB'] = \mathbf{P}[A] - \mathbf{P}[AB] = 0.1$, so that

$$\mathbf{P}[A|B'] = \frac{\mathbf{P}[AB']}{\mathbf{P}[B']} = 0.167.$$

A. 0.1 <u>B. 0.167</u> C. 0.2 D. 0.25 E. 0.333

8° We begin by calculating X. Let us call a number a rank. We must choose two ranks. There are 6 possibilities for the first rank and 5 possibilities for the second rank. If these choices are made, there are $\binom{5}{3}$ ways to choose which dice will have the first rank and which will have the second. Given that a die has been assigned a rank, there is a probability of $1/6$ that it will land on its assigned rank, independently of all the others. The probability that all dice land on their assigned ranks is $(1/6)^5$. All together, this implies that

$$X = 6 \times 5 \times \binom{5}{3} \times \left(\frac{1}{6}\right)^5 = \frac{25}{645}.$$

We now calculate Y. We must choose two ranks. There are 13 possibilities for the first rank and 12 possibilities for the second rank. Given that we have chosen ranks, we choose 3 cards from the first rank in $\binom{4}{3}$ ways and 2 cards from the second rank in $\binom{4}{2}$ ways. The total number of ways to draw 5 cards is $\binom{52}{5}$. This implies that

$$Y = 13 \times 12 \frac{\binom{4}{3}\binom{4}{2}}{\binom{52}{5}} = 0.00144.$$

This implies that

$$X - Y = 0.03714.$$

A. 1.1% B. 1.6% <u>C. 3.7%</u> D. 5.1% E. 8.4%

9° Let W_c be the amount won if Jacob picks the number c. Given that choice, Jacob's expected winnings is

$$\begin{aligned} \mathbf{E}[W_c] &= \mathbf{E}[W_c | X \geq c]\, \mathbf{P}[X \geq c] + \mathbf{E}[W_c | X < c]\, \mathbf{P}[X < c] \\ &= \mathbf{E}[W_c | X \geq c]\, \mathbf{P}[X \geq c] \\ &= c S_X(c), \end{aligned}$$

where S_X is the survival function for X. We calculate that

$$F_X(x) = \int_0^x \frac{3y^2}{1000}\, dy = \left(\frac{y^3}{1000}\right)\Bigg|_{y=0}^{x} = \frac{x^3}{1000},$$

so that

$$S_X(c) = c - \frac{c^4}{1000}.$$

We will now find the maximum for $\mathbf{E}[W_c]$ as a function of c.

$$\frac{d}{dc}\mathbf{E}[W_c] = \frac{d}{dc} c S_X(c) = \frac{d}{dc}\left(c - \frac{c^4}{1000}\right) = 1 - \frac{4c^3}{1000} = 0.$$

This implies that $c^3 = 250$ and $c = 6.2996$ maximizes $\mathbf{E}\left[W_c\right]$. Finally, we calculate that the maximum $\mathbf{E}\left[W_c\right]$ is

$$\max_{0 \le c \le 10} \mathbf{E}\left[W_c\right] = cS_X(c) = c - \frac{c^4}{1000} = 4.72.$$

A. 3.8 <u>B. 4.7</u> C. 5.3 D. 6.3 E. 8.1

10° Let X be the damage due to a major earthquake. Then $(X|Y)$ is normally distributed with mean Y^2 and standard deviation Y. In the course of solving this problem, we will repeatedly use the identity

$$\mathbf{E}\left[X^k\right] = \frac{k!}{\lambda^k}.$$

We compute the expectation of X using the law of total expectation:

$$\mathbf{E}[X] = \mathbf{E}[\mathbf{E}[X|Y]\,] = \mathbf{E}\left[Y^2\right] = \frac{2}{\lambda^2} = 2 \times 15^2.$$

We compute the variance of X using the law of total variance:

$$\begin{aligned}
\mathbf{V}[X] &= \mathbf{V}[\mathbf{E}[X|Y]\,] + \mathbf{E}[\mathbf{V}[X|Y]\,] \\
&= \mathbf{V}\left[Y^2\right] + \mathbf{E}\left[Y^2\right] \\
&= \mathbf{E}\left[Y^4\right] - \mathbf{E}\left[Y^2\right]^2 + \mathbf{E}\left[Y^2\right] \\
&= \frac{4!}{\lambda^4} + \left(\frac{2}{\lambda^2}\right)^2 + \frac{2}{\lambda^2} \\
&= \frac{24}{\lambda^4} - \frac{4}{\lambda^4} + \frac{2}{\lambda^2} \\
&= \frac{20}{\lambda^4} + \frac{2}{\lambda^2} \\
&= \left(20 \times 15^4\right) + \left(2 \times 15^2\right) \\
&= 1012950
\end{aligned}$$

We see that $\sigma_X = \sqrt{\mathbf{V}[X]} \approx 1006.45$, so that the coefficient of variation is

$$c_X = \frac{\sigma_X}{\mathbf{E}[X]} \approx 2.24.$$

A. <u>2.2</u> B. 2.4 C. 2.6 D. 2.8 E. 3.0

11° We must calculate the conditional expectation of R, given that there is an increase in aggregate production. Let I represent an increase in production. We are given the data

$$\begin{aligned} &\mathbf{P}[I|R = 0.035] = 0.45 \qquad &&\mathbf{P}[R = 0.035] = 0.2 \\ &\mathbf{P}[I|R = 0.065] = 0.25 &&\mathbf{P}[R = 0.035] = 0.7 \\ &\mathbf{P}[I|R = 0.085] = 0.10 &&\mathbf{P}[R = 0.035] = 0.1 \end{aligned}$$

We use Bayes theorem to calculate conditional probabilities:

$$\begin{aligned} \mathbf{P}[R = 0.035|I] &= \frac{0.45 \times 0.2}{(0.45 \times 0.2) + (0.25 \times 0.7) + (0.1 \times 0.1)} \\ &= 0.32727 \\ \mathbf{P}[R = 0.065|I] &= \frac{0.25 \times 0.7}{(0.45 \times 0.2) + (0.25 \times 0.7) + (0.1 \times 0.1)} \\ &= 0.636363 \\ \mathbf{P}[R = 0.085|I] &= \frac{0.1 \times 0.1}{(0.45 \times 0.2) + (0.25 \times 0.7) + (0.1 \times 0.1)} \\ &= 0.03636 \end{aligned}$$

With these conditional probabilities, we are in a position to calculate the conditional expectation we seek. In particular:

$$\begin{aligned} \mathbf{E}\left[100e^{R}|I\right] &= 100\mathbf{E}\left[e^{R}|I\right] \\ &= 100\Big(e^{0.035}\mathbf{P}[R = 0.035|I] + e^{0.065}\mathbf{P}[R = 0.065] \\ &\quad + e^{0.085}\mathbf{P}[R = 0.085]\Big) \\ &\approx 105.8. \end{aligned}$$

A. 102.3 B. 103.7 C. <u>105.8</u> D. 108.4 E. 113.0

12° Define a function I by

$$I(m) = \int_0^\infty |y - m| f_Y(y)\, dy$$
$$= \left(\int_m^\infty (y - m) f_Y(y)\, dy\right) - \left(\int_0^m (y - m) f_Y(y)\, dy\right).$$

We take the derivative of I with respect to m

$$I'(m) = \int_0^m f_Y(y)\, dy - \int_m^\infty f_Y(y)\, dy.$$

Since this quantity is 0 for $m = 1.1052$, the probability that $Y < m$ is the same as the probability that $Y > m$. In other words, $m = 1.1052$ is the median of Y. Since Y is a log-normal random variable, we can write $m = e^{\mu}$, so that $\mu = 0.1$. Now, we calculate

$$\mathbf{P}[Y < 1] = \mathbf{P}\left[e^X < 1\right] = \mathbf{P}[X < 0] = \mathbf{P}\left[Z \leq \frac{-0.1}{0.4}\right] \approx 0.401.$$

A. 0.25 B. 0.30 C. 0.35 D. 0.40 E. 0.45

13° We begin by calculating the probability mass function by differentiating F, so that

$$f_X(x) = \frac{3}{2}\left(\frac{x}{2}\right)^2 e^{-\left(\frac{x}{2}\right)^3}.$$

We must find the value of x which maximizes this expression. To that end, we calculate

$$f_X'(x) = \frac{3}{2}\frac{x}{2} e^{-\left(\frac{x}{2}\right)^3} - \frac{3}{2}\left(\frac{x}{2}\right)^4 e^{-\left(\frac{x}{2}\right)^3}$$

Since we are maximizing, we set this derivative to 0 and simplify by cancelling all the common factors.

$$0 = \frac{x}{2} - \frac{3}{2}\left(\frac{x}{2}\right)^4$$
$$= 1 - \frac{3}{2}\left(\frac{x}{2}\right)^3$$

This implies that

$$\begin{aligned} \frac{3}{2}\left(\frac{x}{2}\right)^3 &= 1 \\ \left(\frac{x}{2}\right)^3 &= \frac{2}{3} \\ x &= 2\left(\frac{2}{3}\right)^{\frac{1}{3}} \\ &\approx 1.75. \end{aligned}$$

A. 1.0 B. 1.25 C. 1.5 <u>D. 1.75</u> E. 2.0

14° The correct answer is D.

i. is false. Let Y and Z be independent standard normal random variables and let $X = YZ$. Then we see that

$$\begin{aligned} \mathbf{E}[X|Y] &= \mathbf{E}[YZ|Y] = Y\mathbf{E}[Z|Y] = Y\mathbf{E}[Z] = 0, \\ \mathbf{E}[X|Z] &= \mathbf{E}[YZ|Z] = Z\mathbf{E}[Y|Z] = Y\mathbf{E}[Y] = 0, \end{aligned}$$

but

$$\mathbf{E}[X|Y,Z] = \mathbf{E}[YZ|Y,Z] = Y\mathbf{E}[Z|YZ] = Y\mathbf{E}[Z|Z] = YZ,$$

which equals 0 with probability 0.

ii. is true. We see that

$$\mathbf{E}[X] = \mathbf{E}[1-X] = 1 - \mathbf{E}[X],$$

so that

$$\mathbf{E}[X] = \frac{1}{2}.$$

iii. is true. Since $\mathbf{E}[X|Y] = \mathbf{E}[Y|X]$, the tower law implies that $\mathbf{E}[X] = \mathbf{E}[\mathbf{E}[X|Y]] = \mathbf{E}[\mathbf{E}[Y|X]] = \mathbf{E}[Y]$.

A. ii. only B. i. and ii. C. i. and iii. D. ii. and iii. E. i., ii., and iii.

15° The value of all the coins is \$1, so 50 cents must land in each urn. We will pick one urn and enumerate the ways in which 50 cents can land in it. The admissible events are

i. 2 quarters

ii. 1 quarter, 2 dimes, 1 nickel

iii. 1 quarter, 1 dime, 3 nickels

iv. 4 nickels, 3 dimes

The number of admissible ways to place coins in the urn we choose is

$$\binom{2}{2} + \binom{2}{1}\binom{3}{2}\binom{4}{1} + \binom{4}{4}\binom{3}{3} + \binom{2}{1}\binom{3}{1}\binom{4}{3} = 50.$$

The total number of ways to throw coins into the urns is 2^9. This implies that the probability is

$$\frac{50}{2^9} = \frac{25}{256} \approx 0.0977.$$

A. 0.10 B. 0.11 C. 0.12 D. 0.13 E. 0.14

16° We recognize the moment generating function as the product of moment generating functions M_{X_1} and M_{X_2}, where

$$M_{X_1}(t) = \frac{1}{1 - \frac{t}{2}}$$

is the moment generating function of an exponentially distributed random variable X_1 with parameter $\lambda = 1/2$, and

$$M_{X_2}(t) = \left(\frac{1}{3} + \frac{2}{3}e^t\right)^4,$$

which we recognize as the moment generating function of a random variable X_2 which follows the binomial distribution with parameters $n = 4$ and $p = 2/3$. Since $M_X = M_{X_1} \cdot M_{X_2}$, $X = X_1 + X_2$. We use the law of total probability to calculate

$$\begin{aligned}
\mathbf{P}\left[X > \frac{3}{2}\right] &= \mathbf{P}\left[X_1 + X_2 > \frac{3}{2}\right] = \mathbf{P}\left[X_1 > \frac{3}{2} - X_2\right] \\
&= \mathbf{P}\left[X_1 > \frac{3}{2} - X_2 | X_2 = 0\right] \mathbf{P}[X_2 = 0] \\
&\quad + \mathbf{P}\left[X_1 > \frac{3}{2} - X_2 \middle| X_2 = 1\right] \mathbf{P}[X_2 = 1] \\
&\quad + \mathbf{P}\left[X_1 > \frac{3}{2} - X_2 \middle| X_2 = 2\right] \mathbf{P}[X_2 = 2] \\
&\quad + \mathbf{P}\left[X_1 > \frac{3}{2} - X_2 \middle| X_2 = 3\right] \mathbf{P}[X_2 = 3] \\
&\quad + \mathbf{P}\left[X_1 > \frac{3}{2} - X_2 \middle| X_2 = 4\right] \mathbf{P}[X_2 = 4] .
\end{aligned}$$

Since, in each case, X_2 is known, we simplify to

$$\begin{aligned}
&\mathbf{P}\left[X_1 > \frac{3}{2}\right] \mathbf{P}[X_2 = 0] + \mathbf{P}\left[X_1 > \frac{1}{2}\right] \mathbf{P}[X_2 = 1] + \mathbf{P}\left[X_1 > -\frac{1}{2}\right] \mathbf{P}[X_2 = 2] \\
&\quad + \mathbf{P}\left[X_1 > -\frac{3}{2}\right] \mathbf{P}[X_2 = 3] + \mathbf{P}\left[X_1 > -\frac{5}{2}\right] \mathbf{P}[X_2 = 4]
\end{aligned}$$

We recognize that some of these events are certain. In particular, X_1 is a positive random variable, so $\mathbf{P}[X_1 > 0] = 1$, and

$$\begin{aligned}
&\mathbf{P}\left[X_1 > \frac{3}{2}\right] \mathbf{P}[X_2 = 0] + \mathbf{P}\left[X_1 > \frac{1}{2}\right] \mathbf{P}[X_2 = 1] \\
&\quad + \mathbf{P}[X_2 = 2] + \mathbf{P}[X_2 = 3] + \mathbf{P}[X_2 = 4] .
\end{aligned}$$

Recalling that the survival function for $X_1 \sim E_{\frac{1}{2}}$ is $S_X(x) = e^{-\frac{x}{2}}$, we calculate

$$\begin{aligned}
&e^{-\frac{3}{4}} \left(\frac{1}{3}\right)^4 + e^{-\frac{1}{4}} \binom{4}{1} \left(\frac{1}{3}\right)^3 \left(\frac{2}{3}\right) \\
&\quad + \binom{4}{2} \left(\frac{1}{3}\right)^2 \left(\frac{2}{3}\right)^2 + \binom{4}{3} \left(\frac{1}{3}\right) \left(\frac{2}{3}\right)^4
\end{aligned}$$

which we see is approximately 0.97.

A. 0.91 B. 0.93 C. 0.95 D. 0.97 E. 0.99

17° Let $\mathbb{1}_k$ be the indicator variable for the event that the k-th pair of magnets belong to a contiguous block, so that

$$N = 1 + \sum_{k=1}^{35} \mathbb{1}_k.$$

We have $\mathbf{P}[\mathbb{1}_k = 1] = \frac{1}{2}$, so that

$$\begin{aligned} \mathbf{E}[N] &= \mathbf{E}\left[1 + \sum_{k=1}^{35} \mathbb{1}_k\right] = 1 + \sum_{k=1}^{35} \mathbf{E}[\mathbb{1}_k] \\ &= 1 + \sum_{k=1}^{35} \mathbf{P}[\mathbb{1}_k = 1] = 1 + \sum_{k=1}^{35} \frac{1}{2} \\ &= 18.5. \end{aligned}$$

A. 17.5 B. 18 C. 18.5 D. 19 E. 19.5

18° Let p_n be the probability that there is no rain for n days – in other words, that the first day of rain occurs on the $(n+1)$-st day. We see that $p_n = \frac{12}{11}p_{n+1}$, so that $p_n = \left(\frac{11}{12}\right)^n p_0$. We can find p_0 by solving for it in

$$1 = p_0 \sum_{n=0}^{\infty} \left(\frac{11}{12}\right)^n = \frac{p_0}{1 - \frac{11}{12}},$$

so that $p_0 = \frac{11}{12}$. We see that the number of days with no rain is a geometric random variable with parameter $p = p_0$. We conclude that the number N of days of rain is binomial, with parameters $n = 90$ and $p = p_0$. Let B be the benefit paid. We calculate:

$$\begin{aligned} \mathbf{E}[B] &= 250\binom{90}{1}p(1-p)^{89} + 500\binom{90}{2}p^2(1-p)^{8}8 + 750\binom{90}{3}p^3(1-p)^{8} \\ &\quad + 1000\binom{90}{4}p^4(1-p)^{86} + 1250\mathbf{P}[N \geq 5]. \end{aligned}$$

Of course,

$$\begin{aligned}\mathbf{P}[N \geq 5] &= 1 - \mathbf{P}[N < 5] \\ &= \binom{90}{1} p(1-p)^{89} + \binom{90}{2} p^2(1-p)^{88} + \binom{90}{3} p^3(1-p)^{87} \\ &\quad + \binom{90}{4} p^4(1-p)^{86} \\ &\approx 0.8788.\end{aligned}$$

We can now substitute for $\mathbf{P}[N \geq 5]$ in the expression for $\mathbf{E}[B]$ to find $\mathbf{E}[B] \approx 1200$.

A. 1000 B. 1100 C. 1200 D. 1300 E. 1400

19° Since A and B are independent, $\mathbf{P}[AB] = \mathbf{P}[A]\,\mathbf{P}[B]$. And since A and B are independent,

$$\mathbf{P}[A|B] = \frac{\mathbf{P}[AB]}{\mathbf{P}[B]} = \frac{\mathbf{P}[A]\,\mathbf{P}[B]}{\mathbf{P}[B]} = \mathbf{P}[A].$$

Similarly, $\mathbf{P}[B|A] = \mathbf{P}[B]$, so that

$$\mathbf{P}[A|B] + \mathbf{P}[B|A] = \mathbf{P}[A] + \mathbf{P}[B] = 1.$$

We solve for $\mathbf{P}[A]$ in the equations:

$$\mathbf{P}[B] = 1 - \mathbf{P}[A]$$

and

$$\mathbf{P}[A]\,\mathbf{P}[B] = \frac{1}{7} = \mathbf{P}[A]\,(1 - \mathbf{P}[A]) = \mathbf{P}[A] - \mathbf{P}[A]^2,$$

so that

$$\mathbf{P}[A]^2 - \mathbf{P}[A] + \frac{1}{7} = 0.$$

We use the quadratic formula to solve for $\mathbf{P}[A]$, so that $\mathbf{P}[A] \in \{0.17267, 0.82736\}$. We are told $\mathbf{P}[A] < \mathbf{P}[B]$, so we must conclude $\mathbf{P}[A] \approx 0.173$.

A. 0.173 B. 0.205 C. 0.434 D. 0.759 E. 0.827

20° We begin by finding $\mathbf{E}\left[X|5 < X < y\right]$. We use the formula

$$\begin{aligned}\mathbf{E}\left[X|5 < X < 7\right] &= \frac{c\int_5^7 xf(x)\,dx}{c\int_5^7 f(x)\,dx} \\ &= \frac{\int_5^7 x^4 + x^3\,dx}{\int_5^7 x^3 + x^2\,dx} \\ &= \frac{\frac{x^5}{5} + \frac{x^4}{4}\Big|_5^7}{\frac{x^4}{4} + \frac{x^3}{3}\Big|_5^7} \\ &\approx 6.1556\end{aligned}$$

We find $\mathbf{E}\left[X^2|5 < X < 7\right]$ using similar methods:

$$\begin{aligned}\mathbf{E}\left[X^2|5 < X < 7\right] &= \frac{\int_5^7 x^2 f(x)\,dx}{\int_5^7 f(x)\,dx} \\ &= \frac{\int_5^7 x^5 + x^4\,dx}{\int_5^7 x^3 + x^2\,dx} \\ &= \frac{\frac{x^6}{6} + \frac{x^5}{5}\Big|_5^7}{\frac{x^4}{4} + \frac{x^3}{3}\Big|_5^7} \\ &\approx 38.207,\end{aligned}$$

so that

$$\begin{aligned}\mathbf{V}\left[X|5 < X < 7\right] &= \mathbf{E}\left[X^2|5 < X < 7\right] - \mathbf{E}\left[X|5 < X < 7\right]^2 \\ &\approx 0.32\end{aligned}$$

A. 0.1 B. 0.3 C. 0.5 D. 0.7 E. 0.9

21° Let N be the total number of defective bulbs the Phoebus Group finds and let F be the total amount fined. We see

$$F = \begin{cases} 0, & \text{if } N \leq 3 \\ 100,000N, & \text{if } N > 3, \end{cases}$$

so that

$$\mathbf{E}[F] = 0 \cdot \mathbf{P}[N \le 3] + \mathbf{E}[100{,}000N]\,\mathbf{P}[N > 3].$$

Let T be the life of a randomly chosen bulb. Since the lifetimes are normally distributed, we can calculate the probability that it is defective as

$$\mathbf{P}[T < 1000] = \mathbf{P}\left[Z < \frac{1000 - 940}{35}\right] \approx 0.9564,$$

so that the probability that a randomly selected bulb is defective is approximately 0.0436. The number of defective bulbs Phoebus finds is a binomial random variable with parameters $n = 100$ and $p = 0.0436$. We find, then that $\mathbf{E}[N] = 4.36$. We calculate $\mathbf{P}[N > 3]$ as

$$\begin{aligned}\mathbf{P}[N > 3] &= (1-p)^{100} + 100p(1-p)^{99} + \binom{100}{2}p^2(1-p)^{98} \\ &\quad + \binom{100}{3}p^3(1-p)^{97} \\ &\approx 0.361105.\end{aligned}$$

We substitute these quantities into our formula for $\mathbf{E}[F]$, so that $\mathbf{E}[F] = 157441.95$

<u>A. 150000</u> B. 200000 C. 250000 D. 300000 E. 350000

22° We can find the probability that $X + Y > 3$ by reading off from the moment generating function. In particular, $\mathbf{P}[X + Y > 3] = 0.15 + 0.08 + 0.1 = 0.33$. Notice that these are the coefficients of e^{2s+t}, e^{s+2t}, and e^{2t+2s}. We can calculate expectations using a similar method. In particular,

$$\mathbf{E}[Y|X + Y > 3] = \frac{(2 \times 0.15) + (3 \times 0.18)}{0.33} = 2.545454$$

and

$$\mathbf{E}\left[Y^2|X + Y > 3\right] = \frac{(2^2 \times 0.15) + (3^2 \times 0.18)}{0.33} = 6.727272,$$

so that

$$\mathbf{V}\left[Y^2|X+Y>3\right] = \mathbf{E}\left[Y^2|X+Y>3\right] - \mathbf{E}\left[Y|X+Y>3\right]^2 = 0.2479.$$

A. 0.09 <u>B. 0.25</u> C. 0.49 D. 0.81 E. 1.21

23° Let G be the number of days where the stock price increases. The payoff is $X = 0.08G + 0.05(5 - G)$, so that the expected payoff is

$$\begin{aligned}\mathbf{E}\left[X\right] &= \mathbf{E}\left[0.08G + 0.05(5-G)\right] \\ &= 0.08\mathbf{E}\left[G\right] - 0.05\mathbf{E}\left[G\right] - 0.25 \\ &= (0.03 \times \mathbf{E}\left[G\right]) - 0.25 \\ &= 0.1075.\end{aligned}$$

A. 0.10 <u>B. 0.11</u> C. 0.12 D. 0.13 E. 0.14

24° For a fixed k, $Y_k = -k\log X$ defines a function $g_k(X)$, and we see that ${g_k}^{-1}(Y) = e^{-\frac{Y}{k}}$. The density for Y_k is

$$\begin{aligned}f_{Y_k}(y) &= (f_X \circ g_k^{-1})(y) \cdot \left|\frac{\partial}{\partial y} g^{-1}(y)\right| \\ &= \frac{1}{k}e^{-\frac{y}{k}}.\end{aligned}$$

We recognize that this is the density of an exponential distribution with parameter $\lambda = \frac{1}{k}$. The distribution of the minimum of value is

$$\begin{aligned}F_{Y_{(1)}}(y) &= 1 - \prod_{k=1}^{k=8} \mathbf{P}\left[Y_k > y\right] \\ &= 1 - \prod_{k=1}^{k=8} e^{-\frac{y}{k}} \\ &= 1 - e^{-(1+\frac{1}{2}+\frac{1}{3}+\cdots+\frac{1}{8})y},\end{aligned}$$

so that

$$\mathbf{P}\left[Y_{(1)} > \frac{1}{2}\right] = 1 - F_{Y_{(1)}}\left(\frac{1}{2}\right) \approx 0.26.$$

A. 0.25 B. 0.30 C. 0.35 D. 0.40 E. 0.45

25° The correlation of M and N can be written as

$$\rho = \frac{\mathbf{E}[MN] - \mathbf{E}[M]\,\mathbf{E}[N]}{\sqrt{\mathbf{V}[M]\,\mathbf{V}[N]}}.$$

Since N is Poisson, we see that $\mathbf{E}[N] = \lambda$ and $\mathbf{V}[N] = \lambda$. We can calculate $\mathbf{E}[M]$ using the law of total expectation

$$\mathbf{E}[M] = \mathbf{E}[\mathbf{E}[M|N]\,] = \mathbf{E}[pN] = p\mathbf{E}[N] = p\lambda,$$

and we can calculate $\mathbf{V}[M]$ using the law of total variance as

$$\begin{aligned}\mathbf{V}[M] &= \mathbf{E}[\mathbf{V}[M|N]\,] + \mathbf{V}[\mathbf{E}[M|N]\,] = \mathbf{E}[Np(1-p)] + \mathbf{V}[Np] \\ &= p(1-p)\mathbf{E}[N] + p^2\mathbf{V}[N] = (p - p^2)\lambda + p^2\lambda \\ &= p\lambda.\end{aligned}$$

The only quantity we need to find now is $\mathbf{E}[MN]$. Let $\{M_i\}$ be a sequence of independent Bernoulli trials with parameter p. We can write

$$M = \sum_{i=0}^{N} M_i = \sum_{i=0} M_i \mathbb{1}_{[i \le N]},$$

so that

$$\begin{aligned}\mathbf{E}[MN] &= \mathbf{E}\left[N \sum_{i=0}^{\infty} M_i \cdot \mathbb{1}_{[i \le N]}\right] = \sum_{i=0}^{\infty} \mathbf{E}[M_i]\,\mathbf{E}\left[N \cdot \mathbb{1}_{[i \le N]}\right] \\ &= p \sum_{i=0}^{\infty} \mathbf{E}\left[N \cdot \mathbb{1}_{[i \le N]}\right] = p\mathbf{E}\left[N \cdot \sum_{i=0}^{\infty} \mathbb{1}_{[i \le N]}\right] \\ &= p\mathbf{E}\left[N^2\right] = p\left(\mathbf{V}[N] + \mathbf{E}[N]^2\right) = p(\lambda^2 + \lambda).\end{aligned}$$

We collect terms and write

$$\begin{aligned}\rho &= \frac{\mathbf{E}[MN] - \mathbf{E}[M]\,\mathbf{E}[N]}{\sqrt{\mathbf{V}[M]\,\mathbf{V}[N]}} = \frac{p(\lambda^2 + \lambda) - p\lambda^2}{\sqrt{p\lambda^2}} = \frac{p}{\sqrt{p}} \\ &= \sqrt{p} \approx 0.5916.\end{aligned}$$

A. 0.5 B. 0.6 C. 0.7 D. 0.8 E. 0.9

26° We see that there are 4 ways to throw a 5, so the probability of throwing a 5 is $\frac{1}{9}$. The number of throws until a geometric random variable with parameter $p = 1/9$.

Player A wins if he throws a 5 on the first roll, or if they all throw something other than a 5 on their first throws and A rolls a 5 on the fourth throw, and so on. In this way, we write the probability that A wins as

$$\begin{aligned}\mathbf{P}[A] &= q^0 p + q^3 p + q^6 p + \cdots \\ &= p(q^0 + q^3 + q^6 + \cdots \\ &= p\frac{1}{1-q^3} \\ &\approx 0.3732.\end{aligned}$$

So far, we have calculated the probability that A wins the game. If the players play a sequence of games, the number N_1 of games they play until A wins his first game is a geometric random variable with parameter $p = \mathbf{P}[A]$. Because of the memoryless property, the number of games played after the first win until the second win is a geometric random variable with parameter $p = \mathbf{P}[A]$. The expected number of games played is

$$\mathbf{E}[G_1 + G_2] = \frac{1}{p} + \frac{1}{p} \approx 5.36.$$

A. 3.5 B. 4.0 C. 4.5 D. 5.0 E. 5.5

27° We have the formula

$$\mathbf{V}[X] = \left(e^{\sigma^2} - 1\right) e^{2\mu+\sigma^2} = \left(e^{\sigma^2} - 1\right) \mathbf{E}[X]^2.$$

This implies that

$$\sigma^2 = \log\left(\frac{\mathbf{V}[X]}{\mathbf{E}[X]^2} + 1\right),$$

so that $\sigma \approx 0.3538$. Since

$$\mathbf{E}[X] = e^{\mu + \frac{\sigma^2}{2}},$$

the median is

$$e^{\mu} = \frac{\mathbf{E}[X]}{e^{\frac{\sigma^2}{2}}} \approx 1.4.$$

A. 1.30 B. 1.35 <u>C. 1.40</u> D. 1.45 E. 1.50

28° Let $\alpha = 20$ and $\beta = 10$. We calculate

$$\begin{aligned}
\mathbf{P}[T_1 > kT_2] &= \int_0^\infty \int_{kt_2}^\infty \alpha\beta e^{-\alpha t_1} e^{-\beta t_2}\, dt_1 dt_2 \\
&= \int_0^\infty \beta e^{-\beta t_2} \left(\int_{kt_2}^\infty \alpha e^{-\alpha t_1}\, dt_1 \right) dt_2 \\
&= \int_0^\infty \beta e^{-\beta t_2} e^{-k\alpha t_2}\, dt_2 \\
&= \beta \int_0^\infty e^{-(\beta + k\alpha)t_2}\, dt_2 \\
&= \beta \left(-\frac{1}{\beta + k\alpha} e^{-(\beta+k\alpha)t_2} \Big|_0^\infty \right) \\
&= \frac{\beta}{\beta + k\alpha} \\
&= \frac{10}{10 + 20k}
\end{aligned}$$

so that $k = 3$.

A. 1 B. 2 <u>C. 3</u> D. 4 E. 5

29° We will use the central limit theorem to approximate the probability. Let X be the healthcare cost for a policy. We calculate that the expected total benefit is $500 \cdot 0.85 \cdot \mathbf{E}[X] = 3786750$. We are given that $\mathbf{V}[X] = 12557000$, and we must find

$$\sqrt{\mathbf{V}[500 \cdot 0.85 \cdot 1.07 \cdot X]} = \sqrt{500^2 \cdot 0.85^2 \cdot 1.07^2 \cdot \mathbf{V}[X]}$$
$$= 500 \cdot 0.85 \cdot 1.07\sqrt{\mathbf{V}[X]} \approx 1592080.$$

Let T be the total the company spends. We calculate

$$\begin{aligned}\mathbf{P}[T > 7000000] &= 1 - \mathbf{P}[T < 7000000] \\ &\approx 1 - \mathbf{P}\left[Z < \frac{7000000 - 3786750}{1592079.75}\right] \\ &\approx 1 - \mathbf{P}[Z < 2.01] \\ &\approx 1 - 0.9778 \\ &\approx 0.0222.\end{aligned}$$

A. 0.005 B. 0.010 C. 0.015 <u>D. 0.020</u> E. 0.025

30° Samantha misses fraudulent claims when a batch contains more than 1 fraudulent claim. Let N_j be the number of fraudulent claims in the jth batch. The number of missed claims is

$$M_j = \begin{cases} 0, & \text{if } N_j \leq 1 \\ N_j - 1, & \text{if } N_j > 1 \end{cases}$$

We use the law of total expectation to calculate

$$\begin{aligned}\mathbf{E}[M_j] &= \mathbf{E}[M_j | N_j \leq 1]\,\mathbf{P}[N_j \leq 1] + \mathbf{E}[M_j | N_j > 1]\,\mathbf{P}[N_j > 1] \\ &= \mathbf{E}[M_j | N_j > 1]\,\mathbf{P}[N_j > 1] \\ &= \mathbf{E}[N_j - 1 | N_j > 1]\,\mathbf{P}[N_j > 1] \\ &= \mathbf{P}[N_j > 1]\,[\mathbf{E}[N_j] - 1]\end{aligned}$$

We can calculate $\mathbf{E}[N_j | N_j > 1]$ by solving for it

$$\begin{aligned}\mathbf{E}[N_j] = \mathbf{E}[N_j | N_j = 0]\,\mathbf{P}[N_j = 0] + \mathbf{E}[N_j | N_j = 1]\,\mathbf{P}[N_j = 1] \\ + \mathbf{E}[N_j | N_j > 1]\,\mathbf{P}[N_j > 1],\end{aligned}$$

so that

$$\mathbf{E}\left[N_j | N_j > 1\right] = \frac{\mathbf{E}\left[N_j\right] - \mathbf{P}\left[N_j = 1\right]}{\mathbf{P}\left[N_j > 1\right]}.$$

Since N_j is a binomial random variable with paramters $n = 10$ and $p = 0.04$, we can easily calculate the missing quantities to find that

$$\begin{aligned}\mathbf{E}\left[N_j | N_j > 1\right] &= \frac{\mathbf{E}\left[N_j\right] - \mathbf{P}\left[N_j = 1\right]}{\mathbf{P}\left[N_j > 1\right]} \\ &= \frac{0.4 - \binom{10}{1}0.96^9 \cdot 0.04}{1 - \binom{10}{0}0.96^{10} - \binom{10}{1}0.96^9 \cdot 0.04} \approx 2.115.\end{aligned}$$

We substitute to find

$$\mathbf{E}\left[M_j\right] = \mathbf{P}\left[N_j > 1\right]\left[\mathbf{E}\left[N_j | N_j > 1\right] - 1\right] \approx 0.064832.$$

Finally, if we let $M = M_1 + M_2 + \cdots + M_{20}$ be the total number of missed claims,

$$\mathbf{E}\left[M\right] = \mathbf{E}\left[M_1 + \cdots + M_{20}\right] = 20\mathbf{E}\left[M_j\right] \approx 1.297.$$

A. 1.0 B. 1.1 C. 1.2 <u>D. 1.3</u> E. 1.4

CALCULUS

DERIVATIVES

$$\frac{d}{dx}c = 0 \qquad \frac{d}{dx}cx = c$$

$$\frac{d}{dx}f(u) = \frac{df}{dx}\frac{du}{dx} \qquad \frac{d}{dx}(fg) = f\frac{dg}{dx} + g\frac{df}{dx}$$

$$\frac{d}{dx}(f+g) = \frac{df}{dx} + \frac{dg}{dx} \qquad \frac{d}{dx}\left(\frac{f}{g}\right) = \frac{g\frac{df}{dx} - f\frac{dg}{dx}}{g^2}$$

$$\frac{d}{dx}x^n = nx^{n-1} \qquad \frac{d}{dx}e^x = e^x$$

$$\frac{d}{dx}\log x = \frac{1}{x}$$

INTEGRALS

$$\int du = u + C \qquad \int cf(x)\,dx = c\int f(x)\,dx$$

$$\int f\,dg = fg - \int g df \qquad \int f(x) + g(x)\,dx = \int f(x)\,dx + \int g(x)\,dx$$

$$\int x^n\,dx = \frac{x^{n+1}}{n+1} + C \qquad \int e^x\,dx = e^x + C$$

$$\int \frac{1}{x}\,dx = \log x + C$$

TABLE INTEGRATION

Table integration is a simple, time saving notation for performing integration by parts. It is a handy technique, and definitely belongs in your problem-solving toolbox. We will begin by reviewing integration by parts.

Integration by Parts

Let u and v be differentiable functions. Then *integration by parts* is the process of using the following theorem to compute an integral:

$$\int u dv = uv - \int v\, du$$

The trick in using integration by parts is to recognize that an integrand is the product of a suitable u and dv. Unfortunately, this can be a little bit error prone. For example, consider:

$$\int xe^x\, dx$$

This is how not to do it. Let $u = e^x$ and let $dv = xdx$. Then the integration by parts formula tells us that

$$\int xe^x\, dx = \frac{x^2}{2}e^x - \int \frac{x^2}{2}e^x\, dx$$

This equation is definitely true. But it doesn't help you find the integral. In fact, this integral is harder than the one we started with. We're actually further away from an answer than when we started.

As a general rule, we want u to be a function of x whose n-th derivatives will eventually be 0. We want dv to be a function of x that is easy to integrate. So let's take

$$\frac{x^2}{2}e^x - \int \frac{x^2}{2}e^x\, dx$$

as our starting point. We will do it the "right" way, and set $u = \frac{x^2}{2}$ and $dv = e^x dx$, so that

$$\begin{aligned} \frac{x^2}{2}e^x - \int \frac{x^2}{2}e^x\, dx &= \frac{x^2}{2}e^x - \left(\frac{x^2}{2}e^x - \int xe^x\, dx\right) \\ &= \int xe^x\, dx \end{aligned}$$

Notice that this brought us back to the original integral. Now, we will do this integral the "right way". Let $u = x$ and $dv = e^x dx$. Then the integral equals

$$\begin{aligned} xe^x - \int e^x\,dx &= xe^x - e^x \\ &= (x-1)e^x \end{aligned}$$

This example is pretty simple, but it does indicate a few essential features of integration by parts. Again, we want u to have an n-th derivative that is 0 eventually. And we will have to do integration by parts $n-1$ times, taking derivatives of u each time. And integration by parts can be a little bit error prone. If you pick u incorrectly, you can end up going the "wrong way". If you switch between a derivative of u and dv, you'll reverse back on yourself.

Table Integration

Luckily, there is a great trick, called "table integration" that lets us do integration by parts with fewer errors. We still need to pick the right u and dv, but once we have done that, the method is entirely mechanical. And it's fast and easy. How do you do it? Essentially, tabular integration is a different notation for doing integration by parts. We make a table! The table will keep track of all of the important features, so we don't end up going in circles.

Let's pick a harder function to integrate. We'll integrate $f(x) = x^2e^{3x}$. Our table will have three columns. One for u, another for dv, and a third that will contain either a plus or a minus. Now, the column labelled $\pm$ will contain alternating plusses and minuses, starting with plus. The column labelled u will contain the successive derivatives of u, starting with u, and column labelled dv will contain the successive anti-derivatives of dv, starting with the first anti-derivative v. We can stop making rows when the u column reaches 0.

$\pm$	u	dv
$+$	x^2	$\frac{1}{3}e^{3x}$
$-$	$2x$	$\frac{1}{9}e^{3x}$
$+$	2	$\frac{1}{27}e^{3x}$
$-$	0	—

With the table complete, we are now in a position where we can mechanically read off the anti-derivative of x^2e^{3x}. For each row, we look at the first column to check if it's a plus or a minus. If it's a plus, we add the product of the u column with the dv column. If the first column is a minus, we subtract the product of the u column with the dv column. In this example, the integral is

$$\int x^2e^{3x}\,dx = x^2\left(\frac{1}{3}e^{3x}\right) - 2x\left(\frac{1}{9}e^{3x}\right) + 2\left(\frac{1}{27}e^{3x}\right)$$

INDEX

79888509R00129

Made in the USA
San Bernardino, CA
19 June 2018